NAMING THE OTHER
Images of the Maori in New Zealand Film and Television

by
Martin Blythe

The Scarecrow Press, Inc.
Metuchen, N.J., & London
1994

Based on the author's doctoral dissertation "From Maoriland to Aotearoa: Images of the Maori in New Zealand Film and Television," UCLA, Dept. of Film and Television, 1988.

British Cataloguing-in-Publication data available

Library of Congress Cataloging-in-Publication Data

Blythe, Martin J., 1954–
   Naming the other: images of the Maori in New Zealand film and television / by Martin Blythe.
      p.   cm.
   Includes bibliographical references and index.
   ISBN 0-8108-2741-7 (acid-free paper)
   Filmography: p.
   1. Maori (New Zealand people) in motion pictures. 2. Maori (New Zealand people)—Public opinion, 3. Public opinion—New Zealand.
   I. Title.
   DU423.A1B59   1994
   305.89′94—dc20   94-495

CONTENTS

iii

ACKNOWLEDGMENTS

My deepest thanks go to all those who contributed toward this book in their own unique way. No one could write about New Zealand film without the assistance of the New Zealand Film Archive, the New Zealand Film Commission, and the National Library of New Zealand, so my grateful thanks to their respective staffs—I hope it will be enough to say, you will know who you are. I would also like to give special thanks to the Film Commission for the financial support they provided me with for this book; to Professor Roger Horrocks at the University of Auckland for his steady encouragement over the years; to Clive Sowry at the National Archives for patiently answering my many instant trivia questions; and finally to all those good souls, Maori and Pakeha, whom I have quoted, lambasted, praised, or reproduced in the book's photos.

I would also like to acknowledge that a version of Chapter 3 appeared in the *East-West Film Journal* and a version of the introduction appeared in *Quarterly Review of Film and Video,* by Harwood Academic Publishers, Switzerland with permission.

Here in Los Angeles, there is no doubt that Professor Teshome H. Gabriel of UCLA's Department of Film and Television has his stamp all over this book. No one could ask for a better mentor or for more intellectually stimulating arguments about the naming game. I would also like to thank the Department and UCLA itself for their financial support during my Ph.D., from which this book grew.

Finally, to my family at home in Auckland, New Zealand, and to my wife here in Los Angeles, this book is for you.

Martin Blythe
Los Angeles, 1991

INTRODUCTION: THE GEOGRAPHY OF THE IMAGINATION

> Names, once they are in common use, quickly become mere sounds, their etymology being buried, like so many of the earth's marvels, beneath the dust of habit—Salman Rushdie, *The Satanic Verses.*[1]

Growing up in raingreen New Zealand, the most attractive names and stories for me were set in distant desert lands. My early reading took in the magic of *The Arabian Nights*—Scheherezade, Sinbad, Aladdin; the caravan trails along the Silk Road— Samarkand, Bokhara; John Buchan's *Greenmantle* and Rider Haggard's Africa. The Norse and Germanic legends—Siegfried, Tristan and Isolde, the Valkyries and Valhalla—seemed chilly and doom-ridden by comparison. It was in the tales set in the desert that I found the powers of transformation, rejuvenation, illusion, irony, the power to strike down absolutes, archetypal trickster figures and magicians, messengers and thieves—rather than the immovable and implacable Father or Mother.

I suppose in retrospect, the discovery that my childhood reading was made up in part by British imperial writing has not interfered with my pleasurable memories of such stories. However, it did alert me to the "Fall" of other genres when I encountered them in the social sciences, history, anthropology, and so on. My choice of the Fall metaphor may seem a little grand, but I always did think there was little difference between the popular and academic writing of the British/European imperial era and the American/European writing of the present.

Some stories were always a lot more persuasive than others, of course—the double helix, l'année durée, postmodern implosion— but that was nevertheless the limit of their appeal, as stories. Clearly not everyone will share my view here, but "outside" of these stories there seemed to be no objective referent that I could

1

see other than an inchoate and amorphous reality which allowed itself to be shaped according to the scientific principles applied to find it. Consequently, I now find it difficult to overlook other writers' motives for writing within their chosen institutional, philosophical and ethical frameworks.

My reasons for opening in this way have to do with what I perceive to be the relative decline of film theory as a genre of writing. It is precisely in that it can now be perceived as a genre, with its own imported narratives and myths (auteurist, psychoanalytic, Marxist, feminist, structuralist), and its own syntaxes and vocabularies, that its Fall can be tracked. During the Seventies and early Eighties, film theory (and film culture) constituted a kind of Self, assimilating other intellectual trends for its growth. I am not trying to imply anything shameful here—any academic or popular movement might be described the same way—but sooner or later it threatens to become the "canon," the "tradition." Marxist Screen-speak, the empiricist historians, and the psychoanalytic-feminist alliance had by the mid-Eighties begun to demonstrate the kind of "Terroristic Terminology" that Charles Newman identifies, in *The Postmodern Aura* (1985), with an age of post-modern literary "inflation."[2] Quite predictably, an impasse for film theory and film history resulted, since words and concepts like "voyeurism," "scopophilia," "economy," "power," "commodification," "male hysteria" and "the Classical Hollywood Cinema" constructed yet new versions of the Fall. It was a Fall because the genre confirmed in its own texts what the writers diagnosed in the society at large: a perversion or failure of vision on the one hand and a totalitarian/monolithic institutional enemy on the other. There was no way out except self-implosion and Oedipal blindness.

In the mid-Eighties, a degree of self-consciousness set in among those influenced by literary theory and cultural studies. The introduction of the jargon of Self/Other, center/margins, post-colonialism and post-modernism, essentialism and pluralism, and so on, was timely. With one drawback of course: nowadays it is possible to read of "the Other" as another new cliché being fitted out for size. What exhilaration to wash up on new shores like Robinson Crusoe, to follow new footprints, to consume new sexual fantasies—China, Japan, India, Australia, Brazil . . .

Yet to invoke these terms, Self/Other and so on, is to recall just what many literary theorists were trying to do in the Seventies and Eighties—make our sensitivity to language at least as important as our attention to history, and to remind us that it is vital to understand how and why we name ourselves and others and our world in the way we do. Indeed the significance for me of Roland Barthes' *S/Z* (1974 in English) was in the way it confirmed my suspicions that (mis-) reading as an activity is such a subjective experience that writing ''authoritatively'' about anything can never be more than a dubious pretense.[3]

I like to call this terminology ''the geography of the imagination,'' which is of course really no different from the geography of the world. It seems to surprise many French people that the English call the body of water they share between them the ''English Channel.'' The French have a much more elegant name—they call it ''La Manche,'' which literally means ''The Sleeve.'' Nobody else in Europe attributes it to the English either. Moral: to name is to ''own,'' and to own is to forget origins. So too in New Zealand there is a simmering debate over whether New Zealand should be replaced by Aotearoa, its Maori name. This is popularly translated as ''Land of the Long White Cloud,'' so named because that is how early Polynesian navigators first saw it on the horizon, many centuries before the Europeans arrived. The name New Zealand, by the way, is derived from Nieuw Zeeland, bestowed by Dutch navigator Abel Tasman in 1642.

The Welsh have the dubious distinction of inheriting someone else's name for them. The words Wales and Welsh derive from Walh or Wealas, which literally meant ''foreigners'' to the Anglo-Saxon invaders who pushed the Celts/Britons back into what is now called Wales. To many of the Welsh themselves, however, their country is still Cymru, and they are the Cymry. In a world dominated by the English language, who would know that the Greeks call their country Ellás or Elláda, the Hungarians theirs Magyarország, the Albanians Shqipëri, the Indians Bharat, the Japanese Nihon, and so on? Moral: to be named is sometimes to take the name bestowed by an Other. In New Zealand, the names Maori and Pakeha are used to denote the two main ethnic groups: its indigenous Polynesian people, the Maori, who make up around 12% of the population, and its white, mostly British-derived people, the Pakeha, who make up around 85%. While Maori probably once meant "normal," i.e. "us," Pakeha is a Maori word which probably once meant "stranger," i.e. "them." White New Zealanders have inherited an Other's word for them. Naming (i.e. Self/Other relations) is deeply imbedded in all genres, from fantasy to political economy, travel writing to history, ethnography to literary theory. For example, Tolkien's *The Lord of the Rings* can be read as a modern allegory of the christian Salvation Myth set in the period between Celtic and Medieval England.[4] Tolkien (who was a philologist) has his elves speak something like Welsh; the dwarves sound Norse; the Orcs' names evoke the Westerner's horror of the Turkic and Mongol hordes who swept through Eastern Europe after the disintegration of the Roman Empire; and the Shire might as well be rural England. Moral: all naming is geographically and culturally centered.

And then there are the more pejorative names like "savagery" and "civilization," "cannibalism" and "barbarism." In the New Zealand film *Utu* (1983), set during the 1860s, some of the early sequences show Maori warriors shooting up the crockery, heaving a grand piano off a second story balcony, chopping off the head of the local Minister of the Church, and generally offending British sensibilities. Local reviewers reacted by criticizing what they took to be the negative stereotyping of Maori people. Wrote one, these Maori were shown "reverting to savagery" so that the British authorities would be justified in crushing the rebellion. Not only did those reviewers fail to understand the clever way the film resolves the circle of violence, they assumed that what we see on screen is savagery. My own reading of these scenes was that they were ironic and parodic, and that savagery, like anything else, is in the eye of the beholder. But the main point I want to get at here is that the reviewers found it extraordinarily easy to match these concepts to images they saw in the films. The Word blocks further thought. Moral: names set up an aesthetic that relies upon visual imagery for its force, whether this be romantic, horrific, comedic, or whatever.

So, to restate my point: there is no inherent difference between the principles behind the names discussed above and the structural oppositions of the Western academic disciplines: center and margins, Hollywood, Europe and the Third World, post-modernism and post-colonialism, material and spiritual, Self and

Other, and so on. New Zealand/Aotearoa, Maori/Pakeha, the language of imperialism, colonialism and nationalism: they are all a part of the geography of imagination. As many an anthropologist has argued, the classifications are basically still "tribal" at heart.

*   *   *   *   *

There have always been many New Zealands, never just one: imperial New Zealand, Maori New Zealand, official New Zealand, tourist New Zealand, your New Zealand, my New Zealand. Official New Zealand exists within the framework of nationalism: one small ship-of-a-nation state drifting toward Antarctica with 3.4 million people on board, sailing in search of the obligatory national identity, well stocked with sheep, kiwi fruit, sporting venues, beautiful landscapes, and a sometime great notion of a nuclear free zone. New Zealand is unique in the world in being a mix of a dominant "settler culture" from mostly British origins and a proportionally smaller Polynesian culture who settled the land first. For the Pakeha at least, New Zealand has been most of the things that Britain failed to provide: the promised land, equality, freedom, health, Utopia in the South Seas, and looking back over those one hundred and fifty years to the settlement period and the Pioneer Myth which came out of it, one can well imagine that it must have been a glamorous undertaking for many of its settlers, soldiers and missionaries.[5]

THE TREATY OF WAITANGI

In 1840, representatives of the British government sat down with a number of paramount Maori chiefs to sign the document known as the Treaty of Waitangi. In practice, the Treaty resulted in the formal annexation of what was then becoming known as the "New Zealand colony." So just who were the New Zealanders in 1840? Were they the various Maori tribes or the British settlers? Neither really, but the Treaty of Waitangi made it possible to produce some, just as it became possible to produce some "Maori" and some "Pakeha," since these terms also date from around this time. It was an Oedipal scenario—a family romance whereby the paternal British annex the maternal Maori to produce a "young" New Zealand. As New Zealand writer Michael King has observed, Waitangi (literally "weeping waters") remains the most powerful symbol as far as the national mythology is concerned.[6] During the Eighties, there were endless public debates which turned on whether the Treaty now symbolized the Original Sin of imperial annexation, or the later desire for national integration, or the more recent desire for biculturalism, or the potential for Maori separatism (see Figure 1). Obviously, it can symbolize any and all of these, but the recent impetus has been toward the segregation option (integration in reverse), and whether this is unfortunate or not, the main casualty is the mythology of New Zealand.

THE DOUBLE BIND OF POWER

In the Fifties, Gregory Bateson, and subsequently R. D. Laing, popularized the notion of the double bind, a theory of schizophrenia which suggested that ordinary family relationships in Western culture have a habit of tying people up in knots. In Bateson's theory, a double bind was a no-win situation for whoever happens to be the victim in an unequal power relationship—usually children.[7] For example, Bateson describes the case of a mother visiting her "schizophrenic" son in hospital. The son is caught between two conflicting modes of behavior: when he sees her he puts his arm around her but she stiffens, so he takes his arm away and then she says "Don't you love me anymore?" She in fact punishes him for correctly recognizing that she has set him a trap, and he is powerless to evade it. This kind of double bind situation may not in itself drive a person crazy; the crucial element is not being able to leave the field or point out the contradiction, and children often find themselves in just that situation.

Such double binds also arise whenever Maori and Pakeha are told they are New Zealanders together, united by the national mythology of New Zealand.[8] I do not want to be misunderstood here; I am not claiming that the Maori are not New Zealanders. That would be presumptuous as well as ridiculous. What I am claiming is this: on the one hand, the Maori are declared to be

Figure 1:

Social-historical models for the Integration Myth.

This figure summarizes Pakeha positions vis-à-vis the Maori. It basically follows the social-historical models of the Hunn Report to the Department of Maori Affairs in 1960, which was the fullest theoretical defence of the Integration Myth.

Annexation means assimilating the Maori completely into the Pakeha world. With integration, the overlap implies a desire for rapprochement between the two cultures, but it risks annihilating difference under the banner of identity (this is the basis of nationalism). Segregation stresses cultural difference but risks destroying mutual identity (this is the basis of biculturalism, but when biculturalism is defined as a static model, moving away from nationalist parameters, then it is stripped of its momentum toward exclusion). Exclusion assumes complete cultural difference; it is the final destination of segregation—Apartheid.

It should be apparent from this figure that analogically it provides metaphors of (in-)digestion and engulfment, cannibalism and sacrifice, and that these are two-way processes in that the Pakeha too can engage in atavistic self-sacrifice by imagining himself consumed by the savagery of civilization.

1. ANNEXATION

2. INTEGRATION

3. SEGREGATION

4. EXCLUSION

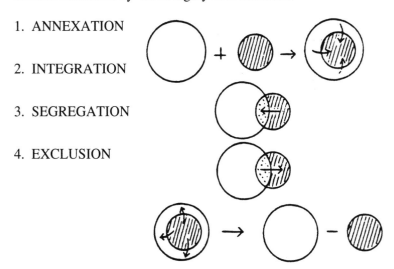

"New Zealanders" by virtue of the Waitangi Treaty of 1840 ("You are New Zealanders and British subjects, entitled to all the benefits which follow from that"). On the other, "New Zealand" is defined along British (Pakeha) lines ("You are Maori, you are different and we don't necessarily want what you represent"). And the second always comes attached to the first—a kind of double play which oscillates between annexation (assertion of nationalism) on the one hand, and exclusion (denial of biculturalism) on the other. The situation is the same elsewhere in the world of course: the Kurds must be Iraqis, Slovenians must be Yugoslavs, Qechua must be Bolivians, Zulu must be South Africans.

Nowadays, anyone who speaks/writes on cultural issues in New Zealand has to deal with the legacy of this double bind. As a result, not only do Pakeha intellectuals continue to design theories "about" the Maori which place them in double binds; Maori install them in return upon the Pakeha, and upon each other. The frontier is a lively place. Credentials are demanded, passports checked, baggage rifled. Mostly it is an exercise in name-calling and bullying, a constant process of prescription and proscription, incitement to revolt and repression when you do. There are still seemingly endless acrimonious debates as to whether Maori culture (a large abstraction in itself) is "oppressed," "marginalized," "developing," "decayed," "reviving," "post-colonial," "oppositional," "traditional," "natural," "spiritual," or any of the other epithets currently in circulation, along with debates as to whether Pakeha culture is the opposite of these. It is a world of linguistic schizophrenia and inevitable cliché.

The response to this from Maori intellectuals has been a clever sleight-of-hand: there is an ambiguity which is frequently present in their writing whenever "New Zealand" comes up. They create a dichotomy between "Pakeha New Zealanders" and the "Maori," attaching the seemingly redundant "New Zealanders" on to the Pakeha but not the Maori.

For the Pakeha these problems are rarely apparent or important, and the usual response tends to be: "Of course the Maoris are New Zealanders." Pakeha cultural producers (writers, filmmakers, historians, anthropologists, photographers, painters) have usually decided to annex the Maori into their own texts rather than to exclude (ignore) them. Two alternatives have then automatically followed: textual integration or textual segregation. Historically, most Pakeha texts have stated their support for integration as a national ideal, yet they have practiced segregation by devoting separate chapters, scenes, or even the whole work to the Maori. In itself this has not been surprising since it reflected the territorial and social distance between the two peoples. However, it also confirms that New Zealand's national mythology still has a huge fault line running through its official texts. Statement and act have not been consistent, and the utopian ideals have been necessary to cover over the cracks.

Integration and segregation are abstract nouns of temporal process, and their momentum as social ideals has been provided by a chronological notion of history expressed in linear narrative. If Maori and Pakeha were not integrated (merged/fused) today, then they would be tomorrow. On the surface, New Zealand's national story has been a utopian historical romance, subscribing to a belief in the pursuit of progress and modernity and, if possible, racial harmony, in an attempt to transcend its oedipal origins. That it has only ever been partially successful is evident from the substantial counter-tradition which has reminded New Zealanders constantly of their original Fall, their exile and drift from the imperial centers, and the greater spiritual authenticity of the Maori in Aotearoa.[9]

The solution, if there is one, is to recognize that if popular culture reduces life's complexities to fundamental absurdities, then intellectuals turn life's absurdities into dazzling complexities with all manner of clever philosophical ''knots'' specifically designed for tying up the reader. Recall Alexander of Macedon's encounter with the Gordian Knot. Alexander entered the town of Gordium with his army in 333 B.C., well aware of the local oracle: whoever could ''untie'' a huge and complex knot wrapped around a chariot pole would go on to become conqueror of Asia. Which of course he did—by way of the sword—thereby gaining enormous publicity value for what turned out to be a very successful military campaign. Now, I have no idea if ''untie'' at all resembles the original word being used in Gordium at the time, or if Alexander ever actually used a sword on it; historians who recorded the event were all in the service of one party or another. Depending on whom you read (history having no ultimate authority), Alexander's taking a sword to its sophisticated coils is either an example of Western pragmatism and positivism overcoming Oriental guile and duplicity, or an example of Western crassness and vulgar opportunism.

I take the view that Alexander, who was educated by Aristotle after all, understood that the ''problem'' was really a semantic one. He could ''untie'' the knot all right, simply by interpreting this term to refer to ends rather than to means; the knot was indisputably untied by the time he had finished with it, even if he did not literally take the time to untie it. Alexander well understood that knots are designed to protect the privileges of their custodians and to embarrass outsiders. He understood that in order to get results, you have to be crass and vulgar according to the prevailing moral, social, and political codes. The problem is, to take Alexander's side in all this can also amount to a justification of imperialism.

If the Treaty of Waitangi is a Gordian Knot, then essentialist solutions are probably too drastic. Much better to wait for the Treaty to outlive its usefulness rather than to abolish its principles or institutionalize it in law. Its power for many Maori still resides in its ambiguous definition, so it is really a question of waiting tactfully for it to lose this power. When that happens, we will no longer be in an age governed by national identity.

The films and television programs discussed in this book are treated as allegories, in the belief that this area of cultural relations has been overly neglected. Back in 1929, Maori intellectual and statesman, Sir Apirana Ngata, wrote, ''The Maori orator delights in allegory.''[10] In my view, it is time that the other orators, filmmakers included, understood that allegory is also what they produce. Films and television programs are not essays on authenticity and inauthenticity so much as allegories of cultural engagement.

Part One, ''Maoriland,'' is a tale of two cultures becoming one. Chapter 1 tells of the imperial romances of Maoriland which were shot by British, American, and French filmmakers in New Zealand during the 1910s and 1920s—*The Romance of Hine-Moa, Under the Southern Cross,* and *Hei Tiki.* They are then contrasted in chapter 2 with the national romances produced by New Zealand filmakers of the time—*The Te Kooti Trail, Rewi's Last Stand.* The former are set in the timeless eternal and employ a Romeo and Juliet narrative of true love overcoming tribal conflicts; the latter are timebound within history and flirt with cross-racial miscegenation in order to produce national unity. Two other derivative genres follow in chapter 3: the ethnographic romance and the tourism romance—the James McDonald films, *Whakarewarewa, The Maori As He Was, Amokura, Holiday Haunts.* Neither of these genres is consistent in deciding whether the Maori are supposed to be timeless or timebound, utopia-bound or fallen, ethnographic or historical, New Zealanders or exotics. They usually have it both ways.

Part Two, "New Zealand," is a tale of one culture becoming two again. Chapter 4 begins with the National Film Unit (Government) newsreels of the Forties in which New Zealand is as united and integrated as it ever gets—the *Weekly Reviews, Mirrors,* and *Pictorial Parades.* Chapter 5 discusses the Fifties, when the tourism romance and the historical romance are prominent, but it is the social problem documentary which marks the most significant new direction as the first cracks appear in the Integration Myth—*Aroha, TB and the Maori People, The Maori Today.* Chapter 6 begins with the early Sixties, when there was some momentum toward segregation in a new Maori arts and culture documentary genre which set out to describe a Maori Fall and switched to the task of identifying a Maori cultural and spiritual essence which could arrest the decay and foster a revival—*Maori Arts and Culture No.1, Tahere Tikitiki, Te Maori: A Celebration of the People and Their Art.* In its final mutation it became the pilgrimage genre—the subject of chapter 7—wherein Pakeha supplicants go off on a personal quest for an elusive Maori authenticity from which an authentic Pakeha identity can be derived—*Tangata Whenua, Race Against Time, Maori: The New Dawn.* The quest ends in a troubled silence.

Part Three, "Aotearoa," is the tale of two cultures and the nostalgia for one. For Pacific Films' *Broken Barrier, Runaway,* and *Pictures* (in chapter 8) and much of New Zealand's leftist coalitions, cross-racial romances and the desire to speak for the Maori ultimately lead to three options: atavism (the Pakeha Fall into Maori culture), suicide, or silence. For Television New Zealand's *The Governor* and the New Zealand Film Commission's *The Quiet Earth* in chapter 9, the result is similar: confusion, guilt, and resignation leading to withdrawal. For many of the Film Commission's conservative films in chapter 10—*Sylvia, Other Halves, Arriving Tuesday,* among others—the solu-

tion is different again: repression of the Maori eruption and even reactionary backlash. Nevertheless, several ways out of the double bind are negotiated in three of the Film Commission's best films (in chapter 11), *Utu, Came a Hot Friday,* and *Kingpin.*
In chapter 12, I have discussed the first contemporary "Maori" films such as *Bastion Point-Day 507, Patu,* and *Ngati*—including what this category might now mean and the difficulties faced by Maori filmmakers in commenting on or resolving the double bind of a national identity.

PART ONE
MAORILAND

CHAPTER 1: NOBLE SAVAGES IN HOLLYWOOD

THE BRITISH EMPIRE

The British Empire is nowadays as absent in "modern" New Zealand as the "traditional" Maori culture it came to civilize— worn away by years of nationalist revivalism, urban gentrification, and corporate capitalism. This absence is a fact of history which New Zealand shares with other ex-colonial settler nations—where the United States' Statue of Liberty, or Australia's First Fleet, or South America's Simon Bolivar and the dream of El Dorado all slide into the fetishized images of international consumer capitalism. In New Zealand, "God Save the Queen" no longer plays at the cinema (this practice was stopped in the late Sixties), and only here and there are the ghosts hanging on. In Auckland, the War Memorial Museum still stands granite-aloof in the center of town, and the Railway Station still hosts the occasional train. But museums everywhere have in the age of the microchip and VCR an almost quaint literalness about them: dried butterflies and birds, old yellow bones and static dioramas— frozen images, dead knowledge. And old railway stations only manage bit parts in films like Nagisa Oshima's *Merry Christmas Mr Lawrence* (as Batavia in World War II).

The British Empire was not only a historical and geographical entity; it was (and is) also a state of mind, an imaginary geography. Between 1840, when New Zealand was annexed, and 1931, when it attained full national status via the Statute of Westminster, the Empire was clearly the dominant state of mind. Because it offered a very definite sense of cultural identity and racial hierarchy, New Zealanders were British and that was that. Accordingly, historians and literary critics have stressed the

15

essentially symbolic nature of the early nationalisms and of
Dominion status in 1907, and the "blooding" of the young
Dominion in the trenches of World War I.

MAORILAND

If New Zealand was British, then something else has generally
been overlooked by the official historians: New Zealand has been
offset by a "darker" (and "feminine") adversary—"Maoriland"
(its other names include "Moa-land," "Kiwi-land," and "Zeal-
andia"). If New Zealand was British but not Britain (colonial but
not imperial), then it was also Maoriland but not Maori-land. New
Zealand shares in the double nature and fracture line that runs
through all settler mythologies, repressed in the interests of
national unity, from Mexico to South Africa to Australia.[11]

From a historian's point of view, Maoriland was a sentimental
and romantic cliché of the British imperial age, that first came into
vogue in the 1880s when it was popularized in the Sydney
magazine *The Bulletin*. Though it never had an agreed upon
definition, it was mainly an exotic and utopian synonym for New
Zealand. It appeared in the titles of innumerable books of poetry,
short stories, and periodicals of the time; for example, Thomas
Bracken's *Musings in Maoriland* (1890), Alfred A. Grace's
Maoriland Stories (1895), Elsdon Best's *In Ancient Maoriland*
(1896), William Satchell's short-lived *Maorilander* magazine
(1901), and the trade union movement's influential *Maoriland
Worker* magazine of 1910–1923.

Most of all, Maoriland was useful in the promotion of travel and
tourism—on postcards, in photography and painting—and these
always featured romantic landscapes populated by exotic natives
(*c.f.* chapter 3). In fact, "Maoriland" was the cable address used
by the Department of Tourist and Health Resorts in its worldwide
advertising.

When Maoriland finally settled into permanent cliché in the
A. H. Reed children's publications of the Thirties, it was no longer
a synonym for New Zealand but the name for a long lost world of
legend, or, at best, a moment in New Zealand's "prehistory,"
with a vaguely nineteenth century air about it. By then its cast of

characters consisted almost exclusively of Maori Noble Savages both fictional (beautiful maidens, princely warriors, and powerful demi-gods like Hinemoa and Tutanekai, Puhi-huia and Te Ponga, Pania, Maui and Hine-titama) and non-fictional (idealized warriors of the "Maori Wars" such as Rewi Maniapoto and the heroes of the battle of Orakau). At its most sentimental extreme, many writers of the time—Johannes Andersen, the Reverend H. J. Fletcher, and even James Cowan—never made Maoriland much more than a synonym for "Fairyland."

Though most historians would rather write the term off completely as sentimental racism, I prefer to think that Maoriland can also refer to those many Maori attempts at reaching a conciliation with the expanding British-Pakeha nation. Thus I would include those figures usually cited by Pakeha historians—Princess Te Puea, Sir Apirana Ngata and the Young Maori Party—but also the more dubiously regarded Te Whiti and Rua Kenana, Ratana and the morehu, and Te Rauparaha and Te Kooti Rikirangi, who came to assume the image of the Ignoble Savage in Pakeha eyes.

Aside from the historical perspective, there is also a literary or philosophical perspective. As such, Maoriland could be said to be "out there," a huge territory which existed without any concept of linear time or history. The Maori were "timeless" in the sense that they supposedly had no concept of time until the Europeans arrived to provide them with one. There is no conflict or contradiction in this world view, since only the European had knowledge of the difference between being in time and being timeless. This generated a plethora of jokes and popular tales about "Maori time"; it also generated an enormous literature devoted to establishing the prehistoric origins of the Maori (Egypt, India), as if some obscure issue of cultural superiority were at stake.

Imperialism and colonialism can best be rendered in a metaphor: the translation of the Westerner's time into the Other's space. The image that springs to mind is the hourglass, a time measurement device whereby a spatial exchange is transacted via a revolution. This was a straight commodity exchange: it forced the Maori into historical time while simultaneously relieving them of their land and culture. These time/space relations required that a horizontal exclusion model (British Empire versus Maoriland) be translated into a vertical repression model (New Zealand over Maoriland), which in turn enabled an integration process to occur—upwards rather than inwards.

After the New Zealand colony was established, there was also a sense in which actually living there—being a "colonial"—had to be justified to the world at large. But the widespread use of Maoriland during this period calls into question whether "New Zealand" was successful as an idea. Maoriland implies that British colonists were strangers in a strange land, a Maori land, and this has become the basis of a disproportionately large literature of Pakeha alienation, repression, exile, and "drift." Since repression models are also revolutionary models, the repressed periodically erupts into violence, hence the simultaneous romantic appeal and objectionableness of Maoriland. As a double figure it was always both New Zealand and not-New Zealand, Maori New Zealanders and Maori rebels, the light and the dark of Manicheism, Utopia and the Fall.

HOLLYWOOD

While the British Empire and Maoriland are perhaps obvious states of mind for anyone who reads a history of New Zealand, there was during this period a challenge from the Americans which is generally overlooked: the Hollywood motion picture. During the Twenties, there was an unprecedented shake-up in leisure entertainment activities as theaters opened all over New Zealand (in the small towns in particular), and the Hollywood studios gained economic control through the practice of block-booking and by providing a reliable supply of product. From 1926 onwards, this resulted in an acrimonious debate within New Zealand's official culture, prompted partly by the British themselves, as to the dangerous effects of American films on the Dominion's British way of life. Hollywood's *Film Daily Year Book* expressed a certain irritation at the controversy when it reprinted comments by official spokesmen such as Sir James Parr, then New Zealand's High Commissioner in London, who announced that American films were "cheap, trashy and harmful."[12]

After considerable agitation for more British films and stricter censorship of American films (the main concern was to protect children from their harmful effects), new measures were introduced in 1928 which brought New Zealand into line with actions taken by Britain: preferential treatment for British films through quota requirements and a preferential film-hire tax. As a consequence, the quota of American films screened in New Zealand dropped gradually from about 95% in 1927 to about 80% by the late Thirties.[13] However, the figures are skewed by many of the British quota films actually being financed indirectly by Hollywood, and most of the long-running and popular films were American rather than British.

Therefore, the case can be made that during the Twenties and Thirties, an era that New Zealand's cultural historians discuss as the formative years of the national identity, there was a crucial three-way collision between British, Maori and American cultures. This took shape around three things: the existing class structure and pecking order versus American egalitarianism; traditional business practices versus the new theatrical entrepreneurs; and the appeal to British history and tradition as opposed to American mythologies of the frontier. For British culture it was a case of stand by to repel the American boarders; for the film-going public there must have been a certain ambivalence in watching Hollywood films (especially westerns) that better expressed the New Zealand settler experience than did the more class-bound British product of the time.

Maoriland was much affected by Hollywood—initially in rural and small-town New Zealand and later in the urban areas. It produced those young Maori who came to town on Friday nights dressed like their Hollywood film heroes, challenging the prevailingly British codes of behavior (let alone traditional Maori codes). In the Eighties they dressed as street-smart hybrids of Rasta, breakdancing, and primitivist exotic. Back in the Twenties and Thirties, they dressed as cowboys and there was much public agonizing over whether Maori parental control was inadequate, whether Maori sexual attitudes were just plain different, and whether films were liable to encourage Maori youth into criminal behavior. In 1936, the Attorney-General expressed his concern to the Minister of Internal Affairs in this internal memo:

> I am not one of those who ordinarily blame the pictures as being one of the causes of crime among youths, but in the

present instance there seems good foundation for the suggestion. The Maori boys dress and act the part of the characters
displayed, who are usually heroes of the wild west films.
That the films do have a strong suggestive influence is thus
clear and that this influence is in the direction of increasing
crime is also clear.

The Censor of the day, W. A. Tanner, rebutted this argument in
another internal memo by recourse to the benevolence of the Myth
of Integration: why impose stricter censorship directed at Maori
youth when it would affect all youth? The Censor also defended
films as developing children's imaginations—an enlightened
view for the day—though he did not think such films could appeal
to "people of education."[14]

For those Friday night cowboys, perhaps American westerns
provided a strategy for imaginatively confronting uptight British
New Zealand? Whatever their motives, their imported internationalism and their "camouflage" challenged the prescribed
identity as Maori. New Zealand's official culture therefore aimed
to tame these Maori within the sentimental images of Maoriland.
This is a key reason for the persistence of the stereotype of the
Comic Maori: it was a way of disarming the threat of a subversive
street culture. Hence those strange creatures of New Zealand's
popular humor, the happy-go-lucky Hori and Henare (along with
all his other names) whom I can remember in offensive Pakeha
jokes as late as the Seventies.[15] This figure has been successfully exploited by several Maori comedians, from Wharepaia in
the Thirties (in Rudall Hayward's *On the Friendly Road*) to the
highly ambiguous comic persona of the Eighties, Billy T. James,
whose very name evokes Hollywood westerns and who in *Came a
Hot Friday* (*q.v.*) plays a Maori who thinks he is a Mexican
cowboy!

*   *   *   *   *

The most striking feature of American, British, and French
films shot in New Zealand between 1910 and 1930 (as opposed to
"New Zealand films") is that they are all set in Maoriland. They
belong to a genre that I have termed the timeless romance, an
imperial and international genre which is quite different from the

historical romance utilized by the nationalist filmmakers. This is not to say that American, British and French filmmakers did not also make historical romances, for they did, but that for some reason the Maori seemed to inspire a large number of timeless romances. This is immediately obvious in the films' titles: *The Romance of Hine-Moa*, *Under the Southern Cross* (aka *The Devil's Pit*), or *Hei Tiki*. Within the timeless eternal live various Maori Noble Savages: Romeos and their Juliets, wise chiefs, and heroic warriors, all quite unlike their European counterparts in that they are not subject to the ravages of time, history, or society. This is Utopia before the Fall, a place inaccessible to all but the most intrepid traveler.

In none of the three films discussed in this chapter is there a Western fictional hero placed inside the narrative. This role is appropriated by the filmmakers themselves, quite literally in the case of *Hei Tiki*. The filmmaker promises his audience that he has undertaken that dangerous yet romantic journey to bring back his treasures for the vicarious pleasure of his audience. The following to-camera introduction from *Hei Tiki*, which is spoken by producer/director Alexander Markey himself, is a particularly representative speech in that it encapsulates most of the familiar images and stereotypes of Maoriland:

> It was my privilege to live four thrilling years among the most extraordinary natives on earth on the North Island of New Zealand, where . . . this record of an ancient people was created. . . . I found the Maoris fascinating, their Isle of Ghosts enchanting, their friendship exhilarating, and I'm keen to share with you the pleasure of my experience with them. Forget your cares and problems for a brief interlude and join me on a voyage to the Isle of Ghosts. You will feast your eyes upon a sight no living white man has seen before.

Markey then goes on to describe how his film is inhabited not by actors, make up, or painted scenery, but by ''the remnants of a vanishing race of native noblemen and women—the stalwart people of Maoriland.'' Such stalwarts include ''Te Rangi, the proud chieftain, and Mara, the lovely golden-hearted Maori maiden . . . and Manui, the magnificent son of the wild bush.''

THE MYTH OF AUTHENTICITY

In order to succeed with international audiences, the genre of the timeless romance had, paradoxically, to sustain the illusion that the fictional ''culture'' or ''world'' presented was not simply the product of some fevered filmmaker's or novelist's imagination, but that there was an actual place ''out there'' on the imperial periphery to which they could travel as tourists. As in many novels, travel writing, and ethnographies, the timeless romance resorts to the Myth of Authenticity, a myth in which erotic/exotic worlds can be constructed as authentically different from European or American cultures by piling up various racial and cultural differences. Authenticity was to the imperial era what Realism has been to the national era—a successor to the idea of Nature but with a more scientific ring to it. Despite the pretensions, this Maoriland was not the timeless world it may have seemed; it was quite specifically positioned in time, in the immediate historical past of the filmmaker and his audience—i.e. the nineteenth century.

So far as the Hollywood film is concerned, the founding figure here was undoubtedly Robert Flaherty. When he shot *Nanook of the North* (1922) he was as aware as anyone of Fatal Impact theories; however, he decided, ''I am not going to make films about what the white man has made of primitive peoples . . . . What I want to show is the former majesty and character of these people, while it is still possible—before the white man has destroyed not only their character, but the people as well.''[16] In effect, Flaherty utilized the figure of the Noble Savage (seen also in *Moana,* 1926) as a critical response to the Dying Race images he saw being confirmed all about him. He provided a model for later filmmakers to follow, with the consequence that in all the timeless romances there is an almost fanatical cataloging of supposedly authentic rituals and practices—songs and dances, moko tattooing, games, and so on—which are inserted into a supposedly authentic local legend.[17] Mostly this was a simple question of budget and practicality since these films were B pictures without identifiable stars, and recording native rituals and adding a voice-over is generally cheaper than staging more elaborate dramatic scenes with expensive actors and sound recording equipment. But these obstacles could also be translated into good publicity on the New Zealand cinema circuit or back in the United States and Europe, and, needless to say, all these films were the subject of publicity campaigns detailing just how many exhausting months and what trying conditions were endured to get the film in the can.

The Flaherty-style timeless romance of the early Twenties may be compared with the films produced by aristocratic tourist-adventurers around the same time, which were recordings of their "heroic" expeditions throughout Africa, Asia, Antarctica, and elsewhere.[18] Then there were the purely fictional studio films of the time, where far fewer pretences are made to scientific authenticity; for example, M-G-M's *Trader Horn* (1931) and RKO's *King Kong* (1933).[19] In these variants the natives are clearly Ignoble Savages and the narrative itself duplicates the intrusion of imperialism. Even M-G-M's excellent *White Shadows in the South Seas* (1928) and Murnau's *Tabu* (1931) only break from the established civilized/savage dichotomy to convert their natives into Dying Savages who have fallen into time and history.[20]

Technically, the latter films are historical romances in that the natives now exist in real and present time (our time), in a space which is accessible to Westerners, whether it is laughable, diabolical, or fallen. The natives themselves do not understand this sense of history because they are as yet unable to grasp Western linear time. Consequently, they are also without the powers of representation. This is their fatal flaw, and why they cannot progress; hence the necessity for imperial intervention. The secret of the timeless romance, on the other hand, must always be that its Noble Savages are not yet corrupted by Westerners nor by irony, and if there is trouble in paradise, it must then be internal to it. The intrusion of a fictional hero into such worlds would cast the shadow of Western technology across the innocence of paradise.

THE LEGEND OF HINEMOA AND TUTANEKAI

The legend of *Hinemoa and Tutanekai* comes close to being the perfect allegorical narrative for Maoriland. The most famous of all Maori legends in the imperial age, it was no doubt popular for the same reasons as Shakespeare's *Romeo and Juliet* in that it told of the all-consuming passion of two handsome young lovers who would die for each other, and the Hinemoa story had the added advantage of a happy ending. By 1931, this kind of legend had become such a Hollywood staple that one film critic referred to it as the "trite archives of love forbidden."[21] Hinemoa and Tutanekai are also "natives," of course, and the story's theme is inter-tribal marriage, so why this legend exerted such a strong appeal in the imperial age invites speculation. Perhaps it catered to a paternal and sentimental humanitarianism on the part of colonial administrators toward their charges, as well as to wider audiences who desired to share in the imperial project. Certainly, if the natives were marrying each other, then they would not be fighting each other, nor fighting British settlers, thus relieving the burden of responsibility for law and order from the administration's shoulders and demonstrating the success of the civilizing mission. For a number of writers, the legend offered a free-spirited and capable young woman (who actively pursues her lover), who could be annexed to feminist purposes as a suffragette heroine.[22]

Allegorically, the Hinemoa legend and the timeless romance genre construct a "feminine" discourse of sacrifice and reconciliation, all stage-managed by an absent father-figure (the filmmaker). After a scenario of inter-tribal male rivalry for possession of the heroine, she is eventually sacrificed to the hero's quest. Ironically enough, the Hinemoa legend promotes racial purity: Maori marries Maori, and that was no doubt consistent with imperial thinking. But while such feminine discourses generally ended happily, the "masculine" cross-racial romances (miscegenation) discussed in chapter 2 did not—the Maori heroine usually dies in the last reel.

I have already referred to at least five figures that were used to represent the Maori in the imperial age: the Noble Savage, the Ignoble Savage, the Romantic Savage, the Comic Savage (Hori, Henare), and the Dying Savage.[23] Literary historians seem agreed

The erotic-exotic: a poster for one of the early film versions of *Hinemoa*, this one from 1914.

that in the hands of Rousseau and Diderot the Noble Savage was used ironically in an attempt to undermine the "noble man" and a hierarchical social order, and that gradually there was a transition through these five figures as colonialism accelerated and native peoples suffered drastic population decreases, even genocides. In the hands of New Zealand and foreign filmmakers in the early twentieth century, however, we see a return to the Noble Savage (and his other incarnations), but they are meant to be taken literally—there is no irony in these films. However, it is doubtful if New Zealand audiences ever took them seriously, and none of these films fared well at the box office. What may have played in Hollywood as a B movie looked like a set of clichés in New Zealand. By the Twenties, "race" as a generic term had generally displaced the terms "savages" and "natives," in keeping with developments in nineteenth century scientism associated with social Darwinism and eugenics, topics which were hotly debated

A metaphor for imperialism? *The Romance of Hine-Moa* (1925) is a Romeo & Juliet melodrama whereby its two lovers overcome tribal enmities through their love. Here Hine-Moa confronts her own people.

in New Zealand.[24] New Zealand audiences demanded something different, and the imperial era was fading.

NOBLE SAVAGES IN HOLLYWOOD

The Romance of Hine-Moa (1925/27) was a British film produced by Sphere Films Ltd. for Gaumont and directed by Gustav Pauli, a Danish filmmaker, photographer and painter. Only the first reel now survives.[25] It was the third of the four versions of the Hinemoa legend and undoubtedly the most stylish. A fairy tale-like story of handsome Noble Savages, it is set against the visual imagery of forest leaves and sparkling lakes designed to appeal to the contemporary fascination with racial and sexual purity and fidelity. Accordingly, the dialogue sub-titles are couched in the language of imagined upper-class intimacies: "Gentle, and famed for her beauty, Hine-moa, daughter of the chief Umukarei, was so prized by her father that he knew not with whom to betroth her."

The film would have had little appeal for working and middle class audiences of the time and was probably aimed at the art houses. Who else would have appreciated a sub-title that claims: "For the first time, a film has been acted entirely by Maoris, who, in less than a century have emerged from savagery and barbary to a high state of civilization." Though these lines nowadays occasion gasps at screenings arranged by the New Zealand Film Archives, there is a humanitarian, if patronizing, discourse at work here—the forthright claims to superior acting ability in the face of otherwise negative discourses on Maori hygiene, work record, lack of success at farming, and so on. Of course, this is primarily a marketing ploy for the film, but it does also suggest imperial and national pride in including the Maori in the joint progressive venture of empire and nation-building. If we have to have some natives, then let us have the best.

Under the Southern Cross (1928–29) has also been known as *The Devil's Pit* (its later U.S. release title), *The Dragon's Pit* (the Canadian title), and *Taranga* (its shooting title).[26] A fairly standard Hollywood B picture, it comes complete with the usual Romeo and Juliet scenario and the requisite exotic rituals and

The Romance of Hine-Moa. Maoriland provided a Victorian idyll of racial purity and pastoral cliché—here Hine-Moa with her Tutanekai.

action scenes. It was shot mainly at Ohiwa, near Whakatane, for Universal Pictures by its assistant director, Lew Collins, after the original director, Alexander Markey, broke with the studio (Markey went on to shoot his own "Maori film" instead—*Hei Tiki*—with private investors). It is "dedicated" to the New Zealand Government.

In the Maoriland of *Under the Southern Cross* it is the mystique of enormous threatening volcanoes, mud and steam, menacing spirits, and oncoming darkness which provide the scenographic backdrop. We could almost be watching *King Kong,* which it predates. The story centers on the romance between hero and heroine, Prince Patiti and Princess Miro, who come from different tribes. It is a fairly conventional domestic romance with an early triangle developing when the deceitful Prince Rangi cheats Patiti out of Miro's hand. True love eventually conquers all and the warring tribes are united. As the foreword states: "This legendary drama concerns the uniting of two warring tribes and the founding of one mighty tribe of Maori warriors."

Alexander Markey's romantic epic, *Hei Tiki: A Saga of the Maoris* (1930/35), aka *Primitive Passions,* is one of the strangest films ever shot in New Zealand, and it has already inspired a second film about it—Geoff Steven's documentary for New Zealand television, *Adventures in Maoriland* (1982).[27]

Hei Tiki's resemblance to *Under the Southern Cross* is immediately obvious. There is the same Romeo and Juliet scenario with a happy ending to unite the warring tribes, the same sense of a virgin bride whose body is contested by male virility, and the same attention given to action spectacle and to traditional rituals and customs. However, there are two significant additions. First, there is a soundtrack, complete with Markey's own to-camera introductory presentation (quoted above). His subsequent voice-over progressively drops out as the narrative gathers momentum, and this has an interesting effect. Obviously Markey could not use sub-titles to convey narrative information in the sound era, but his frequent interruptions come to suggest some distant paternal figure reluctantly releasing his child into the world. Second, there is a considerable increase in the erotic voltage.

The film's story is simple. The heroine is Princess Mara, the "forbidden bride of the tattooed war god." She first appears in the film stepping over the prostrate forms of young men, apparently

Director Alexander Markey adding some finishing touches to *Hei Tiki's*
hero, Prince Manui, in a production shot from this 1930 film.

meant to signify her coming of age. (Scenes like this were
offensive to the Tuwharetoa people among whom it was filmed
because it broke tapu sanctions; other scenes strained affiliations
with the people of the Whanganui River who were used as extras.)
The hero is Prince Manui of an enemy tribe. He embarks on a
spying mission and surprises Mara in the forest and the two
quickly become lovers. He gives her his ''hei tiki''—''a symbol
of earthly surrender,'' thus setting in motion the conflict between
the ''living warmth of the hei tiki'' and the ''cold virginity'' of
tribal tradition symbolized by the mountain volcano in the
background. Personalized bourgeois romance is thus set up to
triumph over the tribe's ''barbaric'' sacrifice of a virgin to the
mountain god. As with *Under the Southern Cross,* there are many
shots of ''traditional'' Maori life—children with tops, stick
games, flax weaving, and steam cooking—all of which convey a
sense of village life as romantic pastoral idyll. But the primary
emphasis is on erotic tension: there are many voyeuristic shots

A production shot from *Hei Tiki,* with the heroine, Princess Mara, on the right.

emphasizing Mara's breasts, especially in one sequence when she slips out to meet Manui in secret.

The climax of the film approaches when, in a lengthy sequence, Manui returns with other members of his tribe and uses technology to deceive Mara's people into believing that he is the war god come to collect his sacrifice. Manui emerges through a cloud of smoke and successfully claims Mara from her father, and so the lovers are able to escape. Before long, their deception is uncovered and a reasonably dramatic war canoe pursuit follows. Mara's father resolves the subsequent conflict by declaring that it must have been the intention of the gods that the tribes unite. He has, of course, just learnt that his daughter is no longer a virgin. Having again resolved the inter-tribal conflict by *deus ex machina* rather than narrative logic, Markey can now return the natives to the forest and their unspoilt romantic idyll.

These three films enable us to form some conclusions about the characteristics of such Noble Savage romances. *The Romance of Hine-Moa* uses a British imperial framework where the ''Maoris

Cast and crew relaxing on the set of *Hei Tiki.*

of New Zealand'' are praised as remarkable for their successful leap from savagery to civilization, which implies praise for the British role in civilizing them, but then proceeds to show the Maori as Noble Savages in a pre-European state of nature. This Maoriland is thus a fantastic (and, needless to say, impossible) prehistoric colony of the Empire. In American films like *Under the Southern Cross* and *Hei Tiki,* on the other hand, the Maori are treated as curiosities from the international menagerie, the consequence perhaps of the United States being unable to celebrate an imperial success with ''native races'' the way the British films could do. This Maoriland is thus a fantastic (but real!) prehistoric land on the outskirts of Western civilization.

First, then, to give it a High Culture spin, Maoriland enabled the humanitarian idealists of the time to preserve their utopian aspirations by preventing native peoples from falling from nature into society and history. It was, in short, designed to prevent the

Maori from becoming fallen like the West itself. This idealism served as an implicit rebuke of the West by holding out a Maori Other who kept intact all the values and aspirations associated nostalgically with nineteenth-century Europe and America before the high-water mark of imperialism, World War I, and the onset of intellectual and technological modernism, an Other who did not suffer doubt because he/she was hermetically sealed within the timeless eternal. Second, however, Maoriland was also a convenient resource for taming threatening images and repressing the material fact of colonization. It annexed all the disparate Maori tribes into one ramshackle category of ''Maori,'' and ideological responses among British, Americans and Pakeha tended to vary not over whether Maoriland existed outside of their own imaginations, but what use they could put it to.

CHAPTER 2: THE BIRTH OF A NATION

Easily the most popular story in New Zealand films and novels, even into the Eighties, features romantic liaisons between Maori and Pakeha. Curiously, they have almost always ended unhappily. Allegorically, most of them are historical romances that work out the national dilemma: how can Maori and Pakeha be brought together in the shadow of the wars that followed the Waitangi Treaty. Instead of the archetypal timeless romances of Hinemoa and Tutanekai made by offshore directors, the nationalist films that developed in the Twenties and Thirties are at pains to demonstrate that the love between a Pakeha man and a Maori woman is a good idea, even if it is hardly practical at that point in the country's history.

The racial romance between a Pakeha man and a Maori woman offered a solution to an existential problem, a means to regain Utopia by marrying the foreigners to the natives. But, in ending on a tragic note or, at best, a bitter-sweet one, these films end up reconfirming the original Fall (exile to the colonies) and an insuperable racial divide.

In the one hopeful variation, half-caste girls (never boys) are recuperated back into civilized society to atone for the original sexual/racial transgression of their parents. Until the Seventies, New Zealand films invariably paired a Pakeha man with a Maori woman, never the reverse, and even with that formula it took until as late as 1952 to produce a happy ending. Aside from *Broken Barrier,* these films were all somewhat literally minded; for example, Rudall Hayward's films generally kill off the heroine at the climactic moment, suggesting that the older paternalism had difficulty in sanctioning even fictional cross-racial romances if they were simply not the norm for middle- and upper-class Pakeha. Given the paternal social structure of the time, if there was some chance of a successful union when the man was Pakeha, there was none when the man was Maori.[28]

It helps to recall, I think, that miscegenation was officially outlawed from Hollywood films by the Production Code from the Twenties until 1954. New Zealand never had such explicit guidelines drawn up, either officially or unofficially. The Cinematograph Films Act of 1916 (little altered in 1928 and 1961) contained only the following prohibition: of "matter that is contrary to public order or decency, or the exhibition of which would for any other reason be undesirable in the public interest." Only in 1976 did this change to prohibit "the extent and degree to which the film denigrates any particular class of the general public by reference to the colour, race, or ethnic or national origins, the sex, or the religious beliefs of the members of that class." This suggests that there was probably no need to pass stricter censorship legislation in the Twenties and Thirties, since no filmmakers really tested the limits of what could and could not be said. Alternatively, perhaps filmmakers and audiences in New Zealand were more prepared than the Americans to accept cross-racial romances in films and novels. Certainly, New Zealand's history has always contained many real-life "romances" of this kind.

THE FILMS OF RUDALL HAYWARD

Rudall Hayward is widely recognized as New Zealand's greatest pioneering filmmaker, and his career spans from the Twenties until the Seventies. This period roughly coincides with the heyday of the Integration Myth, and of all New Zealand filmmakers he has explored the genre of the cross-racial romance more than anyone, extending it to his private life. In his second feature, the historical epic *Rewi's Last Stand* (1925), Hayward began a tradition in film which held out a tentative hope that one day love might triumph at a personal level despite the irreconcilable political differences between British and Maori races. Rewi Maniapoto is the title character though not the hero (that role is reserved for a Pakeha). Rewi himself is the embodiment of the Romantic Savage, a heroic representative of the old-time Maori, doomed to pass from the land after the battle of Orakau as British civilization spreads. Hence the film's title. Only one reel of it now survives.

This early version of *Rewi's Last Stand* falls into the tragic
mode in that just as Rewi is doomed, overwhelmed by the British
Army (the agents of history), so too are the potential lovers
doomed in the fashion of Romeo and Juliet. They are overwhelmed by a narrative in which the warrior code and racial and
sexual differences triumph over ordinary people thrown together
by historical happenstance. The film does not promise much of a
future for bicultural nationhood.

THE TE KOOTI TRAIL

Rudall Hayward's *The Te Kooti Trail* (1927) is an extraordinary
historical epic, rich in the contradictions of the age and a good
guide to the transitional allegiances from empire to nation. Most
importantly, it provides a wide range of stereotyped heroes and
villains. If Rewi Maniapoto has come down in British and Pakeha
histories as the epitome of the heroic old-time Maori, Te Kooti
Rikirangi (like Te Rauparaha) has sired an alternative stereotype
of treachery and violence, and he provides an exotic backdrop for
the film. As Auckland's *Sun* newspaper of 18 November, 1927
remarked: "Mr. Rudall Hayward, in filming historical events in
the romantic career of Te Kooti, murderous rebel or sanctified
saint according to which particular school of Maori thought one
leans to, has done New Zealanders good service. There is a
generation in New Zealand today which knows not Te Kooti. To
many, if indeed, they have heard of him at all, he is something of
a myth, and may be placed in the same class as Hinemoa and
Tutanekai."

The exposition provides an allegory of the nineteenth- and early
twentieth-century Pioneer Myth: New Zealand was an imperial
experiment wherein the "pathways" (to quote the dialogue) were
made safe for future settlers, and the seeds of nationhood were
planted by the unrecognized Lost Legions and heroic individualists gone before. Although the film opens with the prototypical
New Zealand settler soldier, Eric Mantell from England, it soon
displaces him from the narrative center and introduces Jean
Guerrin, to whom the film is dedicated: "I only hope that this
humble epic may awaken a greater public interest in the history of

our dear country, and perhaps cause some suitable monument to be placed on the nameless grave of heroic Jean Guerrin." From this it is possible to infer that Hayward intended *The Te Kooti Trail* to foster a sense of national unity and pride based on a recognition of the nation's historical past. Of course, Guerrin is a little different from Mantell; he is French, not English, and he has married a Maori woman, Irahapeti. She, in turn, is the daughter of a neighboring chief and they live mainly with other Maori— Irahapeti's sister (Monika), Monika's lover (Taranahi), and several others. Hayward's nation-building here is rather on the idealistic side; the little community of Guerrin and Maori friends is described as "a peace-loving and industrious little tribe of brown people friendly to the British."[29]

In the scenes following, the message is clear: Te Kooti and Maori nationalism cannot tolerate New Zealand nationalism and biculturalism where Maori and Pakeha live in peace. Te Kooti's troops attack the little community and kill Guerrin, execute Monika (for refusing to reveal where the ammunition is hidden), and force Irahapeti to marry one of Te Kooti's men. Since, in Hayward's view, nationalism must be preserved, then the only solution, it so develops, must be a military one involving an alliance between British soldiers and Maori kupapa ("friendlies") to eliminate Maori separatism (*c.f. Utu, q.v.*).

Ironically enough, it is Te Kooti's aide, the half-caste Baker McLean (Peka Makarini)—the living embodiment of biculturalism—who is vilified as the evil force in this morality tale. He is almost a diabolical creation. He too was based on a real historical figure, the illegitimate son of Donald McLean, Native Secretary and Native Minister. After being educated in England, Peka returned to New Zealand and joined Te Kooti's rebellion, whereupon he became the literal embodiment of that once most feared and hated phenomenon, the half-caste. Te Kooti, by contrast, remains a shadowy figure, always on the edge of the action, given to quoting biblical apocalypse and quite obviously power-crazed.

As in D. W. Griffith's *The Birth of a Nation* (1915), *The Te Kooti Trail* appears to condemn miscegenation by emphasizing Peka's half-caste status. This strikes a strange note in view of the Guerrin marriage, but it could be interpreted as the unacceptable face of union between Maori and Pakeha—unacceptable when the half-caste identifies with Maori nationalism. Similarly with christianity; its unacceptable side is personified by Te Kooti the prophet, and its acceptable side by the moment when Monika's crucifix transfixes one of Te Kooti's warriors. Since Guerrin has been eliminated, the new prototype for a future Pakeha identity is army Lieutenant Gilbert Mair. On witnessing Peka's handiwork (the execution of Monika), Mair declares, "Well boys, Vengeance is an ugly thing for a white man to speak of, but I swear that I shall never rest until I bring that Bloody monster Baker McLean to Justice." Taranahi, the Noble Savage, has similar desires—"Utu! Utu!"—and the two men successfully combine, British and Maori, to kill Peka. Interestingly, this entails the usual dichotomy between British Law and Justice versus the bloody monstrous Ignoble Savage, but here the white man must lower himself to a "Vengeance" which somewhat resembles Maori "Utu." The implication once again is that British and Maori can be one people, but not biologically within the same person. Since Taranahi is mortally wounded in this encounter, Maori representation in the film is effectively wiped out, leaving the Pakeha in control. Taranahi has the dubious consolation of being able to join Monika in death (via a series of remarkable superimpositions); his spirit can be seen on a faraway hill joining hers while his body lies cradled in Mair's arms. The final image in the film is of Mair's memorial in Rotorua, on which are written the words, "In memory of an English gentleman and soldier who loved the Maori race."

And what of Maoriland? The familiar images do appear in the film, in particular a scene in which Taranahi plays his flute for Monika, and another when the lovers are in a canoe on the river. However, these are immediately followed by the sub-title, "Peace in the valley but far in the mountains the war trails shook 'neath the rush of many feet," as if to suggest that the Maoriland of this Hinemoa and her Tutanekai cannot survive against the warrior tradition of Maori nationalism. The Noble Savage ends up being obliterated by the Ignoble Savage rather than by British imperialism!

Immediately prior to *The Te Kooti Trail*'s release in 1927 it became one of New Zealand's greatest censorship controversies. To begin with, it was held up by the Film Censor, W. A. Tanner, who was sensitive to complaints by a number of influential Ringatu Maori who resented a film being made about Te Kooti's life. It was not helped by Hayward weighing in with the following public statement to the Auckland *Sun*: ''The superstitious Maoris still look on Te Kooti as something approaching a saint. They are objecting to the part he plays in my picture, where he is shown in his true character as a misguided patriot . . . . The Government is paying altogether too much attention to the imagined grievances of the chiefs . . . . What would have been the position in America if the Government had forbidden the taking of Indian pictures which had been the mainstay of their industry, as Maori pictures were to New Zealand?''

Despite all this, when the film was finally released, the reviews were favorable.[30] It is an exciting film, after all, and Hayward's direction, photography, and editing of parallel plot lines are once again excellent. The *Sun* of 18 November pretty much summed up all the key issues when it described it as being about ''a period of national adolescence'' which ''gave a glimpse of a beautiful wooded country upon which the blood of Maori and Pakeha have mingled and rendered it sacred.'' The reviewer was enthusiastic about the Maori cast, somewhat cooler about the ''Europeans,'' and at one point remarked, ''There certainly seemed no grounds upon which the Ringatu people could be offended by this representation of their founder.'' Out of these conflicting points of view, it is pointless trying to identify a unitary Pakeha perspective, but there is undoubtedly a shared assumption that ''New Zealand'' is the proper context for viewing *The Te Kooti Trail,* that Ringatu fears must be overridden in the national interest, and that film companies were crucial in the Dominion's growth toward maturity. Finally, and most intriguingly, these arguments are identical to those raised in the Eighties in defence of New Zealand's ''reviving'' film industry.

REWI'S LAST STAND

Several films later in 1940, Rudall Hayward remade *Rewi's Last Stand* for Frontier Films Ltd, and it now exists only in the foreshortened version known as *The Last Stand,* but both versions are at any rate quite different from the 1925 film of the same name. The latter had raised the tentative possibility of a love story

A poster for *Rewi's Last Stand* (1940) that displays the paradox of the film: while the key art and title focus on the Maori, the film's actual protagonists are British.

between a British soldier and a Maori woman, a love story which like Romeo and Juliet must tragically fail because of an insurmountable racial difference. In *The Te Kooti Trail,* Hayward had identified sympathetically with the cross-racial marriage between Jean Guerrin and Irahapeti, while retaining a sentimental fondness for the Hinemoa-Tutanekai courtship of Monika and Taranahi. The film nevertheless condemned the half-caste Peka, suggesting that the proper recipe for nation-building was British paternalism and Maori subservience. Britain assumed the stereotypical "masculine" role (the Law, justice, rationality) and the Maori the "feminine" (Nature, the emotions, the irrational). There was no suggestion of the reverse being applied. The narrative for the second *Rewi's Last Stand* returns to the cross-racial formula of the first version, and even in 1940 remains pessimistic about its success.

The film was shot in 1938–39, largely in the Te Awamutu area, with considerable local support. Battle scenes were shot near the original site of the battle of Orakau in the Waikato. The film was released in Auckland in April 1940 and the reedited version, *The Last Stand,* screened in Britain in 1949 and then again in New Zealand in 1955.[31]

The film opens with a rolling sub-title which offers clues to the subtle changes in outlook made possible after a period of 15 years:

> In New Zealand after the Maori Wars of the Sixties, men of famous British regiments took up land and became soldier-settlers. Near one of the towns they founded—Te Awamutu—the townspeople filmed recently these pages from rough-hewn history, reenacting on the actual locations the parts played by their pioneering forefathers. In the struggle for possession of this land of promise the "Pakehas" (white men) found the Maoris tough and chivalrous fighters who were often defeated by sheer weight of arms but were never conquered. Today the slowly blending races of white men and brown live in peace and equality as one people . . . the New Zealanders.

This time the emphasis is no longer on dramatizing a famous episode in Britain's conquest of Empire, or on the romantic deeds of victorious British soldiers and their gallant Maori foes going down to defeat. Rather, this time the emphasis is on a trading off

A poster for *Rewi's Last Stand:* the feminine (Maori) figure as sacrificial object.

of Maori and British as joint partners in the nation-building of New Zealand. Even if the Maori once again go down to defeat and the cross-racial romance does not last, the film does not pose the racial differences as irreconcilable. The romance might even have survived had it not been for the war. The film, then, is a more fully developed thesis on the possibility of integration—of common identity despite racial difference—facilitated in this case by having the Maori woman be a half-caste raised among the Pakeha community.

It is April 1863, and the pages of James Cowan's book *The New Zealand Wars* are seen turning, invoking the authority of the Historical Myth (even though the three main characters are fictional). In a sequence reminiscent of John Ford westerns, Pakeha settlers are seen evacuating the Waikato under the threat of war. One of them is the film's hero, Bob Beaumont, a young Pakeha storekeeper. He is fluent in Maori, a confident young man who warns that Tamehana and the other chiefs may not be able to control the Maniapoto war parties, and the scene is cross-cut with threatening close-ups of watching Maori warriors. They are in full tattoo and have come to seize all half-castes before the conflict worsens.

The opening sequence, then, reconfirms a racial difference between the peaceful British and the war-like Maori. No middle ground is tolerated between the two, neither in terms of the land, nor the half-castes who carry the conflict marked on their bodies. What is also clear is that the film's main thematic problem is displaced from the political dispute over the land to the personal dispute over the fate of the local Reverend's adopted daughter, Ariana, a half-caste of aristocratic birth with whom our hero, Bob Beaumont, has fallen in love.

With this displacement to the personal, two questions drive the narrative: what will be the final fate of Bob's and Ariana's romance, and what is the answer to the enigma of Ariana's parentage? Both can be resolved by a (re)union of the Maori woman with a Pakeha man—through Ariana marrying Bob, and Ariana being reconciled with her unknown father. Allegorically, this sets up a dual quest for the nation's future and its origins. It can only be resolved by Ariana's crucial choice later on in the film: whether to side with Male/Father/Pakeha or with Female/Mother/Maori.

Initially, the Maori choice has been rendered the extremist one since it is the Maniapotos who have (supposedly) polarized the dispute by kidnapping all the half-castes like Ariana and eliminated choice. As if to confirm the view that no mediating positions are possible when the Maori are being so stubborn, Bob Beaumont joins the para-military Forest Rangers and is greeted by its captain with: ''We're just plain colonials.'' As with the earlier *Rewi's Last Stand,* the Forest Rangers are presented in admiring terms: they are sarcastic about the so-called ''glorious life'' they lead, but their plain-speaking, down-to-earth heroism is the familiar Hayward prototype for a Pakeha identity, an identity the citizens of Te Awamutu would no doubt have been proud of. It closely resembles the frontier mythology of American westerns and there are several sequences in the film which feature Bob galloping across farm country or through forests, exchanging shots with Maori war parties, all to the accompaniment of the excellent romantic musical score.

The narrative is placed more properly in historical perspective at this point with a shot of Governor Grey's proclamation to the Waikato chiefs, which is overlaid by an anonymous voice-over narration which can only be that of Bob Beaumont in hindsight, reflecting on the events that have already occurred. The effect of this narration is to immediately cast a fateful tone over the action. It proceeds to explain how the Waikato Maori are preparing for war and then, more curiously, it states: ''Ariana had taken her *rightful* place as a tribal leader in entertaining the visitors'' (my emphasis), which emphasizes her Maori lineage. A negative interpretation might have it that Bob is rationalizing the future failure of the narrative to bring the couple together, as if to say that Ariana was Maori after all, so how could it have worked? In the meantime, Bob manages to find Ariana down by the river away from the village (this scene is accompanied by the love motif on the soundtrack), and he escapes down river with her. Before long they are discovered and pursued by the warriors in a war canoe chase sequence. This forces Ariana to make her crucial choice: should she go with Maori or Pakeha, mother or father, feminine or masculine?

Ariana's choice between Bob and her Maori people is essentially a tragic one, and, metaphorically, it was the choice many Maori people faced during the era of the Integration Myth. Bob is

Excerpts from a *Rewi's Last Stand* poster that reflect the two tensions in the film: war story (masculine) versus love story (feminine).

keen for Ariana to meet one of the Forest Rangers, the avuncular
Ben Horton, and it will turn out that Ben is her long-lost father.
This would justify her return to Pakeha society by invoking blood
ties on patriarchal grounds just as the Maniapotos invoked her
matriarchal bloodline. However, Ariana chooses her Maori side:
"Maori women fight beside their men . . . . I can't change what is
in me . . . . For us there can only be now."

This dialogue implies several things about Hayward's construction of the double bind. First, that Ariana, and by implication
Maori culture, tend to think collectively, in a belief that the land
must be defended collectively. Compare this with Bob, and by
implication Pakeha culture, which tends to think individualisti-
cally and hires impersonal military professionals to fight its war.
Second, it is implied that Ariana ought to recognize Bob's love
and abandon the Maori cause altogether. That she chooses not to
means that her romantic Maori nature overcomes her British
commonsense. Certainly, she is a tragic heroine for choosing
commitment to a lost cause rather than opting out for selfish and
individualistic reasons, however history will roll right over her.
Third, her argument sounds like racial and biological determinism
("I can't change what is in me"), and thus it is the Maori who
appear to be the more stubbornly inflexible.

After having displaced the political to the personal, only now
that it is too late does the film reverse its strategy and sacrifice
personal destinies to political destinies. The film commences a
historical overview for the oncoming battle of Orakau. It provides
newspaper headlines and an animated map to suggest documen-
tary-like historical data, over which can be heard Bob's hindsight
voice-over: "In nine months most of the tribes were defeated and
dispersed. The danger to pioneer settlement was over."

The Orakau sequences run through the entire last third of the
film. They begin with cross-cutting between the Waikato and
Maniapoto preparing their trenches (including Rewi's famous
"Last night I had a dream. I saw a kite falling"), and the British
military coolly discussing tactics, again underlining the racial
contrast between the emotional Maori and the rational British.
What follows is a masterpiece of realist editing and war photography, supported by a musical score that whips up the tension with
great booming sounds and taut strings. British troops with their
bayonets and moustaches attack the Maori trenches and are mown

down in the crossfire against the thunder of guns and explosions all across the battlefield. The British retreat, leaving the broken bodies of the dead of both sides. When Maori reinforcements arrive and perform a haka (war chant), Bob Beaumont's voice-over returns to restore order with a mention of the warriors' "savage spirits" (echoing the earlier Rewi). Again, this tends to reveal more about Beaumont's interpretation of events than the film's since there is no reason why the authority of the film should coincide with its protagonist. If anything, because the battle is shot mostly from within the Maori trenches, this tends to encourage identification with the "savage spirits" of the Maori! However, the film then switches allegiance to the British trenches and the two most celebrated scenes of the Orakau siege follow: Tama Te Heuheu creeps through the lines to find water for the dying, and during the ceasefire, Rewi Maniapoto declares (translated as), "Friend, I shall fight you forever, forever." General Cameron's response: "What glory can there be in killing men like these?"

The final storming of the Orakau defences is most moving: Maori women fighting with blood on their faces, men on crutches, children in there too. The next scenes are carnage: a warrior is bayoneted in close-up, the cavalry ride down the fleeing defenders, and both Ariana and Tama are hit, Tama fatally as he fights a rearguard action. The music wells up and Bob finds Ariana just before Ben Horton (her father), and, though it is not entirely clear, it would seem that Ariana dies in Bob's arms.[32]

Hayward's decision to shoot the most dramatic sequence in the film so as to show this carnage makes for a highly ambiguous non-resolution to the film. After the personal dilemmas being given first priority in the narrative and then all hopes dashed with Ariana's fatal choice, a massacre might have been expected. But how is it possible to celebrate the Maori warriors' valor and courage as one is massacring them? They are only defending their land and culture after all. Did not the British, for all their heroism and restraint, commit excessive atrocities in subduing Maori resistance? Was it necessary to kill women and children? (Back in 1925, the program notes for the earlier *Rewi's Last Stand* had tried to rationalize this with a ludicrous disclaimer that the Maori women were short-haired and so indistinguishable from the men.) Most of all, did the British not provoke this tragedy in the first place? Technically speaking, historians now tend to blame not the British Army (General Cameron was a model of deliberate tactical indecisiveness), but the rapacious land-hungry settler-colonists who were pushing for war. But either way the film's violent climactic scenes can generate a sense of moral outrage in its audiences, suggesting that the "Maori Wars" were less the heroic struggle of empire than the bloody tragedy of a nation's origins, admittedly a relatively contemporary idea. A disturbing tremor ripples back through memory to the opening sub-title which speaks of peace and equality as one people—the New Zealanders.

Hayward's film, for better or worse, undermines its own premise; to return to this version of history for guidance in the national experiment—for "origins" means (re)discovering a tragedy. Ariana chose her Maori side; the British retaliated with a massacre!

The release of *Rewi's Last Stand* was not in the most encouraging of circumstances. In 1940, New Zealand and Britain were at war with Germany and in neither nation was there much interest in a film which cast doubt on the legitimacy of the imperial age, the morality of warfare, and romances across the barrier. Certainly, at a private screening in Wellington, it received a generous tribute from the influential British documentary filmmaker, John Grierson. According to the press of the time, "Mr. Grierson said that it was more important that New Zealanders should have produced that film than that they should see a hundred films from Hollywood. Not that good films were not made in Hollywood, for they were, but because in this film they had just seen, a nation had expressed itself."[33] If a nation had indeed expressed itself, then it was expressed through the familiar double bind and the film's viewers would have had to grapple with it.

Rewi's Last Stand's thesis in essence is this: given the ambiguous status of half-castes in the film, the willingness by both sides to claim them forces the inexorable double bind of Waitangi, in which one must be British or Maori but not both. In this New Zealand there is no joint contract. In choosing her Maori side, Ariana effectively rejects her British side and is forced to pay for it with her life. In a sense she is triply punished since she rejects both her paternal lineage, and a future bicultural marriage with Bob, and she loses her life. That is not a narrative resolution designed to please audiences. How could one celebrate a joint nationhood when one was implicated (however indirectly) in the death of one's lover? It would be over forty years before a film appeared with a more accommodating reconciliation; that film was *Utu* (1983).

CHAPTER 3: ROMANCES IN MAORILAND

The links between tourism and ethnography are by now well-known. Particularly since Claude Lévi-Strauss' masterpiece, *Tristes Tropiques* (1955), many anthropologists have begun to examine these links against the wider context of European and American imperialism in the eighteenth and nineteenth centuries and the gradual "democratization" of both practices in the twentieth.[34]

So far as New Zealand is concerned, tourism and ethnography were there from the beginning. The main period of racial conflict was over by the late nineteenth century, and the transfer of exotic trophies, totems, and legends from Maori custody to newly established Pakeha museums, private collections, and literary anthologies virtually complete. Not only did these trophies provide excellent devices for attracting tourists (and ethnographers) to New Zealand, they also provided a reservoir of images on which to build the burgeoning postcard industry and early tourism films. The Maori were, from the beginning, a key part of that package, and at the turn of the century Thomas Cook Tours were advertising them in the following way: "The Maoris, whose presence, together with their strange habits, customs, and legendary lore, adds greatly to the interest of a visit to New Zealand . . . . They are undoubtedly a splendid race, although, unfortunately, the type met with along some of the well-worn tourist routes presents anything but a fair representation."[35] Already within this passage—well before the explosion of mass-market tourism—can be read the archetypical tourist's (or ethnographer's) frustration at witnessing the paradox of his activity: tourism destroys the very authenticity it desires.

As the transfer of Maori space (land and taonga/treasures) continued in exchange for time ("progress"), this necessitated at least some token preservation of Maoriland before it died out completely. There were two favorite locations for this and they

This model village tableau from *Amokura* (1928) captures one of the dilemmas of late imperial filmmaking. Tourism films, like ethnographic films, contradict the authenticity they desire.

both resembled frontier zones. The first was the model village of Whakarewarewa near Rotorua—the most filmed location in New Zealand—which came complete with its own geology, archaeology, and anthropology. The second was the Whanganui River—extremely popular at the time for its river boat tours—which provided the primeval Bush virtually untouched by human habitation. Furthermore, if Maoriland was on display in model villages, in thermal areas, on river boat tours, and in museums, then primarily it was arranged visually, implying that tourism and ethnography were processes by which a moving spectator imbued life onto what was essentially dead or frozen in time because it was static. The tourist or the ethnographer moved through time and in time, resurrecting a life for objects and places almost lost to time and not yet pressed into the service of progress (i.e. pastureland). It was all an illusion, of course, for Maori and mixed Maori/Pakeha communities were dotted all over New Zealand and they were not dying out by any means, despite periodic epidemics of influenza.

There is a strange paradox here: if the Maori were as exotic as the land itself and therefore a source of tourist income, then this also tended to imply that much of the land was "theirs." Although colonialism was a process for wresting the land from the indigenous people, it was also predicated on a strict demarcation of "theirs" from "ours." For one thing, if this demarcation was not maintained, then the Maori could no longer be useful as a tourist or ethnographic resource. For another, there was never any alternative to this anyway, since Pakeha New Zealand and Maori New Zealand occupied different territories. Necessarily, Maoriland was useful as a point of comparison: it demonstrated that contemporary Maori had abandoned Maoriland's "barbaric" ways and now the rest of New Zealand could be subjected to the system of property acquisition and ownership that arrived with colonization. Advertising of the period was directed as much at prospective settler-farmers as it was at the leisured or ailing tourist. In the publicity books available at the time, many of them published by the Department of Tourist and Health Resorts, the appeal was always three-pronged: to "the tourist, the health-seeker, and the home-seeker."[36] While tourism photography specialized in waterfalls, bush scenes, and erotic/exotic Maori, and most of the business advertising was for traveling rugs, cigarettes and tobacco, hotels, and shipping companies, there was also regular advertising by land and real estate agents seeking to attract more British immigrants and investment.

If there are differences between the grand tour-ism of the upper-middle classes and the early ethnographers, then it was only a question of the degree to which they spent time annexing Maori culture and translating it into the space occupied by their writing. Some tourists went home and wrote voluminous books about the highways and by-ways of Maoriland; early ethnographers were like long-term tourists motivated by the same fascination as the day-tripper, except that they went to almost obsessive lengths to match it to a prevailing ideology. Film likewise belongs with these two practices. As a technology which developed historically at exactly this time, it might have been made to order for them. Far more than writing, film technology and its narratives amount to the almost complete reduction of space to time and thus resemble their contemporaries, the telephone and the airplane.

In the preceding chapters, I drew a distinction between the

timeless romances of imperial Maoriland and the historical romances of national New Zealand. The former excluded the Maori from present space and time, the distance being traversible only by the filmmakers' conjuring tricks. The latter annexed the Maori into British space and time but placed them both ''on the margins'' and ''behind'' the progressive British/Pakeha. The subject of this chapter is two further genres which straddle these two contradictory ideas without ever resolving them. For this reason, the films discussed here can be read equally as tourism romances and as ethnographic romances, though for the sake of keeping their intentions clear I have bracketed them off from each other (see Figure 2).

The key to the tourism romance or travelogue is the juxtaposition side-by-side of two separate worlds. The first, Maoriland, is a world outside time, a lost world even, into which the tourist may

Figure 2:

Timeless and historical romances, ethnographic and tourism romances.

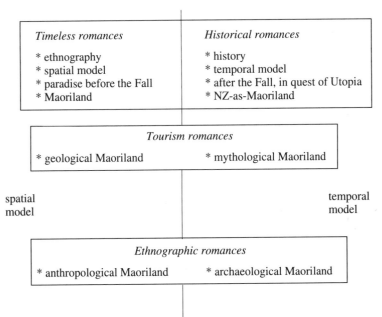

step briefly and tantalizingly before returning to the luxury and comfort of the nearby hotel, and the hotel is, of course, in New Zealand in real and historical time. The thermal area around Rotorua was the favorite location for this: Maoriland hisses and bubbles and its geology is profoundly unstable, but in nearby New Zealand the hotels are havens where one can obtain a cup of tea and a good night's sleep.

Much less common is an alternative in which the two worlds are juxtaposed temporally rather than spatially, where New Zealand physically displaces Maoriland. Instead of offering Utopia as a tourist attraction, this narrative offers the Fall, making use of the romantic legends drawn from Maori mythology.

Ethnographic romances also have both spatial and temporal options: either they juxtapose the timeless world of Maoriland as next to (or within) present-day historical New Zealand, and the ethnographer ventures into it on his anthropological mission of salvage and recovery; or they banish Maoriland to the past before the New Zealand of today, which only the archaeologist can recover. Usually they try to do both and so confuse themselves.

Both tourism and ethnographic romances are founded on the contradictions of the Historical Myth: do the Maori live in Maoriland or New Zealand? Do they live in the historical past or the ethnographic present? Do the films record the reconstructed past or the soon-to-be-lost present? An archaeology or an eschatology? As we shall see, neither the James McDonald films nor the Government Publicity Office films of the Twenties and Thirties ever resolved this contradiction. The Maoriland they represent is assumed to be in a state of terminal cultural decay, with both genres being haunted by the fear of lost authenticity. But did this imply that the Maori were fast becoming New Zealanders, and did it also necessitate repressing the whole regrettable weight of colonization? These were, of course, questions for a later age.

THE FILMS OF JAMES MCDONALD

James McDonald began work for the Dominion (now the National) Museum in 1904, and by 1907 he was also shooting "scenics" for the Tourist Department. The four films "about" the Maori that he made for the Museum from 1919 till 1923 are now regarded as the highlights of his career. They were intended to be part of a larger series, with further expeditions planned to Taupo, the Bay of Plenty, Rotorua, and the Urewera, but these never took place. The expeditions consisted of the Museum's ethnologist and Director, Elsdon Best, the Librarian at the Alexander Turnbull Library, Johannes C. Andersen, and McDonald. The films fall into two groups: in the first two, a hui (ceremonial occasion) serves as a starting point from which to record informal demonstrations of "traditional" activities. The other two are confined solely to the demonstrations themselves. There is no evidence that the films were ever edited into exhibition copies, although apparently some of the footage was shown publicly just after it was shot.

Essentially, the McDonald films are products of the Eighties as much as the Twenties in that they were restored and assembled for public screenings between 1981 and 1985 with titles and sub-titles based on McDonald's original notes. Historically, they preceded the main surge in government filmmaking and were never more than "occasionals" shot by enthusiastic mavericks operating on the margins of government. Although the government of the day could see the benefits of tourism publicity, it was not especially interested in preserving on film the "traditional" activities of a race who were supposedly abandoning their old ways and becoming "modern" New Zealanders. Furthermore, there was the more negative view around that the Maori were a drain on the taxpayer.

Stylistically, a number of things are apparent from what survives of the films. First, there is no narrative structure as such and the camera remains static. The action moves in and out of frame, suggesting a decision by McDonald not to intervene too obviously in the activities being filmed. Andersen and Best themselves frequently appear in frame and there is a good deal of banter and humor between the "subjects" in front of the camera and those off-camera. Dogs and children wander past in the background or observe in the foreground, and the effect is the kind of unself-conscious and relaxed rapport usually associated with Home Movies. Second, and pulling against the informality, is the serio-comic business of recording ethnographic "facts." This is partly the effect of using sub-titles to provide the names of the

James McDonald took this photo while shooting the material that has become known as *Scenes at the Rotorua Hui* (1920). It shows welcoming ceremonies for the Prince of Wales.

people being filmed and the bare minimum of descriptive information about what they are doing, and partly the effect of many of these people looking directly at the camera, even bowing to it to end a scene. In the tension between these two perspectives—between insider knowledge and objective representation—can be read one of the anthropological dilemmas of the age: can a relative insider formulate an objective picture of a culture?

Significantly, until Television New Zealand's *Tangata Whenua* series in 1974, these were the only films ever produced under the auspices of the New Zealand Government in which the film-makers themselves appear, and perhaps that only goes to suggest that these were the last films on Maori themes for some fifty years in which there was substantial Maori imput. Certainly they were made partly at the insistence of a Maori member of Parliament, Sir Apirana Ngata, and so occupy a peculiar existence at the bicultu-

Scenes at the Rotorua Hui: anthropologist Elsdon Best (left) observes demonstrations of Maori string games.

ral edge between a Pakeha-controlled technology and the Maori subjects of the film. In that sense, the films in the Eighties and beyond are a window into the past and the future, particularly for those Maori whose tipuna (ancestors) and tribal areas appear in them. These films are not simply "historical records"; they are also Home Movies—both literally and figuratively. From 1922 onward, unfortunately, government and independent filmmaking resumed the master narratives of empire and nation, against which the Maori were measured. If the McDonald films have benefited from never being edited into release prints with sub-titles (except recently), then it is precisely in their ambiguously "silent" status that their appeal resides. They evoke neither a timeless eternal nor the historical past.

It would help at this point, I think, to ask what the McDonald/Best/Andersen expeditions wanted from these films. The work of Elsdon Best, for example, is now generally placed in the transition period between the nineteenth-century "armchair" anthropologists such as James Frazer, who relied almost solely on the reports of others from the imperial margins (travelers, government offi-

Scenes of Maori Life on the East Coast (1923): this photo taken at Waiapu on the East Coast shows women with traditional moko making kete (flax bags).

general and the nation's past in particular as a justification for its own existence. It assumed that ghosts in the machine are better than no ghosts at all.

A sign of the increased interest in all this is that G. H. L. Pitt-Rivers of the British functionalist school accompanied Best on one of the Whanganui River trips. Pitt-Rivers was looking for evidence to support his modernist thesis of global disintegration:

> Close study of the world of reality gives no assurance of any present tendency towards integration, harmony, and unity, but reveals a contrary tendency towards disintegration and the dissolution of aggregates, whether of empires, nations, races, creeds, or classes.[39]

Predictably enough, Pitt-Rivers' book is concerned mostly with "cultural decay," and his Maori chapter is titled "Culture Clash in a Maori Village—Some Observations on the Passing of the Maori Race and the Decay of Maori Culture." In it he expresses what seems like disappointment at finding Maori culture on the Whanganui River rapidly adapting to Pakeha ways!

> I hoped that I might be privileged to observe, not exclusively with the eyes of a stranger and a twentieth century European, but that I might, with his assistance, gain something of perspective and peep back through borrowed spectacles into the intimacies of history that is past, and attempt to understand the viewpoint of a forgotten as well as of the present Maori generation.[40]

What he finds is three distinct generations of Maori where the decay has indeed set in with the erosion of the Maori tapu system (sacred values) and mana (prestige) of the chiefs, and where "the younger generation are guarded from all knowledge of their pagan past."[41]

It is tempting to interpret Pitt-Rivers' analysis as not much more than the discovery that it was British imperial power that was decaying rather than Maori culture. Curiously, it is the Maori in this scenario who do not have a collective memory, and it is their culture which is supposedly decaying because there is not the technological sophistication to record the data which constitute a memory. Hence the necessity for anthropologists, just as there would one day become a necessity for historians, archivists, and literary theorists.[42]

GOVERNMENT FILMMAKING IN THE TWENTIES & THIRTIES

New Zealand Government Publicity Office interest in things Maori was relatively late in coming and was as much as anything an attempt to capitalize on the general interest in Maori themes shown by independent and foreign filmmakers from 1925 onwards and peaking around 1928. Earlier, in May 1922, the Publicity Office had taken over the Photographic and Cinematographic Section of the Agriculture Department so as to be able to produce more scenic films for tourism promotion. This usually extended to shooting newsreels of visits by famous people and paeans to the nation's triumphant agricultural and industrial progress. None of the films made before 1925 now survives. By 1926, the Publicity Office was making one reel a week for M-G-M release, a practice which would be discontinued in 1930 with the advent of the talkies.

As far as Maori themes are concerned, the Publicity Office did shoot *Maori Hui at Tikitiki* in 1926, presumably an ethnographic study of contemporary Maori celebrations (it does not survive). Then followed some early tourism romances: *Whakarewarewa* (1927), *Valley of Enchantments* (1930), and *New Zealand's River of Romance* (1930). These identify a tourist spot and enumerate the local glories, the emphasis being on leisure activities—sports, boating cruises, strolling in the thermal areas, with relatively little attention paid to the mundane details of accommodation, dining and entertainment, and transportation. The main ethnographic study of the period, the five-part *The Maori As He Was* (1928), was also shot around this time, as was the unusual Maoriland legend, *Amokura,* shot in 1928 but not released until 1934.

After 1930, the output of Government films drops off steeply, a consequence of the Depression and the necessity for soundtracks, and in June 1930, the Government Publicity Office was transferred from the Department of Internal Affairs to the Department of Tourist and Health Resorts.[43] The leanest year was 1932, when only two films were produced. By 1934, a tentative stability had been achieved and several films released in that year (out of eleven or so) were on Maori themes: the ethnographic romances *Ka Mate!* and *Maori Days,* the sound version of *Amokura,* and (in 1935) *Holiday Haunts.* In late 1934, there also began the first of the *Maoriland Movielogues* series to deal with Maori themes: numbers *5* (1934), *9* (1936), and *14* (1939). Maoriland is used in these titles as a synonym for New Zealand, and of the three or four items in each episode, one might be on Maori themes.

First, the tourism romances. In *Whakarewarewa,* a group of tourists is shown around the "old-time Maori village" by a contemporary Maori maiden dressed in traditional costume. The tourists see the famous Hinemoa-Tutanekai gate, Pohutu geyser, steam cooking, and so on, and the guide draws their (and our) attention to the pertinent information in the guidebook. The narrative structure juxtaposes a primitive past (Maoriland) next to the modern present (New Zealand) so that tourists can jump back

into history and ''see'' how early Man lived in primitive times—
the steam cooking, canoe travel, storehouses. Once one enters
Maoriland, one has left history, stepped out of it into the timeless
eternal, only to return to history on leaving for the hotel or golf
course nearby. The Maori guide serves as the link between the two
worlds. In that sense, national tourism romances colonize Maoriland for themselves, preserving it within New Zealand. ''New
Zealand'' in these films is not a state of mind so much as a
geographical location which has existed throughout history, once
formerly under Maori sovereignty and now a Pakeha-dominated
modern nation with oases of timelessness preserved for tourists.

The evolutionary historical model anchors these films in a
self-fulfilling and self-justifying circle, its message being that the
romance of history underpins New Zealand's pride in nation-
building. ''We'' got where we are today by moving from this form
of ''picturesque barbarity'' to modern civilization, and we have
preserved places like this as scientific evidence of that fact. This
does not mean that the films consign contemporary Maori to the
romantic past; as government films they would of necessity
subscribe to the thesis that the Maori were moving into the
twentieth century very successfully. However, this evolutionary
model has the effect of positioning Maori culture within the
double bind of the Integration Myth: the Maori must either be
identified with the lost past of Maoriland or move into the
Promised Land of New Zealand. Not surprisingly, the contemporary Maori has to disappear aside from the Happy Maori of
Whakarewarewa in *Valley of Enchantments* in which ''dusky
native children'' dive for pennies tossed from a bridge by tourists.
These images are sentimental and nostalgic rather than racist, but
in confining the Maori within a tourist framework (as guides,
Maoriland maidens and warriors, and children), their status as
New Zealanders was still obviously in doubt in the films of the
Twenties and Thirties.

The ambiguous identity of the Maori is even more apparent in
independent filmmaking of the period, which otherwise followed
the same principles as government filmmaking. Newsreel-style
historical romances were shot to commemorate visits by famous
people and historical events of national importance such as *Prince
of Wales in Maoriland* (1920), *Waitangi Celebrations* (1934), and
Maoris Demonstrate Their Goodwill and Loyalty at Waitangi

(1934). Other films were more regional in outlook, blending the
newsreel with the tourism romance, for example *Historic Otaki*
(1921). Some film-makers aimed to showcase the offbeat and the
exotic, as in *Journey Into Rua's Stronghold* (1928). There were
also the conventional tourism romances, for example those shot
by the American Fox Movietone News around 1930: *Rotorua NZ:
Penny Diving, The Maori: Everyone Bathes on Washing Day at
Rotorua,* and the film fragment known as "Koura Fishing."
Operating quite separately from everyone else during the Thirties,
Jim Manley shot footage of the building of several giant Maori
canoes to participate in the Waitangi centennial of 1940.

It is in the tourism romances of Fox Movietone News that these
films come as close as any to justifying charges of racism. For
example, *Rotorua NZ: Penny Diving* is a two-minute fragment
consisting of Maori children diving for pennies tossed by Pakeha
tourists. It nowadays comes across rather badly, the voice-over
enthusing, "Wildly, gamely, they scramble for the pennies of the
Pakeha, pennies from heaven." There is also a shot of a young girl
jumping in while the voice-over maintains, "Maori maidens,
graceful naiads of the stream, and talking of springs, how's this?"
and the shot is run in reverse. Straining after catchy phrases
produces some execrable clichés. The same can be said for *The
Maori: Everyone Bathes on Washing Day at Rotorua,* another
two-minute fragment. It shows a Maori family bathing and the
cheerful if paternal voice-over states: "Rotorua, New Zealand—
an earthly paradise with hot water laid on, and the Maoris love to
bathe in these warm springs. Men, women and children together,
with no costumes and no false modesty. Like most things in life,
bathing is fun to these happy children of the happy isles." Mum
says, "Come on in, the water's fine," and when Mum and Dad
dunk each other, the voice-over makes a reference to the Dying
Race mythology: "Now we know what they mean when they say
the Maori is becoming submerged." The film concludes with their
son and daughter doing the same and the voice-over states: "And
here are the water babies—a shampoo for little boy brown . . . but
he's got to take it. Never mind son, in future just keep away from
water and masterful women."

I accept that many readers will find these films racist, however
I think this overstates the case. After all, these Movietone News
films are fundamentally no different from other films of the time,

which forces us into the proposition that genres and narratives used by Pakeha cultural producers at this time were, or were not, inherently racist. There can be little doubt now that they were intended to be facetious, and certainly they were ethnocentric in the sense that they were Pakeha-centered, since they date from a period when there were few alternatives to this point of view. However, if racism assumes a hierarchical value-system which places the Pakeha above the Maori, then it is difficult to read this off directly in the films. If anything, the reverse conclusions can be drawn just as easily. After all, the Maoriland tourism romances sketch a Noble Savage Utopia in order to wax enthusiastic about the supposedly wonderful carefree life and material comforts of the Maori which the Pakeha tourist can share in. This suggests a nostalgia for the old imperial fixities when the Maori were (supposedly) authentically Maori, before the ravages of Western history and technology. Therefore, the success or otherwise of these films depends on the degree to which any viewer is prepared to accept that the Maori on screen are/were typical of all Maori, and this is not unambiguously provided for within the films themselves.

The argument can be better made perhaps in reference to the Government Publicity Office's *Holiday Haunts* (1935), a gem of a film which is replete with the contradictions of the age. The first half is a showcase for Whakarewarewa and its Happy Maoris; the second is a showcase of Pakeha tourists visiting other local sights.

In the opening to the "Maori" half a jaunty Pakeha voice-over asks, "Want a guide? Want a guide? Of course we want a guide to show us Rotorua and New Zealand's thermal regions. And who wouldn't with a guide like this?" . . . and the film cuts to a Maori maiden. The sequences which follow include the Hinemoa-Tutanekai gate, penny-diving, geysers with Maori maidens strategically placed in front of them, boiling mud pools, and Maori cooking and washing in the steam pools. The film's voice-over generates highly ambiguous cultural collisions with these images which are at once paternalistic, ironic, and affectionate, especially over the matters of cooking and washing, and they automatically key the film into decades of Pakeha moralism over Maori hygiene! It is all intended to be droll of course; the voice-over remarks that the steam pools "make housekeeping easy" and "gas bills are quite unknown," and then, over a shot of an elderly kuia (grandmother) doing some cooking it adds, "Luncheon will be served in twenty minutes." Over a shot of children and adults in a steam pool, the voice-over declares, "Washing day is held here on Monday . . . or Tuesday, or Wednesday, or any other day. It makes no difference." While on the one hand these juxtapositions evoke the stereotype of Happy Maoris without a care in the world, and serve as the utopian reproof to a timebound Pakeha work ethic, the intention is nevertheless to promote the "getaway-from-it-all" of tourism discourse. Furthermore, some images, such as a naked Maori naiad and smiling children playing cute for the camera, distantly echo the "coon humor" of the time. No Pakeha woman would ever be so filmed and the shots are obviously staged.

The "Pakeha" half of the film begins with the local golf links (it includes a "thermal hazard"), diving, and bowls. Significantly, the film is equally droll in its treatment of these Pakeha. The sight of Pakeha golfers on the green and another sub-title which reads, "The ladies are waiting with the tea-cups," followed by a shot of the "ladies" waving to the camera, has a humorous self-consciousness about it which is underwritten by the innocence and enthusiasm of the period. The film then goes off to a Maori Wishing Tree with some tourists dutifully tramping around it to the tune of "Here We Go 'round the Mulberry Bush." A bathing sequence follows, demonstrating that "New Zealand girls do not believe in lunching off a lettuce leaf and a lemon in order to keep their schoolgirl figures." By such devices the film attempts to build a confidential and informal relationship with its target viewer—tourism must be fun, it seems to say. Certainly this encourages charges of paternalism, both sexually and culturally, but the film seems to be equally droll toward the Pakeha tourists with their strange golfing attire and cups of tea, and it is ironic about its own self-importance as a narrational authority.

In the tourism romances discussed above, Maoriland exists as an erotic/exotic land of geological and anthropological wonders which is spatially rather than temporally separate from Pakeha New Zealand. It therefore remains accessible to the modern tourist just as it does to the ethnographer. *New Zealand's River of Romance* (1930) offers the alternative temporal narrative and belongs more properly to the genre of the historical romance in that the Maoriland it portrays is no longer accessible except in films. Like the lost world of the archaeologists and romantic fiction writers, Maoriland is swept away by New Zealand within the narrative structure! The film was designed to promote river-boat tours on the Whanganui River and it begins with a clumsy dramatizing of Fenimore Cooper-style romance: "Long ere the white man reached New Zealand, the river was a highway for the slender canoes of Maori braves"—and two Maori braves are demonstrated paddling their canoe. With wild gesticulation and painted moko (tattoo) they evoke Maoriland, but the characters and costumes jump around without much sense of continuity or chronology, and they are finally swept away by scenes of a modern paddle steamer and a canoe-racing carnival.

This use of the historical romance exactly matches that of the official historians who between the Twenties and the Fifties all but abandoned the Maori at the siege of Parihaka in 1881, aside from a brief mention of their "venturesome daring" in World War I.[44] The Maori simply did not exist as such presumably because as New Zealanders their Maori identity became invisible. Significantly, this was also the time that romantic legends of Maoriland were beginning to mushroom in Pakeha writing. Therefore, set alongside the blank in official histories, the only conclusion to be drawn is that not only did "Maori history" cease around the same time that the creation of the Dominion of New Zealand nominally converted settler colonists into nationals, but that the only history the Maori were to be entitled to was in romantic legends. This has the effect of consigning Maori culture to the past and of leaving the momentum of domination with the Pakeha.

So what kind of Maoriland legends were the Maori to be left with? An interesting example is the Government Publicity Office film, *Amokura* (1928/34). Its opening titles describe it as "A romance of Old New Zealand" and "A legendary love story of New Zealand's Maori people"; however, the setting is quite definitely Maoriland in its Fairyland incarnation, not old New Zealand. The story tells of a young Maori maiden, Amokura, who has the misfortune to be tattooed in the manner of a man because her father really wanted a boy. She is able to experience "no joy of womanhood" until she falls in love with Turi, the flute player. Upon hearing her prayers the god Tane removes the moko for one season and Turi's pity blossoms into love. When the season is over, Turi's love remains constant, so Tane removes her moko

Amokura: Turi the flute player.

forever and the lovers find happiness: "My children, you have stood the test. For true love dies not like the fading flowers. Amokura, the tattoo is removed forever." Delightful as the legend is, the film serves as an implicit criticism of traditional moko: "Her dark eyes look sadly out from a face whose beauty was marred by the heavy lines of the tattoo."

It could be argued that the New Zealand Government stands in here, allegorically, as a benevolent father figure supervising the Maoris' abandonment of supposedly savage customs like the moko. On the other hand, the film, which was shot in Rotorua in 1928, was not released that year because it did not seem likely to fill hotels with tourists. How could it do so when it suggested that New Zealand was still wild and uncivilized? Surviving copies date from 1934 when it was finally released (in shortened form, with a lush orchestral score and, most unusual for the time, a woman's voice-over) to ease the dearth of new product.

Ethnographic films also continued intermittently. The most important was the five-part ethnographic series, *The Maori As He Was* (1928), which was named after Elsdon Best's influential book of the same name. According to *The Dominion* newspaper of December 12, 1927, the series was designed "to serve as a historical record of the dawn of civilization in the Dominion . . . for screening in all parts of the world," and the headline reads: "The Maori Race: Historical Record in Film Form." In short, not

A production shot from *Amokura:* Maori subjects, Pakeha filmmakers, but who is the audience?

ethnographic but historical. But as if to contradict such claims to historical truth, the article also claims that the series will portray "every phase of daily life among the Maoris, including their arts and crafts, their customs and superstitions, the preparation and cooking of food, war dances and exercises." Unless the Maori are no longer to be known as Maori but as New Zealanders, then this implies The Maori As He Is. So where does this leave the contemporary Maori of 1927: in the historical past or the ethnographic present? The contradiction is also evident in what is essentially an identical article in *The New Zealand Sporting and Dramatic Review* of a week later which headlined this same piece with "New Government Film: Life Among the Maoris."

The films themselves sometimes support this ambiguity when women carrying reeds from a lakeshore wear Western clothes and performers in the poi dance sport flapper hairstyles. The same applies to the sub-titles. Some are fairly respectful, emphasizing the ingenuity and skill of the Maori, sometimes with a touch of lugubrious humor: "The sewing circle where nimble tongues vie with nimble fingers." However, many of the sub-titles in parts IV and V are excessively sentimental and key into legendary Maoriland: "Keeping Maori blood at fighting heat, the thumpings and jumpings of warrior braves."

PART TWO
NEW ZEALAND

CHAPTER 4: GOVERNMENT NEWSREELS & THE INTEGRATION MYTH

ONE HUNDRED CROWDED YEARS

In 1940, New Zealand celebrated the one hundredth anniversary of the Treaty of Waitangi. As part of the celebrations, the government planned a film of epic proportions never before seen in New Zealand: *One Hundred Crowded Years* (1940). This little known and little seen epic was shot by the Government Film Studios, and it took years of preparation, a huge cast of Maori and Pakeha, and many expensive sets and costumes. It probably would have had some considerable impact on the New Zealand public had it not been overtaken by World War II.

In terms of the argument advanced here, *One Hundred Crowded Years* was the last gasp effort of a decaying government filmmaking institution, and so marks the end of an era. As World War II gripped the national imagination in 1940, domestic concerns seemed ultimately to be of less importance than the global picture. The past would have to be deferred for the urgency of the present, and new ideas, new narratives, and new institutions would be called for. To be fair to the film, however, it also showed signs of what those new ideas would be, particularly in its narration, which sounds as if it has been influenced by American newsreel series such as *The March of Time* (which began in 1935). There is a brash confidence about it which is new for local productions, and one could say that *One Hundred Crowded Years* points to a transition from the imperial romances discussed in the last chapter, where allegiance had been exclusively to Britain, to the national romance asserting independence along the lines already taken by the United States.

The dedication of the film is instructive. As in *Rewi's Last*

One Hundred Crowded Years (1940) rather pompously commemorates the hundred years of nationhood that followed the signing of the Treaty of Waitangi in 1840 (dramatized here).

Stand of the same year, it is conveyed by the pages of a book turning, moving the reader into the story:

> To New Zealand's pioneers who came forth from Britain's ordered ways to the wildness of an untouched land, through trials and dangers they toiled and struggled to hew from the wilderness a fair heritage for their children . . . . And they fulfilled their purpose. One hundred years have passed and we who come after remember with grateful pride those brave men and women, our pioneers.

New Zealand's Pioneer Myth was generally organized around these familiar dualisms of Man/Nature, law/disorder, civilization/ wilderness, and so on, in much the same way as the American Frontier Myth. Such a single-minded pursuit of the colonial life usually necessitated repression of the Maori threat other than in vague references to the "trials and dangers" encountered in the early years.

Structurally, the film goes on to lay out the romantic official version of the nation's history via dramatizations in period costume: foggy London streets where men talk of emigrating to New Zealand, the Waitangi Treaty, the immigrant ships, early settlement and trade, the ''Maori Wars,'' gold, public works, welfare state legislation, and agricultural prosperity. Then, two-thirds of the way through the film, almost as if the filmmakers ran out of money, there is a quite striking shift within the genre from period drama to present-tense newsreel, where a paternal Pakeha voice-over narration summarizes the nation's triumphant technological progress over footage of cities, ships, railways, and so on. It later shifts again when a Maori speaker appears in frame, surprisingly, to present a report on Maori progress and the Integration Myth.

I mostly wish to draw attention here to the film's Maori thesis. After establishing the ''Maori problem,'' a Maori speaker directly addresses the camera in the same epic style:

As a foundation for nationhood, *One Hundred Crowded Years* never doubts that the first contacts between Maori and Pakeha must have been amicable.

> The impact of Western civilization a hundred years ago calls
> for drastic and imperative adjustment in the economic life of
> the Maori people, and in consequence, a transitional period
> had to be endured. My forebears discarded some of their
> tribal customs. In this period differences and disputes arose.
> Happily those days are past and our two races now live
> together in harmony.

The introduction of a Maori speaker to pronounce judgment upon
national integration and history was a striking innovation for the
time. The speaker goes on to remind the viewer that Maori
"individuality" and culture must be respected and sustained as
the "expression of something deep within us." He concludes:

> But music and dancing and art are not enough for this
> modern world. We need also such things as our native land
> development scheme and the adaptation of modern farming
> . . . . There is a reawakening among the Maori people and a
> realization of the need to meet the Pakeha at his own game.

The Pakeha narrator then returns once again to recapitulate the
Pioneer Myth and to exhort the present-day New Zealander to
share in "the undaunted spirit that was theirs."

The fact that the narrative of *One Hundred Crowded Years* is
divided against itself produces a curiously schizophrenic effect.
The first two-thirds sets out the traditional historical romance—
legends and tales in which the heroic pioneers and warriors are the
subject of history, represented by the Pioneer Couple. The last
third of the film deploys something entirely new—a justification
of the national progress in factual, statistical, scientific terms, a
version of the historical romance where the nation itself has
become the subject of history. When colonial history produces a
national culture, a space is wrested from the march of time.

This schizophrenia is consistent with a trend within the historical writing of the time. Then, as now, there were two genres
available to the cultural historian: the historical and the cultural.
The historical approach produces a chronicle of stirring events
from the nation's past and resembles fiction narratives; these
books were generally written to exhort the local readership with
tales of the great pioneers, missionaries and savage warriors, and
they were very much in vogue in New Zealand schools during the

It is difficult to imagine these dedicated soldiers from *One Hundred Crowded Years* lasting more than five minutes against Maori snipers, but then it was more photogenic this way.

Fifties and Sixties. The cultural approach produced anthropological categories such as farming, politics and religion, and resembled scientific, commercial and tourism interests; these were more suited to attracting an overseas readership, and they continue to provide the framework for travel guidebooks. If both of these options were inherited from the nineteenth century, then the most striking thing they display is exactly this split between the temporal and the spatial. Just as the Maori appeared to live within both the historical past and the ethnographic present, this reflected what can only be an essential confusion about where the Pakeha lived in space and time.[45] Even at best, if the supposition was that the Pakeha was riding the tideline of history represented by the British Empire and was therefore ''ahead'' of the Maori, then it was offset by the original lack of land which the Maori quite clearly possessed. So if colonization was a system for the translation of time into space, nationalism became a process for filling in the topography of that newly won space. In W. P. Morrell's *New Zealand* (1935), for example, the first half is a historical chronicle, the second is a cultural survey, and it could be said that his colonial history actually produces a national culture.[46] When this space has been wrested from the march of time, then a nation is finally born.

THE WEEKLY REVIEWS

It is always a pleasure, I think, to discuss films that somehow transcend the petty ideologies so often associated with national identity, not the least of these being racial and ethnic differences defined by time/space metaphors. For a brief period during World War II and in the years immediately following, there are films made by Pakeha New Zealanders that, for a change, do not convert the Maori into "natives," and do not lament their lack of "progress." The Maori represented in the *Weekly Reviews* signify, above all, the pride felt by Pakeha New Zealanders for the

The drive of *One Hundred Crowded Years'*s narrative is toward the establishment of the prototypical pioneer couple. It is from this imperial myth that we have inherited the modern nationalist myth of Man Alone.

Maori during those years. What, after all, was more worthwhile than bringing the nation's two races together in a commitment to unity, identity, and racial harmony as a war of global proportions threatened to engulf everyone? If there is a key tenet of successful nationalism, it is unity across diversity. There is nothing inherently objectionable about a national identity; it is simply that so often the way it is defined causes frictions, exclusions, and identity crises.

The *Weekly Reviews* were an anthology series produced by the National Film Unit for screening each week in New Zealand cinemas between 1941 and 1950.[47] Each one consisted of three or four topical items, and, in that they pictured New Zealanders both at war and at peace, they were the film equivalent of the print or radio news. However, they represent much more than this: they were designed, quite intentionally, to be a propaganda weapon. The National Film Unit's first producer, Stanhope Andrews, wrote in 1952: "In June 1941 the War Cabinet appointed me producer and manager, to organize a National Film Unit and to produce a *Weekly Review* of New Zealand activities at home and abroad. The terms of reference were broad enough to cover any eventuality. They were 'to further the war effort'."[48] Whatever this meant, the *Weekly Reviews* turned out to be the Film Unit's finest films in its nearly 50 years of service. Their signature tune, "On Parade" (from *Sweethearts*), and their "Marching Men" titles (during the war years) are distinctive cultural icons of the period.

The predominant film genre during the Forties was the newsreel, so it was natural that the *Weekly Reviews* would adopt the newsreel style. It was not a new genre of course, being essentially a variant of the historical romance. However, the sense of urgency engendered by the war demanded a hard-headed realism set firmly in the present tense, and that was the newsreel's greatest strength. No place here for the timeless eternal or for striding manfully into the future. Therefore, tourism and ethnographic romances completely disappeared; there was no need to invite tourists to New Zealand in a world at war, and ethnographic research had never been more than an academic luxury. The tourism romances would eventually reappear around 1950 as the world was made safe for tourists, and the ethnographic romances would mutate into their present form (the "pilgrimage genre") throughout the Fifties and

Sixties. Reporting the news would of course be assumed eventually by television, but before this happened, the newsreel spawned a variety of interesting new sub-genres including the social problem documentary (along with its close kin, the educational or instructional film) and the arts and culture documentary, which are discussed in subsequent chapters.

The *Weekly Reviews* certainly impressed the critics. Writing in the periodical *Landfall* in 1955, P. J. Downey praised them because they quickly found ''an authentic New Zealand tone . . . . Audiences were delighted to see reflected on the screen the face of workmate and acquaintance, and in the background the New Zealand landscape, with its distinctive conjunction of rolling pasture and raw hillside, awoke a faint sense of affectionate familiarity.''[49] In dramatic terms, this was usually expressed via a heroic protagonist, the ''Kiwi,'' a new phenomenon who appeared on the scene at this time. Thus the *Weekly Reviews* were generally film versions of the Man (or Woman) Alone myth. Like much of the fiction of the time, John Mulgan's prototypical novel, *Man Alone* (1939), told the story of a rugged individualist in conflict with Nature, the State, and his fellow men and women.[50] The *Weekly Reviews,* however, revitalized the myth with tales of heroic individualists out in New Zealand's backblocks—literally alone, rather than spiritually—lighthouse keepers, meteorologists on outlying islands, district nurses and country doctors, village schoolteachers, lifesavers and construction workers, and the Maori New Zealander. It is a centripetal design, integrating the most remote New Zealand communities, however small, into the greater community of the nation.

None of these communities is concerned with the anxieties of individual identity or a sense of place—they are just too busy. Whether for the war effort or for the national interest, these Kiwis are seen pulling together, led by the dedicated professionals of the welfare state. Derek Wright, who joined the National Film Unit in 1947, has said, ''Of course we all had a tremendous pride in our country then. It was the aftermath of war and the returning ex-servicemen had this tremendous urgency to get up and do things.''[51] Perhaps the characters in the *Weekly Reviews* resemble the heroes of *One Hundred Crowded Years*'s strident song of progress; however, they are also fleshed out a little more, in keeping with the tendency away from mythic or analytic narrative toward the psychological realism which had been developing in the prose of Frank Sargeson and other fiction writers. It would seem then that a national identity as such can be described at a time when a stereotype or archetype, be it the Yank or the Aussie or the Kiwi, settles into a set of familiar and distinct characteristics like the stereotypical French or German or English.

In being produced for the domestic market, the *Weekly Reviews* had a mandate to cover the Maori contribution. Therefore the editions of the war years incorporate Maori people at work in the national interest, not as Maori *per se* but as Maori New Zealanders. For example, three of the main "Maori" *Weekly Reviews* of the war years revive the code of the warrior and celebrate Maori heroism in war: *Weekly Reviews 112, 209,* and *232. Weekly Review 112* (1943) is a Special Edition recording the ceremonies at Ruatoria in honor of Lieutenant Ngarimu, who was killed in Tunisia but received a Victoria Cross for his actions. There is a huge crowd in attendance from nearly every "native settlement in New Zealand," all together for the first time since the war "took the young men away from the pa [village]." The highlight is Ngarimu's father speaking in both Maori and English: "He loved his country so well that he was glad to fight for it." The narration is respectful, and probably accurate when it asserts that "today tribal differences and old quarrels have been set aside. Lt. Ngarimu is regarded as belonging not to one tribe but the whole Maori people." Just as the nation was united across the color barrier, so too were the Maori tribes united in the Maori Battalion and its common purpose.

Weekly Review 232 (1946) is a Special Edition recording the return to New Zealand of the Maori Battalion after the war. It opens with an enormous hangi (feast) being prepared at Porirua amid the fires and smoke, and the waiata (songs) and thoughtful faces create a sense of intimacy and expectation. One of the next shots—the troop ship *Dominion Monarch* out in Wellington Harbor—is one of the most poignant in New Zealand film. When the voice-over comments: "For the Maori people, this is the ship they have been waiting for," the moment is enhanced by cross-cutting between the ship and the waiting faces. Subsequently, the wharf serves as the marae (meeting place) for the traditional welcoming ceremonies, and Acting Prime Minister Mr. Walter Nash, Members of Parliament, and former commanders of the

Battalion are present. Dining follows—again spectacular shots—
and the final scenes show welcome home ceremonies at Ohau and
Ngaruawahia. These scenes too are particularly moving, as kuia
(women elders) enfold their returning warriors, and the narration
concludes: "Men of the Maori Battalion are home. In the years to
come, their deeds will be told again and again, so long as Maori
blood endures."[52]

The same sentiments can be found in the newsreels featuring
the New Zealand Maori rugby team, *Weekly Reviews 362, 363,
410* and *459* (1948–1950), where Maori skill and national pride
become synonymous, and in *Maori Village* (1945), an incidental
shot by the *Weekly Review* team when they were in Rotorua to
film the visit by English entertainer Gracie Fields. Significantly,
the narrations in all these films—and they are very well written—
emphasize the unity and sense of pride felt by the entirety of
Maori culture. There is no attempt made to place this in turn
within "New Zealand" as a whole. They are Maori and they are
New Zealanders (Maori New Zealanders), rather than Maori or
New Zealanders or different tribes depending on the occasion.
These films are among the finest expressions of the Integration
Myth and even of a kind of bicultural nationalism. The pride felt
by Pakeha New Zealanders in the Maori contribution remains
implicit; in a historical context when "being a New Zealander"
was obviously the prime value, this is simply accepted by the
films and not problematized. Inevitably, there is some reliance on
the Romantic Savage in defining Maori cultural difference, but
the *Weekly Reviews* treated their Pakeha warrior heroes much the
same way. It was war-time after all.

In the post-war years, the *Weekly Reviews* dealing with Maori
subjects gradually returned to the conventions of the historical
romance proper. There were, of course, the strictly newsreel
editions, for example those recording the opening of a new
meeting house (*Weekly Reviews 321, 420*), and those recording
tangis, funerals, and obituaries (*Weekly Reviews 88, 168, 458*). In
others, however, New Zealand began to regularly displace its old
antithesis, Maoriland, once again. For example, *Weekly Review
280* (1947), aka *Patterns in Flax,* juxtaposes older traditional flax
weaving by hand (Maori) with newer machine weaving (Pakeha),
in order to demonstrate New Zealand's technological (i.e. historical) progress. Maoriland as archaeological site also reappears

after 1948, in *Weekly Reviews 378, 389, 446* (*c.f. Notornis Expedition,* 1950), and Maoriland as quaint legends reappears in *Weekly Review 395.*

As the newsreel evolved, its most interesting new form was the social problem documentary, and this genre came to dominate discussions of contemporary Maori. It reasserted the differential of old and new, antiquity and modernity, the primitive and the progressive, where the Maori play catch-up with the Pakeha. No longer was it a question of historical inevitability, as one might find in Rudall Hayward's films, but of an obvious digital choice between health and sickness, education and ignorance, good farming and bad farming. There are basically four *Weekly Reviews* on Maori themes which belong to this social problem genre: *257, 324, 332,* and *402.* In each one a separate "problem" is posed which requires attention from the nation's professionals.

Weekly Review 257 (1946) is a "Newsclips" edition, in which the fourth item celebrates the work of a Pakeha district nurse in the 90% Maori area around Te Araroa on the East Coast. It is all about heroic individualism, Woman Alone rather than the usual Man Alone. In a landscape evoking Hollywood westerns, the district nurse's grey car fords rivers in grand style—"she travels to places where the only road is a river bed" and she "often completes the job on horseback." Her main target: tuberculosis. She checks out the babies, scrubs the younger children ("she has looked after them since they were born"), arranges for nourishing school lunches at a cheap price, and checks their hair for lice. As, silhouetted against the sky, she rides away at the end of the film, the voice-over says, "She is a lone figure but she is too busy to be lonely. She is trying to bring the health services of the cities to the backblocks. And it's a job that needs much determination and courage. This is 1946 but district nurses in areas such as this have all the spirit that the pioneers ever had" (*c.f. Weekly Review 332, Sylvia,* and *Ngati, q.q.v.*). Anonymity, selfless service, the audio-visual style of the western: these are the trademarks of New Zealand's newsreel genre at its most innovative and imaginative. Nevertheless, the genre is also inherently m/paternal in that Maori health is perceived to be a problem in relation to the city-dwelling Pakeha, and it requires the "pioneer spirit" of heroic doctors, nurses, teachers, and scientists out in the "backblocks" who can assist the Maori to catch up with the Pakeha. Scientific discourse of this kind was sustained in National Film Unit films well into the Fifties, when it was displaced by a renewed interest in Maori arts and culture.

Weekly Review 324 (1947), aka *Maori School,* is the second such film but it has a little more charm because it has Maori people at its center. It establishes Maori education as its social problem and then proceeds to demonstrate that such problems can be overcome with the right commonsense attitude. It opens at dawn in Manutahi as a Maori farmer sees his two children off to school on horseback. The school is in Ruatoria in the valley below and it is run by the Native Schools Branch of the Education Department. The film has its heart in the right place: "To learn by doing is the first principle of modern education" and "growing up should be serious and delightful," so senior students are taught Maori, carving and tukutuku weaving. Nevertheless the main theme of the film is in adapting Maori interests to modern New Zealand. When the narration asserts, "The children are growing up to be good citizens, managers of their own home," the children are shown learning cooking and cleaning, making beds, and cleaning windows in a model cottage. When the film visits former students now out in the community—model citizens, a policeman, bus driver, and butcher—the narration sums up with: "At Manutahi, the school is the center of a progressive farming community and the whole land is a classroom."

A third social problem film is *Weekly Review 332* (1948), a Special Edition aka *Backblock Medical Service.* It is set in the Hokianga district, where "cooperation has built a service that answers the needs of the backblock country," and it begins as "the familiar white cars of the district nurses go out from Rawene Hospital to the scattered settlements of the area." The nurses and doctors are all Pakeha, the patients mostly Maori, but the narration is soft, respectful, and unobtrusive, and the cameos of patients and their families are not patronizing. Obviously, the district nurse has a difficult job; she has "to deal with social problems as well as those of medicine. Problems of society, of how people live and what they eat." The second half of the film is a mini-narrative of a district nurse answering an emergency call which turns out to be acute appendicitis, and the child is stretchered to a boat and taken to hospital. The film has an excellent score and evocative landscape photography, the combination of which is reminiscent of westerns, yet touched with a trace of Alfred Hitchcock and film noir.

Unfortunately, as the Forties begin to near their end, the cheerful optimism declines and impatience sets in. In *Weekly Review 402* (1949), the third item is titled "Maori Rehabilitation: New Farms Beside the Wairoa." The Huramua Estate of the Carroll family is to be broken up into smaller farms for former members of the Maori Battalion and their families, and the Estate will provide them with on-the-job training until they are ready to assume ownership. The film shows men at work on tractors and grubbing scrub, mustering and tending vegetable crops, and relaxing at tennis. It also shows a model Maori mum in her modern home. The narrator's tone is optimistic and encouraging: "If all housing were as good as this there would be a great improvement in the health of Maori children."

Even if the message here is relatively restrained, it becomes much more overt in subsequent years as the social problem genre expanded. For example, in the *New Zealand Mirror* anthology series of 1950–1954, some of the *Weekly Review* footage was reedited for overseas consumption with a crass new soundtrack narration. The Huramua footage reappears in *New Zealand Mirror 10* (1951), where the lines quoted above are refashioned into: "One of the country's headaches: the housing conditions of the Maori people." Another line stresses that this rehabilitation scheme is "paid for by the Government" and that it is a "generous" one. The tone here is patronizing and this tendency is generally typical of the difference between the *Weekly Reviews* of the Forties and the *New Zealand Mirrors, Pictorial Parades,* and one-off documentaries from the Fifties and Sixties.

THE NZ MIRRORS & PICTORIAL PARADES

The year 1950 was one of considerable change at the National Film Unit. In January, the *Weekly Reviews* were suspended so that the Unit could concentrate on covering the British Empire Games in February. The same month, producer Stanhope Andrews resigned, and his writings of the period suggest growing disenchantment with the bureaucracy in which the Unit was becoming increasingly embroiled: "Quietly and skilfully the Film Unit was deprived of its identity and became another Department, or a branch of one."[53] Accordingly, in July of 1950, the Government announced its intention to transfer the National Film Unit to the Tourist and Publicity Department, where it had been before the war and where it has remained ever since.

In August, the last of the 459 *Weekly Reviews* was released and a national institution came, as it had to, to an end. In its place, the Unit split its production output into tourist and publicity films for overseas consumption—for Britain in particular; and departmental and instructional films for domestic use—for the Soil Conservation Council, the Transport Department, the Health Department, the Army Department, and so on. Also from around this time, the first initiatives began in producing films for foreign governments, for British and American television, and for international film festivals; there was also a move into 35mm color film and a huge increase in 16mm processing for sales of films to the general public and for use by Government Tourist Bureaux.

One of the first projects, then, was to reedit *Weekly Review* footage for the *New Zealand Mirror* series. This series was aimed at the British tourism market and it ran to 27 issues. The Maori items selected for inclusion were usually the evocations of Maoriland, supposedly universal in appeal and either heavily nostalgic or given to superficial ethnography, mythology, and archaeology. Although later *New Zealand Mirrors*—numbers *13, 14, 21*—used new material, the narratives remained substantially the same.

Much the same can be said of the *Pictorial Parades,* a monthly anthology series of newsreel items produced by the National Film Unit between 1952 and 1971 for circulation within New Zealand. Initially, they were also intended to provide material for the *NZ Mirrors*—after some re-editing and a new narration—but they went on to outlive them, running to 250 issues. The *Pictorial Parades,* too, were shot mostly in black and white, although from 1958 onwards, some items and even whole films began to appear in color. As with the *Weekly Reviews,* there were the conventional newsreel items recording the opening of new meeting houses (*Pictorial Parades 106, 109, 173*); artistic and sporting items (*74, 103, 108, 128*); and Maoriland archaeology/geology (*76, 141*). As far as Maori themes are concerned, the most interesting are probably *Pictorial Parades 17* and *18* (1954), which were Special Editions devoted to the Royal Tour of New Zealand in that year by Queen Elizabeth II; and *Pictorial Parade 36* (1955), the second item of which showcases Ardmore Teachers' College and focuses mainly on young Maori trainees.

The best of the series is *Pictorial Parade 114* (1961), aka *Visit to Motiti*. This film records the visit of an Auckland primary school class to Motiti Island in the Bay of Plenty. As its young Pakeha narrator explains it, the visit is intended as a Social Studies trip, "to live with a Maori tribe on an island." Because the narrative physically resembles the romantic quest for knowledge in exotic climes, and because the schoolboy's first-person narration is concerned mostly with his own and the class's subjective experiences, the film is devoid of the usual narrational authority of official discourse. The Maori community is backgrounded as a result, but in foregrounding its own narrational perspectives instead, the film has a charm and humor and wit that are missing in other *Pictorial Parades.*

Finally, because we will be moving on to the role of the cultural historians in the next chapter, it is worth noting that by the Fifties, there were no nationalist histories of the kind published today, aside from periodic updates of the Condliffe-Airey *A Short History of New Zealand* and A. H. Reed's non-academic *The Story of New Zealand.* Stylistically and generically, both of these histories had their roots in the imperial era. They are historical romances—"chronicles"—divided up into broad groups of events and shuffled through in chronological order, and with a specifically economic and political focus. Other historical writing of this period was equally specialized—military, regional, and so on. However, the times were changing, and from the Sixties on, it would be possible for the historians to say with confidence that the nationalist era had indeed begun. We were now "New Zealanders."

CHAPTER 5: CRACKS IN THE WALL—
THE SOCIAL PROBLEM
DOCUMENTARY

It was probably inevitable that the tourism romance would return to favor in the Fifties after its ten years out in the cold, metamorphosing out of the "scientific expedition" films of the late Forties.[54] This may imply that I dislike the genre, which is not the case. However, tourism romances presented a terrible dilemma to filmmakers and critics of the time: how could one convert them into something satisfying and challenging aesthetically? The institutional changes at the National Film Unit after 1950 meant that there was a steady increase in the supply of Tourist Department finance available to shoot them, but this was hardly satisfying to the artists within the film community.

Aside from making prohibitively expensive fiction features (and Pacific Films did produce *Broken Barrier* in 1952, *q.v.*), filmmakers had just two options. The first was to aestheticize the tourism romance, as John Feeney did in his four films at the National Film Unit (discussed below); the second was to transform the newsreel into social problem or educational/instructional films for various government departments. Corporations such as the Caltex petrol company were not averse to funding either option if a Caltex station could be inserted somewhere in the film (*c.f. The New Zealanders*, 1959).

Thus it was asked, Could a tourism travelogue ever be considered "artistic"? Could a social problem or educational film be "artistic"? Could the genres be analytically distinguished from one other? Could corporate sponsorship be reconciled with artistic integrity? Many of the debates turned on whether they were all aspiring toward the "documentary," touted by John Grierson as "the creative treatment of actuality" but still eluding a more precise definition. Certainly everyone knew what the tourism romances looked and sounded like. There were only three produced by the National Film Unit on the subject of the Maori, either wholly or in part: *Meet New Zealand* (1949), and its later incarnation, *Introducing New Zealand* (1955), *Thermal Wonderland* (1950), and *Rotorua Radius* (1953).[55] The first of these is an excellent tourism romance; the other two resemble the Maoriland romances of the Twenties and Thirties, juxtaposing historical time (Pakeha New Zealand) next to the timeless eternal (Maoriland). Independent filmmakers, meanwhile, were also shooting tourism romances: Lee Hill, Robert Steele at Neuline Films, and Roger Mirams and John O'Shea at Pacific Films. Hill produced the bizarre Maoriland fantasy of the erotic/exotic, *Land of Hinemoa* (1950); Steele, the conventional ethnographic romance, *The Maori Ancient and Modern* (1950); and Mirams and O'Shea, the erotically charged *Dances of the South Pacific* (1954, *q.v.*).

It helps to remember that in the years after the war and throughout the Fifties there was an enormous increase in High Culture discourse on the state of the arts and culture in New Zealand. While painting and literature received excellent coverage, there are, to my knowledge, only a few articles of film criticism *per se* (mostly in the periodical *Landfall*), and those few deal with National Film Unit documentaries and documentary aesthetics in general.[56] They confirm the split in the prevailing aesthetics of the time alluded to above. On the one hand there was the materialist school of thought influenced by European Marxism, socialism, and modernism, discussion of which is deferred to later in the chapter. On the other, there was the individualistic and romantic subjectivity of the pictorialist school, in which John Feeney can be included. For example, in 1958, Maurice Shadbolt (himself a National Film Unit director) could write that Feeney's films "cannot be considered in isolation from the New Zealand literary mainstream. In his use of myth and symbol, and his exploration of the strange New Zealand landscape, his work is close in mood and feeling to, for example, the mysticism expressed in the essays of Holcroft, or the poetry of Brasch."[57] Despite the mystical strain, or perhaps because of it, Shadbolt's literary mainstream subscribed to a liberal humanist aesthetic of psychological and spiritual authenticity, the function of the individual artist as expressive agent, and romantic nostalgia associated with "exploring" the landscape of New Zealand.

JOHN FEENEY & THE HISTORICAL ROMANCE

In the National Film Unit productions of the early Fifties, the
landscape assumed a greater importance than it ever had in the
Weekly Reviews, almost coming to stand in for the prototypical
New Zealander who lived in it. For P. J. Downey, writing in 1955,
the National Film Unit had otherwise betrayed its promise with
the "trivia" of the *Pictorial Parades* and the "picture postcard"
travelogues in which he detected the heavy hand of the Tourist
and Publicity Department. He argued that "as long as the
filmmakers concentrate their attention on delineating the face of
the land they produce work that is beautiful and satisfying," and
he singled out Feeney's films for praise. Here were the first signs
of an aestheticized tourism romance which rapturously celebrated
the land itself, as the American documentarists of the Thirties,
particularly Pare Lorentz, had done for the United States. In the

The Legend of the Wanganui River (1952): history may be rendered in
narrative form but the cigarettes and short pants have a contemporary
flavor.

place of the great rivers and mountains of America, these New Zealand films drew on Maoriland's geological and mythological traditions, and they are more than simply tourism romances in that the commercial imperative is considerably downplayed. The narrative structure, of course, is still the familiar one of the nation's progress into modernity—wherein New Zealand displaces Maoriland—and the films are more aptly characterized as historical romances. In fact, they come as close as anything to the most complete expression of the nation-as-subject, and, appropriately enough, cinema-going in New Zealand reached its all-time peak during these years.

John Feeney's *The Legend of the Wanganui River* (1952) was the first of four films he made for the National Film Unit, and perhaps his finest. It is a river-as-hero story (*c.f. NZ's River of Romance* and the later *People of the Waikato*). It opens on the Volcanic Plateau as a voice-over narration tells the legend of how Mount Taranaki quarreled with the other mountains and carved his path to the sea, down what is now the Whanganui River. Clouds and flutes give way to a Maori elder telling this story to his mokopuna (grandchildren), which in turn gives way to a spectacular sequence of thunder and lightning and volcanic eruptions. The Pakeha narration then resumes, telling of the streams which feed the river and the tribes who live along its banks. The photography here is excellent: reflections on the water which evoke memories, illusions, the past; and there are point-of-view shots as if the viewer were one of the Maori travelers on the river, which are then juxtaposed with extreme high-angle shots to create a sense of the timeless eternal. The flute accompaniment provides a pastoral ambience and the narration declares: "For centuries the tribes of Aotea had daydreamed on its waters, listening to the song of the tui, studying every leaf and fern, and weaving legends around the whirlpools and rapids of the enchanted river."

However, the music becomes brooding, the screen fills with images of broken canoes, deserted meeting houses, and the bush creeping in, and the narration intones: "Up the river came the white man . . . and the river ran with blood." Maoriland gives way to New Zealand: the bush is cleared, sheep appear, and there is a touch of bag-pipes in the music: "Steamers now ply where once Maori warriors swept along in hundred-man canoes, and to the bush valleys came tourists from other lands." The film reaches

The Legend of the Wanganui River: the two river banks reflect different histories. On the left, native forest; on the right, farmland for sheep grazing. Maori/Pakeha.

the city of Wanganui, where the nostalgic mode is dropped for the Integration Myth: "And here, working alongside the Pakeha are the river Maoris of today, some wearing their army berets from Tunisia and El Alamein." The film then concludes with: "The earth mother sends out her river, out into the western sea, into the hands of the sea-god, Tangaroa, and the winds of the ocean. . . . " The film was very well received, both critically and popularly; as Maurice Shadbolt observed in 1958, it "used a myth and made a poem."

In terms of the argument so far, *The Legend of the Wanganui River* is a historical romance celebrating the nation's as yet incomplete journey toward Utopia. It begins with the timeless eternal in the luxuriant but lost world of Maoriland. The Pakeha, on his arrival, destroys paradise but, paradoxically, his technological and economic know-how promise that paradise can be regained. Maoriland fades away into historical time. Analogically, this is also a narrative of how the Pakeha raped the Maori, offset by the Integration Myth. The gods and demi-gods of the

Hot Earth (1954): Mount Ngauruhoe in permanent eruption provides a metaphor for Maoriland's eruption into Pakeha New Zealand.

opening and closing legends stand in for history and the Christian God who oversees the nation's soul. However, the film seems to be fascinated not by the promise of New Zealand but by the loss of Maoriland. It has, overall, a narrative structure of the Fall rather than Utopia. There is a strongly mystical strain, especially within the metaphor of the river's ultimate dissolution in the sea, symbolically a refuge from the clangor of the world. Arguably too, this metaphor is a sexual one, in keeping with the rape metaphor and the masculine displacement of the feminine.

In subsequent films, Feeney demonstrated his versatility with this genre of the nostalgic historical romance. He produced one film which is almost the reverse of his Whanganui River film: *Pumicelands* (1954), aka *Pictorial Parade 23*. It celebrates the heroic sacrifices and struggles of New Zealanders in turning the "sterile" pumicelands into prosperous and fertile farmland. Utopia this time, rather than the Fall. Another of his films, *Kotuku* (1954), is an elegy for the loss of Maoriland, which he situates in the "secret" lagoon of the rare kotuku (white heron). A third, *Hot Earth* (1954), treats the Volcanic Plateau's thermal region using the same narrative devices as the Whanganui River film. It is more properly an "aesthetic" documentary, rather than a tourism romance, and it portends the later fiction films of Aotearoa where a Maori Other threatens continually to erupt into the narrative structure. But back in the Fifties, the presence of Aotearoa is detectable only in the gradual release of steam and the occasional tremor in the body of the landscape.

THE SOCIAL PROBLEM DOCUMENTARY

The social problem documentary represents the other emergent genre of the period and it grows out of the public service tradition associated with the British documentary movement. The latter produced films for Grierson's Empire Marketing Board Film Unit (and subsequently the GPO Film Unit) during the Thirties. They successfully found a way to attract finance from both government and industry on the grounds that their films were a form of public

Hot Earth showcases some of Rotorua's famous trademarks: picturesque Maori seen cooking in the boiling pools.

service, and it was this model that undoubtedly motivated Stanhope Andrews' *Weekly Review* team in the Forties, though its legacy can be traced back to the imperial era. It also motivated the Historical Branch of the Department of Internal Affairs when in 1945 it published *Introduction to New Zealand,* which was mainly addressed to Americans: "The people who have lessons for us are not M-G-M or Cecil B. de Mille but Grierson (whose advice on a brief visit was very useful) and Cavalcanti. Seeing ourselves on the screen, we can become more conscious of our own individuality as New Zealanders, and not merely of the scenery we own and of the news."[58] By the Fifties, this latter tradition identified itself with the social and psychological realism evident in the *Weekly Reviews.* Initially characters had been allegorical types, political issues were privileged over personal issues, and science and technology mattered more than art. The social problem documentary attempted to maintain these polarities while the rest of New Zealand filmmaking became more self-consciously aestheticized.

The most sophisticated description of what the social problem documentary was or ought to be, for New Zealand, was proposed by writer and professor M. K. Joseph in 1950:

> To record is not enough, and so we exclude the newsreel and travelogue. True documentary records and interprets . . . . [It] begins when it shows, not the country itself, but how people belong in the country, and what they do with it . . . . Taking it a step further, documentary shows people in their relation to their work. It is when we come to the wider social issues that a certain limitation seems to apply . . . . Very seldom does the film in this country take the further step into the realm of social criticism . . . . Yet there are fundamental problems crying out to be tackled—films on full employment and incentives, on the Maori in the cities, on the wharves, on the new needs of education.[59]

Joseph is calling here for attention to specific social problems of the welfare state, but very few of the films in the rest of this chapter match up to his exacting manifesto, which amounts to a rejection of both the tourism romance and the generalities of the national historical romance. The four social problem *Weekly Reviews* discussed in the previous chapter match most of Joseph's requirements, except perhaps the vital role of social criticism.

A major stumbling block for such films would be that sharp and specifically targeted criticism automatically drives a wedge into the idea of national unity and identity. To stigmatize a "problem" rather than to sing the nation's praises always draws attention to discrimination, class divisions, complacency in the nation's bureaucratic apparatus, and the existence of constituencies within the body politic—Maori, trade unions (the crucial union-breaking waterfront strike occurred in 1951), and the sick—whose affiliations might be other than the national interest. The existence of the social problem documentary offers tacit recognition that the New Zealand historical romance, with its narrative of progress toward Utopia, always repressed other narratives—for example, the Fall of the Maori (and other potentially divisive constituencies). This latter tragic narrative was, for the time being, offset by the healing powers of the Integration Myth, and there were few signs that the repressed would erupt into presence to plague Pakeha New Zealand as they would in the Eighties. Still, the cracks in the Integration Myth are visible back then in the films where the "problem" is first bluntly acknowledged.

When social problems were targeted at all, they were in films commissioned by an arm of the government (health, education, etc.) or private organizations involved both in public service and self-promotion (Red Cross, Plunket Society, Blind Institute, NZ Soil Council, NZ Water Safety Council). These were mostly educational and instructional in nature and though they have a problem-solving narrative structure, they are inversions of what Joseph had in mind, in that the problems are usually solved to the greater glory of the government or the particular private organization.[60] In the private sector, Pacific Films produced *Towards Tomorrow* (1956), a "plea to Maori parents to use the opportunities for better education open to their children," and the Presbyterian Church commissioned *Taina—Younger Brother* (1954), about their work among the Maori in the Whakatane area. In the Sixties, the National Film Unit produced *As the Twig Is Bent* (1965) for the Maori Education Foundation, and *To Live in the City* (1967) about urban drift and its problems. Finally, Hayward Film Productions contributed *English Language Teaching for Maori and Island Children* (1971). By and large, these films draw their authority as truth-tellers from an incipient scientific discourse, identifying the problems and proposing solutions.

Aroha (1951): a beautiful publicity shot that neatly visualizes Aroha's choice between Maori and Pakeha solutions: she gazes off left away from the ancestral figure at right who is aggressively staring down the camera.

There are three National Film Unit documentaries that pretty much sum up the range and power of the new genre. The first was Michael Forlong's impressive film, *Aroha* (1951), which frames its social problem through a fictional device and may be compared with the Pacific Films feature, *Broken Barrier* (*q.v.*), of the following year. It mostly takes the form of a first person flashback told by Aroha, the daughter of an Arawa chief. As the film opens, she explains to an imaginary viewer that the celebrations we see are for her wedding. As the film goes into flashback, Aroha is seen studying at university in Wellington and living at a Maori Girls' Hostel. At university she has Pakeha boyfriends, while at the hostel she stands accused of becoming a Pakeha and rejecting her Maori friends. Aroha replies, "But today we're living in a Pakeha world. Some say we should keep apart but we can't grow up as two separate races in the same country." The scene shifts to

Aroha: there is something about the cheerfulness and quiet concentration in this photo that evokes the spirit of racial harmony that the *Weekly Reviews* promoted, but 1951 was a turning point for the worse.

Rotorua as Aroha arrives on the bus. She sees Tahu at the local garage and agrees to see him at the dance that night. She only plans to stay the weekend but her plans change on finding that her father is ill with a brain tumor. She goes to the dance anyway. There Tahu advises her to stick to the old Maori ways, and again she replies: "Why should I bury myself in the country because I'm a Maori? There's no need to. Maoris are not kept out of anything."

At this point Aroha is urgently called away by the news that her father is much worse. Against the wishes of the tohunga (a religious-spiritual figure), she prevails upon her father to enter hospital. Tahu is impressed with Aroha's mana (prestige), but she replies: "I know that here they have the knowledge to make my father better, and it's sensible for us Maoris to make use of that knowledge." Fortunately her father recovers (seemingly a little too quickly) and the film returns to the present moment. Aroha remarks in the voice-over that the Pakeha guests do not really understand how much had really been at stake in all this. The motivation for her marriage to Tahu remains vague, but it appears to be a "Maori must marry Maori" message as a trade-off for Aroha's many Integration Myth pronouncements and the medical message that Pakeha doctors can be just as useful to Maori as tohunga. The final eloquent sub-title reads: "As the Maori people remember their past in singing and dancing their future lies waiting. It will take the form they desire, for it is theirs to shape as they will . . . theirs to form for their descendants and their race."

Tuberculosis and the Maori People of the Wairoa District (1952) was the first fully fledged National Film Unit social problem documentary. It was made for the Health Department with the assistance of Turi Carroll and the local Maori Tribal Executive. The film opens with scenic shots of the Wairoa district—outlying marae, local people, waterfalls, street signs, Mahia ("our historic place of refuge")—and is accompanied by a waiata (song). This local ambience and Carroll's narration key Maori viewers into the film. The narrative then shifts to a monthly meeting of the tribal executive in Wairoa, where TB is under discussion, and this segues into a film-within-a-film: *TB: How It Spreads*.

From this point on, a series of voices alternately controls the narrative. The first is an internationalist medical voice putting TB in global perspective. The second belongs to one of the district nurses, and the visuals show a Maori nurse visiting a family and the TB isolation huts. She identifies the two main problems as overcrowding and poor diet. Carroll then intervenes to state that the Pakeha "gives himself more space to live in," and that "his wife feeds him pretty well." The third voice belongs to a doctor, and a mobile X-ray clinic is shown as one of the positive steps being taken to combat "the enemy TB" ("the lungs are a battleground in the fight against the disease"). Some Maori families who have gone for check-ups are praised for having done so.

In the next section, several Maori villages are contrasted. Te Reinga, a ramshackle settlement, is criticized for doing nothing ("in such conditions disease is a certainty"). Its inhabitants own a lot of farmland and forest so there is no reason to live like this. By contrast, Huramua is a success story (*c.f. Weekly Review 402*). "Perhaps more typical of Maori progress is Iwitea," once like Te Reinga but now improving because of rebuilding. Milk, cheese, eggs, vegetables and eel are praised as good foods: "Well-fed children have the best chance of fighting off TB, should they ever become infected," and, "It is not people's fault if they have TB, but it would be their fault if they passed on the disease to their children or grandchildren." Appeals like this are made directly to camera by Carroll and they seem particularly effective. He concludes: "This TB is an enemy that kills too many of our young people, but it is not an enemy we need fear since we know we can defeat it by better housing, better feeding, and personal care." The film is a fine example of what can be done when Maori consultants and advisers have more than a token involvement in the film production process. It would have screened in cinemas all over New Zealand where Maori health was in some way threatened, and its varied and informative style make it good entertainment as well as a powerful message film.

If *Aroha* and *TB and the Maori People* were made for domestic audiences, *The Maori Today* (1960) clearly was not. Superficially it is an orthodox Tourist and Publicity Department social problem documentary aimed at overseas audiences. However, it is paternal in the extreme, on the one hand praising the Maori for doing their best to make up the lag between the two cultures, and on the other implying that the problems may be insurmountable. It begins with

The Maori Today (1960): two areas where Pakeha filmmakers think the Maori are failing: education and technical trades. The mood in 1960 was grim.

the Integration Myth: the narrator states "Maori or European, it makes little difference"—one can be a photographer, a cabinet minister, or a timber stacker—and "a man's work can't be measured by the color of his skin." The film then makes a brief acknowledgment of Maori culture but defines it in purely material terms—as language, carvings, songs and dances—and then disposes of it to the past: "The past is revered but for members of the tribal committees, today's living is the concern."

The film at length identifies its primary problem: "There's still a third of the Maori population living in poor conditions." After averring that the education system is not the cause of the problem, it highlights two causes: urban drift and the problems of rural farming. Urban drift is diagnosed in patronizing terms: "Learning to live like townsfolk is not easy," and "If the Maoris are to keep pace with their fellow New Zealanders, more of them must enter the skilled trades." The narration then severely criticizes Maori farming methods and recommends consolidation of small holdings into larger ones, and government supervision through the Department of Maori Affairs. The final comments deserve quotation in full:

> [The Maori] will always be sought after when brawn is needed, but to carry respect in the community they must also be in demand when skill is necessary, otherwise all Maoris will be accepted as only fit for unskilled labor. But to retain the age-old traditions is essential in the shift to modern living. To take pride in their past gives a sense of security in these changing times with their subtle problems. In less than a hundred years they're trying to do what it's taken Europeans 2,000 years to do. The young people and the older people too, can be proud of what has been achieved in their adjustment to the 20th century, and their fellow New Zealanders can share that pride with them.

The film may be distinguished, if for no other reason because it represents the first full-scale cultural survey—in film—of the social and economic conditions of the Maori, and regrettably it is a negative one. It is the nationalist equivalent to the imperial *The Maori as He Was* of 1928, and perhaps it is no surprise that it was released in the same year as the Hunn Report to the Government, which strongly recommended integration of the Maori into the

Pakeha New Zealand nation. In the years since then, the social problem documentary has become both more humble and more subtle in its claims to present the historical truth, but in a political climate where such direct cultural commentary can quickly become offensive, the survival of this genre would appear to be dependent on its being adopted by Maori filmmakers and television producers. For a Pakeha to be so forthright in the Nineties is asking for trouble.

THE NATIONALIST HISTORIANS

In this final section, it is important to key the discussion into what the historians were saying about integration by 1960, since they evidently had views similar to the National Film Unit and the Hunn Report. For one thing, there were no fewer than two major national histories published within a year of each other: Keith Sinclair's *A History of New Zealand* (1959) and W. H. Oliver's *The Story of New Zealand* (1960).[61] Sinclair and Oliver belong to a generation of academic historians who grew up during the Thirties and Forties and who took it for granted that by 1960 we knew who "we" were, where we came from, where we were going, and what part the Maori would play in this historical romance.

By way of contrast, the earlier imperial historians (William Pember Reeves, Alan Mulgan, A. H. Reed) were more concerned with the cultural differences between Maori and British; Sinclair and Oliver, however, are more concerned with asserting the national differences between New Zealand and Britain.[62] Rather than adopt a simple linear chronology and gallery of individualized heroes, or a checklist of anthropological themes, they draw on the analogy between the young New Zealand nation and the prototypical New Zealander, the Kiwi. Gone is the nostalgia for the disappearing primeval Bush and the Pioneer Myth; in its place there is an identification between the rugged pragmatic Kiwi and the strange and beautiful landscape "he" has found himself in. In keeping with the wresting of space from time, the new national identity was now conceived of as a cultural essence whose topography must be mapped. If we can place bookends on this period after 1960, then it concluded with W. H. Oliver's *The Oxford History of New Zealand* (1981), the same year as the tour of New Zealand by South Africa's rugby team, the Springboks, when the country was convulsed by a psychological civil war. Taken as a whole, the period from 1960 until 1981, along with its academic ideological supports, displays conspicuous attempts to write the national story from a self-consciously realist and psychological point of view.[63]

This raises the question, Where did the Maori fit into the new historians' concept of New Zealand? In his idiosyncratic and entertaining history, Keith Sinclair constructs New Zealand as a kind of war zone in which various competing and conflicting interests fight it out for the destiny of the nation's identity, which appears to date from World War I. His cast of characters includes Pioneers, Cow Cockies, Red Feds, and Maoris, each of whom achieves a temporary dominance, and his conclusion by 1980 (in a revised edition) is optimistic: "By about 1940, if asked to identify themselves, most people born in New Zealand would without hesitation have said that they were New Zealanders."[64] This is qualified, however, by New Zealanders' regrettable historical amnesia: "But it must not be supposed that any considerable number of New Zealanders devote any considerable energy to ransacking history or, indeed, literature for clues to explain their present situation. In general they have had little sense of their past in the new land"—and this is where the historians themselves join the cast, to remind us of (or invent for us) our past.[65]

For Oliver the rationale is similar: it is provided by the quest for Utopia which motivated nineteenth-century British settlers to come to New Zealand, by the relative failure of that quest in the twentieth century, and its displacement into the quest by New Zealand's artists and writers for "self-understanding." While just as reliant as Sinclair on a general notion of History as ultimate authority, Oliver prefers to stress the artistic imagination and myth-making which consciously shapes our lives. In the end though, his thesis is much the same as Sinclair's, and whether the national psyche is "historical" or "fictional," cheerful or troubled, it is certainly there, it being the historian's stern task to diagnose its psychological condition and push for a stronger more mature identity.[66]

What then are the historians' options vis-à-vis the Maori?

Integrate them into the text of each chapter, or enforce the segregation of separate chapters, or ignore them completely? Sinclair chose to integrate them. Perhaps this was the most honorable option in the Fifties, but the effect can be read now in two ways: either Sinclair has rehabilitated the Maori into twentieth-century history or he has colonized them thoroughly, turning them into brown-skinned New Zealanders. Oliver, on the other hand, chose to segregate them into a separate chapter ("The Two Races"). Is he simply being honest in recognizing that the Maori have not been integrated into New Zealand or is he preaching integration while actually practicing segregation?

Their attempt to integrate the twentieth-century Maori into their twentieth-century texts was a political decision which directly confronted the by-then reified mythologies of the Happy Maori, the Lazy Maori, and, to a degree, the Social Problem Maori. They substituted these with a revamped Historical Maori. Perhaps it was better to integrate or segregate the Maori than to ignore them completely as most of their predecessors had done? Perhaps, too, it was better to position the Maori historically in time than to consign them to the timeless eternal as the imperial romances had done? If the only viable options available to Sinclair and Oliver were integration or segregation, who in retrospect would judge which was the better option? There is no answer to that question beyond the recognition that it is the Historical Myth itself which generated this dilemma, and it is the same Historical Myth which, in the late 1830s, required the British Crown to decide whether New Zealand should be annexed totally, partially, or not at all. In a later chapter, we will revisit the historians to see how the Historical Myth fared in the contentious Eighties.

CHAPTER 6: SEGREGATION BEGINS— THE ARTS & CULTURE DOCUMENTARY

The three genres discussed in the previous chapter continued to be very much the dominant triad throughout the Sixties and Seventies. The tourism romance had returned little changed and the historical romance was now at its artistic peak, and in both genres there was a predisposition toward telling the history of New Zealand as the story of a landscape humanized. However, it was to be the third genre, the pessimistic social problem film, along with its variant, the educational/instructional film, which would persist most strongly into subsequent decades.

When this social problem genre was applied to the Maori, the narrative theme usually adopted—progress toward Utopia—now seemed of diminished use. Curiously, the narrative became inverted so as to produce the regress of Maori cultural decay. No longer did this mean Maori tardiness in keeping up with Pakeha New Zealand, as it had done in the Forties and Fifties. By the Sixties it had begun to mean discovering something fundamentally wrong with the culture. Thus once more the shadow of Pitt-Rivers and Fatal Impact had returned and Maori culture was to be split off from the New Zealand nation.

CULTURAL DECAY OR CULTURAL REVIVAL?

It is no coincidence that at the exact moment when the Myth of Integration became most widely talked about, the beginnings of a new segregationism appeared, based around this notion of cultural decay. This is not the paradox it seems: integration was promoted in equal proportion to the perception of its failure, and Pakeha professionals were tasked with diagnosing where the failure (i.e. decay) had occurred. Not simply in the traditional areas of hygiene, education or farming, since these were all by-products of Pakeha invasion, and decayed teeth, decayed minds, and decayed farming equipment could be repaired by technology, science, and money. Maori decay was to be fixed within something essential to Maori "culture" (in the wider sense of the term), and in the films of the Sixties, this essence was determined to be within the "arts and culture" (in the narrower sense of the term): carving, tukutuku (weaving), songs and dances. These were the anthropological beliefs, practices, and skills that were entirely specific to the Maori and which supposedly marked them off as authentically different from the Pakeha. Now that these were dying out, salvage was necessary: by reviving the carving, the tukutuku, songs and dances, Maori decay could be arrested.

Not surprisingly, this was also the point at which the social sciences became geared up to investigate the phenomena of urban drift and rural decay. In a sense, ethnography was succeeded by sociology and ethnographic photography by photo-journalism, but the institutional impetus was the same: salvage and recovery of a disappearing culture of authenticity.[67]

From all this sprang a new genre of "arts and culture documentaries," some of them optimistic, some of them pessimistic, but all of them couched in the generalist terms of the Maori as a whole. Where *Aroha* and *TB and the Maori People* had refrained from generalizing about "Maori people" and what they ought to do, *The Maori Today* had been a different matter. It had been part of a new mood, offering many problems and few solutions. The new arts and culture genre of the Sixties took as its mandate the quest for those solutions. However, just as in earlier decades Maori cultural decay had been a subject of intellectual debate, so too with its perennial double, the narrative of Maori revival and renaissance. If Maori culture was decaying, so too it could revive. These are, of course, the narratives of the Fall and Utopia discovered beyond the Fall, an archaeology and an eschatology. The problem in the early Sixties lay in ascertaining whether Maori art and culture was meant to be decaying or reviving!

Viewing the films of the period, it is possible to reconstruct the structural and formal problems which presented themselves. For example, what exactly was this cultural essence within the Maori and their art and culture that was in decay? Was it in the people themselves or in their artistic creations? How could it be made to generate a revival? Was it secular like "inspiration" and "skills," or more religious like "spirit"? Could it be equated with "identity"? Was it universal or specific to the Maori? Was it further divisible to the level of iwi (tribe) or hapu (sub-tribe)? Was it more "authentic" than the Pakeha arts and culture imposed upon it? What was the relationship between this cultural essence and history? When narrativized, would Maori arts and culture be placed within a New Zealand national story or an international one? Was it "traditional" as opposed to "modern"? What role did this leave for National Film Unit filmmakers if it was not their revival? These questions will have to be examined in piecemeal fashion, partly because such matters can never be grasped as a whole anyway, and partly because there is little consistency from film to film.

Suffice it to say that Maori cultural essence was conceived initially through the secular humanism of Western art aesthetics and universal history, with artistic inspiration driving the physical and material practices of cultural production. This inspiration was universal, implying that Maori cultural essence was not qualitatively different from that of the Pakeha. The model is a Realist one: it presupposes that "Maori culture" could be identified analytically, and then, working backwards, the sources of inspiration could be represented to the parties most interested in saving it. Yet the arts and culture documentaries were always predestined to be a conservative and nostalgic discourse. When Realism commenced its period of High Culture dominance at this time, the model was already beginning to give way—Maori were migrating to the cities in large numbers, precipitating debates about "integration" and the "national identity," and Maori culture was being abandoned faster than the intellectuals could identify it. By the Eighties, the Realist model has reversed almost completely—inspiration has become a timeless spirit, the materialist model of cultural production has given way to an abstract religious discourse, and history itself has been ousted by culture.

OLD MAORILAND REVISITED

Dances of the South Pacific (1954) serves as a useful introduction to the genre. Directed by Roger Mirams and John O'Shea at Pacific Films, it features the dances of Maori New Zealand, Tonga, Fiji, Samoa, and Tahiti, respectively. It is an unusual film for New Zealand filmmakers for a number of reasons. First, by lumping all Pacific peoples (including the Maori) into one, it uses the more rare imperial/international framework. This is most obvious in its use of books, maps, and memoirs of eighteenth- and nineteenth-century explorers that open and close the film and link the various sequences together (*c.f. Hei Tiki*). At times the narration reproduces the Noble Savage mythology it finds in the memoirs: the fear of the lurking dark side (the Fijians "can still look as frightening in full regalia . . . as did their forebears who were notorious cannibals''), and the fear of lost authenticity (on Manahiki can be seen "the authentic movements of the early primitive dances''). Cultural essence is still preserved in such places.

The film is also unusual because it begins with a fictional device. It follows a young Tongan woman living in Pakeha New Zealand who "has assumed the manners and tastes of European life" because, today, "The old Maori has gone. Only an echo remains." After some sequences of traditional Maori performances ("Today Maori culture is a concert item for ceremonial display''), the young Tongan woman serves as the basis for an excursion to Tonga and various other Pacific islands, but then abruptly drops out of the story and leaves the paternal narrator in control.

A third feature is that some of the shots are highly erotic, including an extraordinary opening title shot. The filmmakers are romantically engaged in an erotic/exotic fascination with the dancers, both male and female. The film's visual style is as passionate and intimate with its subject as the narration, which speaks of the "passionate, pulsing climax of the dances of the South Pacific,'' and which quotes lines from the explorers' memoirs to the effect that "the wahines dance . . . in such a manner as to excite the desire of the opposite sex,'' when this would seem to apply best to the desire of the filmmakers.

Finally, there is the familiar dichotomy between the "traditional" and the "modern," whereby the film proposes that "the Polynesians slip into their new-found place in the civilized world" while it devotes its own attention to recording them "renewing their ancient arts." As such, the film is not necessarily contradictory, but it does confine "South Pacific culture" (like "Maori culture") to something produced only on ceremonial occasions and for the pleasure of outside observers. This is as conclusive a diagnosis of cultural decay as any.

Later films would adopt all these strategies but the eroticized one: 1) spatially, they are internationalist in outlook because they categorize South Pacific/Polynesian cultures within the world art historical scene; 2) temporally, they again split the traditional (Polynesian) and the modern (Western); and 3) they utilize a frame story with Maori heroes who wish to revive the culture by rebuilding a meeting house or forming a performance group. As in the imperial/international films of the Twenties, they are nostalgic for the songs and dances of Maoriland which are performed only on ceremonial occasions, yet they also accept the inevitable momentum of the modern.

There is one film, it should be mentioned, that utilizes the nationalist integration framework instead: *Song and Dances of Maoriland* (1959) by Robert Steele. As usual, New Zealand displaces Maoriland, which lingers only in memory:

> Times have changed. The Maoris have accepted new surroundings and new beliefs. Their original chants have been superseded by songs with European and American tunes. But their natural sense of harmony is still heard . . . (and) the natural dignity of the people is reflected in their art, which is both utilitarian and decorative. The old tools are discarded now but the ancient designs remain as they have always been.

The surviving traces of Maoriland and cultural essence can be found here in the references to a "natural sense of harmony" and "natural dignity." The narration is haunted by the possibility of losing authentic Maori differences forever since, historically, Pakeha New Zealand would have to be to blame for this. Yet Pakeha New Zealand is not held accountable to the same historical change, and in this way contemporary Maori are rendered "more natural," in preparation for their conversion in the Eighties into "more spiritual." The narration tries hard to be complimentary in the only frames of reference it has left—the Maori as natural man—but the effect is peculiarly remote, in keeping with the fact that the film was made for the Tourist and Publicity Department.

The classic film of the genre is *Maori Arts and Culture No.1: Carving and Decoration* (1962), written and directed by Ronald Bowie at the National Film Unit.[68] It is a much more complex film which takes as its central problem the fact that "the native arts have languished, almost disappeared." It opens with the loss of Maoriland: a lush orchestral score, followed by a harp, and expressionistic orange/red light bathing Maori "art objects" in the Dominion Museum. One impression this gives is that the objects are not simply decontextualized but dead. The narration then states that "these early people had an inborn sensitivity to match the style of decoration to the everyday articles they ornamented." It seems that when those early people died out they took their inborn sensitivity along with them and only the everyday articles now remain. Unfortunately, their "meaning" remains obscure. For example, the carved handles of canoe paddles: "The meaning of this ornamentation is obscure. We wonder how much of it was thought to be magic, and how much was merely decoration." This is hardly a promising start; with so little to go on, how can the film offer up recommendations for the hoped-for revival of Maori culture? Of course, the film provides the "art objects" with fairly specific meanings anyway by dividing them into the utilitarian function of "magic" versus the "merely decorative" function. What then was this magic if decorativeness alone is not sufficient? The film is not forthcoming with answers.

Instead, the film assumes that there must be an original or foundational system of design codes (for objects such as the canoe paddle carvings), which the original artists worked with and which can explain later applications such as these carvings. However, this is to start with the design codes as the "effect" and then generate the meanings and functions as a "cause," or, rather, it takes the objects as the cause in order to generate origins as an effect. The vision-quest in *Maori Arts and Culture No.1* is acknowledged as a lost one anyway: the origins "have been lost in the smoke of many fires" because, according to the narration and the publicity sheet, the Maori had no written language. To be fair, the film does concede its own explanatory problems, but the intention is nevertheless to render the art objects accessible to secular and rational inquiry in order to assign them fixed meanings.

So if the art objects themselves provide no solutions, what of the Maori themselves? Early on, the film shows the planning, construction, and opening of a new meeting house at Waiwhetu, eventually concluding that:

> It's in and around these community halls that are found most of the art forms which have survived from the vast rich field of Maori culture, for here they are still functional . . . . The spirits of the ancestors and gods have departed, and with them the skills of the ancient carvers. But a new art form is emerging, less artistic perhaps, but with a clear social purpose. And as the younger people feel the lift of a fresh inspiration, New Zealand Maori art may once again achieve greatness.

These statements assume that Maori "art" is a specific category within Maori "culture"; that some "art forms" survive because they are still "functional"; that the "spirits" and "ancient skills" have been lost; that a new art form with a social function is emerging; and that Maori art presently lacks "inspiration" (i.e. "inborn sensitivity"?) and "greatness." The film resigns itself to leaving inspiration and artistic greatness to the Maori themselves; thus it concedes that it is unable to pass on suggestions to Pakeha and Maori art experts. Those Maori who are awaiting the lift of inspiration will have to look elsewhere to recover the lost skills, even though the inspiration that drives them is supposedly universal.

It was simply a sign of the times that this otherwise well intentioned film did not bother to get a Maori perspective on its subject. Cultural difference is denied, historical identity affirmed, and Maori art and culture placed within the same aesthetic as the greatest works of European art and culture. We are left with yet another version of the Fall, but redeemed by the promise of future resurrection and salvation. This process is identical to that of depositing the artifacts in the first place in museums where art critics can save them for the museum-going public. Once decontextualized and recontextualized within a museum setting, the quest continues apace for their lost original meanings, rather than the new ones attendant on being museum "art objects," or "taonga" (treasures) for that matter.

There is an imperative within the institutions of Western art aesthetics—museums, art galleries, films—that art objects be represented in the most visually stunning terms possible. *Maori Arts and Culture No.1* (like the *Te Maori* exhibition of 1984–87) uses an expressionistic lighting and camera style (as well as soundtrack) to construct a technologically enhanced mystique around the art objects now that their original meanings do indeed seem dead. At best, it is a mystique designed to resuscitate the presence and threat of "violence" and "savagery" discovered there by earlier commentators on the Maori. At worst, the film (like the museum) sanitizes those features of cultural difference which might relativize its own values. Consequently, the history of how the art objects happened to become "art objects" in the first place is repressed. As the years pass and the exotic passes into the merely familiar, it becomes necessary to conceal the fact that the art objects are dead through a process of museumification. Such a dreadful fate is hardly conducive to a national cinema of progress, which is why the film conceals it with its technology and scientific theory, in the process "saving" the art objects. For good reason, Maori people are calling for the return of their taonga, though it may be too late to save them either way.

The earlier *Songs and Dances of Maoriland* co-opts (annexes) the Maori into its own national progress myth, and it is unsentimental about the loss of Maori art and culture. Things have got better and will continue to do so, and as compensation the Maori will retain their "natural sense of harmony," their "natural dignity," and their memories. *Maori Arts and Culture No.1,* on the other hand, is an attempt to redeem the Maori by transcending mere national limitations to an international and universal plane of history.

Again, it might be asked, What other alternatives were provided for back in the Sixties by the Myth of Integration? Certainly, it would be hard to construct an optimistic mythology of Otherness around TB, illiteracy, and poor farming methods, but art and culture always promised to be a different story. Carving, tukutuku, songs and dances are, like sport and war, signs of a cultural equality attainable if not actual. Since the National Film Unit partially justified its existence on the grounds that art and culture were socially desirable activities, so Maori art and culture could be co-opted on the same grounds. During the next few years, there was an unprecedented surge in Maori song and dance films and animation cartoons, most of them aimed at a growing international television market which was requesting Maori material.

By way of contrast, it is worth mentioning *Arts of Maori Children* (1965) by Hayward Film Productions, a film which avoids the rhetoric of decay and revivalism by demonstrating that Maori art and culture continue to change dynamically with the times. Maori and Pakeha school children are shown learning to explore Maori aesthetic styles—traditional and modern—under the encouraging eye of Para Matchitt, Arnold Wilson, Selwyn Wilson, and other Maori artist-teachers. The non-stop narration does not seek essentialist definitions of what Maori art and culture is; it assumes that it is a relativistic process involving a "fusion" of influences. For example, Arnold Wilson is interested in combining "contemporary trends with the work of his ancestors. To be a living force, each generation has to express its own period in its own way." Essence is expressed here as "a living force" but it is equated with "each generation" rather than something which has been lost to the past. This is consistent, too, with the repetition of Hayward's favorite theme, that the two races will become one. In a lengthy sequence on Te Kooti and the Tuhoe Ringatu people, integration is promoted as a social ideal: the meeting house ridge-pole carvings "symbolize a prophecy by Te Kooti that the Maori would intermarry with the European and eventually become one race." Therefore, as for the nation, so too, for art and culture. Yet, Hayward's historical model is finally an essentialist one too, in that it seeks the integration of the two races into one nation. It promotes the genealogy of the Maori New Zealander rather than the genealogy of the New Zealander or the citizen of the world.

THE FLIGHT INTO SPIRITUALISM

Despite a slight falling off of interest in things Maori during the late Sixties, there was renewed interest in the early Seventies, and it developed in association with counter-culture internationalism and a reaction against the uniformity of the Holyoake era. One consequence was a reconsideration of the national archetype of Man Alone, in the form of a "back to the roots" quest for New Zealand's historical and spiritual authenticity. The Maori appeared to offer genuine possibilities in this quest and these years saw the atavistic rebellion by eminent poet James K. Baxter at Jerusalem on the Whanganui River; the ohu commune movement; the rise of radical groups like Nga Tamatoa and the Polynesian Panthers; the early flourishing of Maori language teaching in schools and universities; and finally, the renewal of the land protests, quite aside from the Vietnam War demonstrations and the Kirk Labour Government. Within High Culture, the desire for authenticity was still mostly a secular one because, despite the great impact of imported pop metaphysics of the time, it was a decade presided over by the liberal historians in the twilight of their hegemony. This desire was expressed through a concern with individual and national identity and a place within history; not a spiritual identity *per se,* but a secular historical identity, a place to stand. If culture had come to the Maori, so too had history come to the Pakeha.

Independent and National Film Unit production also gained a new lease on life by feeding off the explosion of discourses on New Zealand history that ensued. A new generation of auteurist-inclined filmmakers made their appearance; Alternative Cinema co-operative was established in 1972; initial steps were taken toward establishing a New Zealand Film Commission; television underwent massive reorganization and began producing a series of historical dramas; and many ambitious National Film Unit documentaries on the state of Maori arts and culture also date from this time.

On Maori themes, there were now two major historical narratives and genres available in the Seventies: the arts and culture documentary and the social problem documentary. They offered the familiar dichotomy between culture and history respectively. The first of these was the essentialist and separatist tradition inherited from *Maori Arts and Culture No.1: Carving and Decoration,* which specifically located the narrative of erosion and decay within Maori arts and culture themselves. It was by now widely recognized that many of Maoriland's great meeting houses were in a bad state of disrepair, that the last kuia moko (women elders with chin tattoos) were dying, and that "traditional" arts and culture had been co-opted by Pakeha traditions. A number of films appeared to investigate this and propose solutions. Some are in the tragic mode: Reynolds' *Into Antiquity: A Memory of the Maori Moko* (1971) and the National Film Unit's *Te Rauparaha* (1972); others are tentatively optimistic: the National Film Unit's *Two Weeks at Manutuke* (1971) and *Two Artists* (1972), and Hayward Film Productions' *Matenga: Maori Choreographer* (1972); and some, which introduce spiritual essence into the mix, are highly ambivalent and fractured: the National Film Unit's *Tahere Tikitiki* (1974) and *Marae* (1974) in particular, but also Trilogic's secular *Two Rivers Meet* (1977). Pacific Films' *Tangata Whenua* series of 1974 (*q.v.*) contains probably the most fully developed working out of this thematic, because of its interview strategy.

In later films, there are signs of a growing confidence in the story of the Maori revival, with Pacific Films' *Te Ohaki O Te Po* (*From Where the Spirit Calls*) (1978), and the National Film Unit's *The Adze and the Chainsaw* (1981) and *Te Maori: A Celebration of the People and Their Art* (1985). All three are celebrations of the spiritual essence hinted at in the early Seventies, but quite different from the artistic "inspiration" and "skills" called for back in 1962. What was once a universal aesthetic in the earlier films was by now narrowed down to a more specific Maori variety—"Maoritanga." This narrative became very persuasive because its aspirations for Maori culture were, finally, religious and utopian. It afforded Maori culture the opportunity to regain its lost glory from before the Fall, and as Utopia came closer, so the historical narrative of cultural revival would slow. Maori arts and culture would aspire toward a timeless eternal once again, and spiritual essence would triumph over secular history. Necessarily, this meant simultaneously promoting Maori segregation and separation. It could not be otherwise: to stress an inner Maori spirit and essence was also to promote something to which the Pakeha was not privy. Therefore, in the Seventies, the key Maori vocabulary optioned for Pakeha use included the relatively secular and accessible ''Maoritanga,'' ''aroha,'' ''mana,'' and ''whenua''; by the Eighties, a more overtly spiritualized vocabulary was in vogue, including ''wairua,'' ''mauri,'' and even ''tapu''—all of them not quite out of reach of Pakeha bent on using them for themselves.

It is a strange irony, therefore, that a national institution like the National Film Unit should end up promoting Maori essentialism but it has.[69] In fact, its films reproduce a phenomenon of the Twenties when visiting imperial filmmakers constructed an exotic Other supposedly uncontaminated by their own self/culture. The National Film Unit experienced a religious conversion, a Fall of its own into Maoritanga. Perhaps the main reason for this is the fact that many of the National Film Unit's roles were usurped by television, and as the Myth of Integration went into decline, its films turned mystical, nostalgic, and narcissistic.[70] The secular gave way to the religious, and history—the myth sustaining nationalism (and the National Film Unit)—began to dissolve into a transcendental abstraction.

The second main genre was derived more directly from the social problem documentary and it concerned itself with rural economic decline, depopulation of rural marae, and the migration of young Maori into the Pakeha cities. Accordingly, this more historical genre told of the Maoris' latter-day Fall into alienation and hardship. Some films, like the National Film Unit's *Children of the Mist* (1974), and the later *Te Kuiti-tanga: the Narrowing* (1980) and *Maori* (1981), belong to this tradition, as do *Turanga-waewae: A Place to Stand* from the *Tangata Whenua* series and most Television New Zealand documentaries. They implicitly subscribe to the battered Integration Myth, attempting to preserve an Olympian authoritative position from which to comment. However, their eventual failure is evident in the fact that their argument collapses and they end up taking refuge in either silence or outright defiance. This genre is totally unwilling to accept the exclusiveness of a separate Maori spiritual essence or the slide into atavism; it holds still to secular history and nation triumphing over religion and culture.

These divergent genres do have things in common. They both

propose: (1) a campaign to rebuild the meeting houses with assistance from the Historic Places Trust, Maori artists, and Pakeha restoration experts; (2) encouragement for Maori artists, carvers and weavers to experiment with a fusion of Maori and Pakeha/internationalist aesthetic styles; (3) encouragement for alienated young urban Maori to return to their ''roots'' (*c.f. Roots,* the enormously popular American television series of 1977); and (4) the establishment of urban, inter-tribal, and multi-cultural marae. But the two genres are also mirror reflections of each other: Utopia and the Fall, an archaeology of pure origins and an eschatology of future failure.

As the Seventies commenced, one of the first films to resume the historical narrative of cultural decay was *Into Antiquity: A Memory of the Maori Moko* (1971). The film was written by Kristen Zambucka, narrated by Maori intellectuals Selwyn Muru and Mere Penfold, and directed by Wayne Tourell for Reynolds Television. It is clearly nostalgic for Maoriland (''antiquity'') and its warriors, prophets and maidens, and it does not anticipate a cultural revival: ''This is the passing of an age. These kuia or old ladies are the last of the old-time Maori. When they pass, they take with them a whole world of experience, a part of the heart of Maoridom. Much of the Maori cultural heritage will die with them.'' So much for the future survival of Maori culture.

A similar film is John King's *Te Rauparaha* (1972), which he wrote and directed for the National Film Unit. It is a much praised but highly ambiguous and ambivalent representation of the myths associated with the warrior chief Te Rauparaha. Although the narrational center keeps shifting through multiple points of view, the dominant voice is that of an authoritative narrator who puts the myths into historical (i.e. final) perspective: ''Here was a man, caught between the past and the future,'' which is to say that history rolled right over him and the Maori fell into time. ''Magic had gone from the land. Progress invaded the hills . . . . Hour by hour we gain a sense of history.'' By placing all this in the tragic mode, the film demonstrates the very historical model of decay without revival that it laments. However, it is more complex than this since there are re-enactments of supposed historical events which are presented in a highly expressionistic style. The screen fills with blood, there are unsettling multi-layered superimpositions and dissolves, discordant music and strange shrieks, and

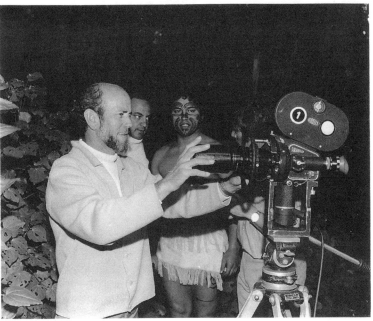

Te Rauparaha (1972) is typical of the resurgence of things historical in the filmmaking of the 1970s. Revisionist interpretations of Maori and Pakeha figures became the norm.

Tahere Tikitiki (1974): carving one of the great canoes sustains the link between the present and the past.

voices which announce that Te Rauparaha "was small with an immense brain, and hooded eyes like a serpent, and the magic power to walk into the arms of death and stay alive." It also revels in talk of "massacres" and "bellies filled with human flesh." The overall effect is distancing, despite—or perhaps because of—the film's attempt to create different subjectivities, including Te Rauparaha's, and it could be said that the film is not so much an oblique celebration of Te Rauparaha's excesses and transgressions as an allegory upon the deficiencies of historical analysis, including its own.

If there are signs here of a fracturing in the historical model, then they are more pronounced in *Tahere Tikitiki: the Making of a Maori Canoe* (1974), written and directed by David Sims for the National Film Unit. The film records the construction of a giant canoe (waka taua) commissioned by the Maori Queen—from the felling of totara trees to the final launching eighteen months later. It opens with a traditional invocation by master carver Piri Poutapu as the trees are selected, and the Maori narrator (Harry Dansey) speaks of this being "a sacred moment . . . invoking the past in the present . . . a path bound back to antiquity." It is a

Tahere Tikitiki: the completed canoe before its launching on the Waikato River.

moment which provides "that sense of belonging, when your ancestors are present, and being proud of a civilization which for the Maori leads back through the great ocean migration from Hawaiiki and beyond." Henceforth, the world of the construction and carving is intercut with the world of on-going daily life at Turangawaewae marae, at the freezing works, and at the pub.

Therefore the main structural dichotomy of the film is between the sacred and the secular. This is also equated with "private" and "public," "traditional" and "modern," "spiritual" and "physical," and, needless to say, the additional analogy can be made between "Maori" and "Pakeha." *Tahere Tikitiki* is probably the first National Film Unit film to pass beyond the Integration Myth and begin an overt dichotomizing of Maori and Pakeha cultures. With the launching of the canoe at the end of the film, "the two worlds [which] stood apart" are again in harmony. The canoe exists as "the physical proof, [the] perfect embodiment of a spiritual concept."

It would seem then that the "origins" and "inspiration" sought for in *Maori Arts and Culture No.1* and the films of the Sixties have been superseded by a "spiritual concept" or essence,

Tahere Tikitiki: a celebration on the marae before the launching.

associated here with the laws of tapu. The film elects to define it
no further but it would seem to be the creative force which
generates all cultural production. At this point, the National Film
Unit begins to drop Maori culture out of history once again into
some sort of timeless eternal, even if the only attempt at actually
evoking the mystique of tapu and spiritual essence occurs in one
short montage sequence. This occurs immediately prior to the
launching of the canoe and it is reminiscent of both the opening of
Maori Arts and Culture No.1 and the *Te Maori* exhibition
advertising.

   Culture and spiritual essence are even more closely identified in
Te Ohaki O Te Po (*From Where the Spirit Calls*) (1978), though
history does remain the primary organizing myth. The film is
written and directed by John Reid and produced by Pacific Films
for the New Zealand Historic Places Trust. It opens with shots of
a dark and shadowy forest and carved faces (Maoriland) before a
voice-over intones, ''The spirit lessened and was no longer strong
. . . but it never died. As the old people summoned up the spirit of
their ancestors, the old meeting houses summoned them back
once more.'' This is the classic description of cultural decay while
promising that revival is at hand. The reason: restoration of two

historic meeting houses, Rukupo of Manutuke, and Rongopai of Waituhi, to be carried out by supervised groups from all generations and drawing on the advice of the elders, influential Maori artists like Para Matchitt and Cliff Whiting, and even a Pakeha conservator.

If the arts and culture documentaries were now successfully demonstrating the triumph of the spirit over history, the social problem documentaries were still retaining the pessimism of the social realist tradition they emerged from. For example, *Te Kuiti-tanga: the Narrowing* (1980), directed by John King for the National Film Unit, identifies the loss of Maori (Ngati Maniapoto) culture as its problem and goes on to describe it in the tragic mode of the Historical Myth: "Maoritanga, the cultural heritage of New Zealand's Maori people, is fading in the European lifestyle introduced by English Pakeha settlers." Initially, it describes this problem in terms of the effects, for example as new behavior patterns ("sharing is giving way to individual enterprise") and as confused identity ("One day our children choose to be Pakeha, the next day they choose to be Maori"). The root cause is determined to be Pakeha power: "Somehow the Pakeha is in control of all the power structures." The education system is singled out as the main offender because it has made English the first language of Maori children.

However, the film is also a case study of one town, Te Kuiti, known locally as "the narrowing," and from this case study generalizations about Maori culture at large can be made (*c.f. Children of the Mist*). The plight of the town and its economic problems are sketched in terms of the declining job opportunities and erosion of family structures as the young people move to the cities. For the Maori community there is the additional problem of the meeting house being too close to the main railway line. The townspeople are seen banding together to overcome all these problems but the film's dominant tone is one of pessimism. Only in the rediscovery of Maoritanga, the film seems to argue, can cultural revival get underway, but, in keeping with the fact that this is a social problem film, no references to "spirit" are invoked. Instead, in its second half, the film focuses periodically on one man, Eddie, to demonstrate his as-yet tentative potential for future leadership. Despite Eddie's lack of confidence with the Maori language, other elders encourage him in his desire to help and his quiet dignity is impressive. This helps slightly to mitigate the film's pessimism.

Maori (1981) is much more gloomy. It was produced by the National Film Unit for the Ministry of Foreign Affairs for exhibition abroad, and it gained notoriety after it was attacked by "Maori nationalist" Atareta Poananga. Her criticism is mostly justified: the film is a repeat of *The Maori Today* (*q.v.*) with its by-now archaic narrative of the Maori-as-social-problem, even if it does end with a mention of "a future rich with promise." It initially covers history (how Maoriland was displaced by New Zealand), and traditions (portrayed sentimentally and reminiscent of the photo series known as *Washday at the Pa,* a controversy in the Sixties). Then follows a survey of "problem" areas associated with the Maori: education, labor, land, urbanization, and the erosion of traditional values. These sections almost entirely exclude Maori speakers despite the fact that the narration frequently invokes "We Maori people." Worn out stereotypes are recycled: "We are called the people who sing—spontaneous singing of Maori action songs is always a feature of parties at home," and almost no attention is paid to the subtleties of context because the narration remains relentlessly generalist. The film is thus an unintended elegy on the Integration Myth, futilely calling for its implementation while diagnosing its failure, and thereby segregating the Maori from New Zealand. There are no credits on the film.[71]

With *The Adze and the Chainsaw* (1981), however, the National Film Unit's quest for the ahistorical spiritual essence of Maoritanga is resumed. The film was researched by Judith Wright, directed by Pat McGuire, and narrated by Dougal Stevenson, none of whom is Maori. It celebrates contemporary Maori artists, from the traditionalists like Kaka Niau to the innovators like Arnold Wilson and Para Matchitt, and it also covers the so-called "decadent" art of Rongopai marae and its restoration, the abstractions of Ralph Hotere, and the carving of the Rotorua Arts and Culture Institute. The Pakeha narration is given to somewhat portentous pronouncements (in standard television newsreader style), but it tries to avoid the cultural decay/revival narrative and at times even attacks it: for example, the restoration of Rongopai is "part of a living culture. It is for others to see something romantic in decay."

The film then embarks on its quest for the spiritual essence of Maoritanga in order to assert that it is flourishing today. The Maori artists interviewed all speak not of loss and identity crisis, but of their mauri (life force), or the responsibilities they have taken on in passing the "sacred knowledge" on into the future. However, the narrative is already overdetermined by the early exposition which is couched in terms of Fatal Impact and the repression of nature (Maori) by technology (Pakeha). Despite the use of the past tense, hopes for cultural revival are anchored in the persistence of nature's power:

> Before Europeans, before machinery and farms, there was a time when life and nature were woven legend. The Maoris of New Zealand saw in nature a magic power—the force which was both mysterious and sacred. It was an inspiration in all aspects of their life. They saw in nature more than just beauty; they saw a violent and creative power. To be moved by nature's exhilarating power is to begin to understand the Maori concept of the world and the inspiration of their carving.

This is actually the opening voice-over and it is juxtaposed with images of contemporary farm life and of a baby's birth, associating the Maori with nature, artistic creativity, birth, and spirituality. In this familiar double bind, Pakeha culture is by implication saddled with technology, desecration, and a general lack of the above. The film's narration is strongly religious and influenced by the Myth of the Fall (*c.f.* John Feeney's films) and it idealizes the pre-European Maori. With a slight fillip, it would produce a discourse of confession, guilt and self-implosion; instead it takes up the defence of what it at one stage calls "Maori nationalism," so where this places the filmmakers (and the National Film Unit) is highly ambiguous, to say the least.

A second qualification concerns the film's conclusion, in which Kaka Niau—arguably the film's hero—is interviewed. The interview breaks off as the narration tells of him being at work in Kawerau, "carving his finest meeting house," but he cannot be filmed because this would violate tapu. Thus the film actually acknowledges the limitations of its position and its own lack of power to represent Maori spiritual matters. This acknowledgment casts a long dark shadow over all National Film Unit attempts to represent Maori culture, including its own. The momentum is toward silence (at the very worst), and atavism (at the very best).

Te Maori: A Celebration of the People and Their Art (1985) was produced by The National Film Unit and Thomas Horton Associates to capitalize on the *Te Maori* exhibition of 1984–87. It demonstrates where the impasse described above has led—not to silence or atavism but to a pastiche of older narrative styles and genres. The historical master narrative of Maori cultural decay and revival continues unabated, but it is now confused as to whether cultural/spiritual essence and history are any longer reconcilable. The film opts for both and so confuses itself; however, it seeks to evade the contradiction by dissolving it into snappy audio-visual fragments and impressions. This tactical evasion is understandable given that the film's primary intention seems to be "celebration"—but celebration by whom and for whom?

First, there is the narrative of cultural/spiritual essence. *Te Maori* is clearly a film made by outsiders but it wants to have things both ways: its title acknowledges immediately that it is about "them," and the "Te Maori" consciously invokes the double meaning of (a) the people and (b) the exhibition, a doubling which is restated in the film's sub-title. However, the film's narration (credited to its American producer, Thomas Horton) is spoken by Maori host Don Selwyn, who switches between third person and first person as he delivers the following:

> Now for the first time, the Maori people have allowed their ancient arts and sacred treasures to leave New Zealand. This is the story of those treasures. Our taonga whakairo, me nga moko, our Maori culture, our Maoritanga. Here we will tell you in our own words and in the words of our ancestors, of the thousand year history of the Maori.

This language is designed to publicize the exhibition for international audiences (that it might appeal to Maori audiences in New Zealand is probably proportional to their capacity to identify with an outsider's perspective). Why else is it important to mention the "thousand year history of the Maori" and how "ancient" the "treasures" are unless to imply at least equal status on the tree of knowledge? Certainly the narration makes no mention of taha Maori: wairua, mana, tapu, whakapapa, and only tosses in the few Maori words for exotic effect.

Unlike *Maori Arts and Culture No.1,* in which the "art objects" look dead, *Te Maori,* like the other publicity for the exhibition itself, seeks to imbue a life and presence in the "taonga" by audiovisual means. The taonga appear in snappy jump-cut close-ups, in dissolves and superimpositions, in chiaroscuro lighting and accompanied by a narration which orates romantic and imperial clichés: "traditional incantations," "the pathway through dimly lit halls," "sacred art treasures," while the images thrust themselves forward with all the style of a contemporary rock video. Is this an improvement on *Maori Arts and Culture No.1,* or merely an updating of the technology and aesthetic norms to match an international corporate-controlled mass media market with its large appetite for exotica? The taonga themselves are treated with just as much "reverence," "respect," and "love" (to quote the narration) in the earlier film, as indeed they were when they were first exhibited in museums under electric lights. In fact, it could be argued that contemporary audiovisual technology does not so much restore life to the taonga or enhance their "essence," as make them further dependent upon external forces for their power and appeal to contemporary audiences.

The essence is only mentioned once as such in the film, but it is there in the many references to "spiritual," "sacred," "nature," a "shining vision which has touched the hearts of all." Such English-language religious vocabulary belongs to the voice of Western art aesthetics, which has generally required the separation of the spectator from works such as these *Te Maori* exhibits. It seeks to persuade us that certain works of art are universal and timeless and that one may gain a feeling akin to religious experience as one stands before them. Such a judgment has to be highly ambivalent: on the one hand, in being extended to Maori art objects this is high praise; on the other, it again consigns them to the timeless eternal as if they date from a time when the Maori knew no time. The film is simply not interested in trying to explain terms like "wairua" or "mauri."

Having rendered the art objects timeless (ahistorical), there is, then, the question of history. The concluding narration (spoken to camera) asserts:

> For the Maori the future is the past. The past is now and the
> future. Although our departed ancestors have died, they are
> still with us . . . . Through the *Te Maori* art, we extend our
> hand, hoping that people will come to know and respect the
> heritage of our ancestors, living, dead, and unborn, who are
> as near to us as yesterday, and never further than tomorrow.

In this formulation, Maori culture apparently conflates past,
present and future time. If this is indeed the case, having collapsed
Western time frames into one (the present or a timeless state?),
how does this square with the "thousand year history of the
Maori" mentioned at the film's beginning, which was clearly
meant to be chronological and evolutionary? Elsewhere, the
narration states that "for over twelve centuries the Maoris have
lived here in Aotearoa," and "over 2500 years before the birth of
Christ." In addition, the *Te Maori* film argues that for many
Maori people who have drifted away from traditional backgrounds, their tragedy has been a Fall into the "relentless assault
of progress":

> Young Maori living in large cities must adapt to a dominant
> European culture. For many, never having learnt their Maori
> language, history or tribal values, they live somewhere
> between two cultures, neither white European nor secure in
> the odyssey of their own people.

These contradictions were symptomatic of the new tack taken
by Pakeha film and television documentaries on the Maori in the
Eighties. More hesitant with the earlier master narratives of
history and culture, the narration now merely evoked them with
fragments and pastiche. It is noticeable that this film, *Te Maori,*
cannibalizes earlier National Film Unit productions such as
Tahere Tikitiki and *The Governor* (*q.v.*) to demonstrate (respectively) "culture" and "history." Not that this is a new practice:
the National Film Unit has regularly recontextualized its own
archival footage, but this may be one of the first examples of the
archives being used instead of contemporary footage because the
National Film Unit has itself built a tradition, an official version
which carries its own authority.

Te Maori also demonstrates the shift in the National Film
Unit's policy of joint sponsorship of topical films. Where once it

was the New Zealand Government which would have funded such a film, now it is the corporations—the *Te Maori* film was funded by Challenge Corporation, just as the exhibition was funded by Mobil.[72] Accordingly, and appropriately with the decentering that this process brings (one government, many corporations), the narrative itself is fragmented and impressionistic. It keys into the clichés of popular debates about what ''Maori culture'' is supposed to be, and, for better or worse, completely blurs the issues. It also suggests that cannibalism has become a dominant mode of Pakeha knowledge production.

CHAPTER 7: THE PAKEHA PILGRIMAGE DOCUMENTARY

During the Seventies and Eighties, it gradually became apparent in New Zealand that ''history''—linear or otherwise—was also a myth. Perhaps this is always a natural consequence of any political context in which a nation becomes confused about its destiny and its sense of direction and turns introspective. In New Zealand films, the social problem documentary and the spiritual essence documentary were joined by yet a third form, the pilgrimage genre, and it has become the final refuge for a Pakeha liberal humanism which, driven by a guilt complex derived from history, desires to renounce its authority and cede it to the Maori.

At the same time, the pilgrimage genre desires to establish a new Pakeha self-identity in the reflection this provides. It is a two-way exchange: I acknowledge the Other as having an authentic Self grounded in this land (tangata whenua, i.e. ''People of the land''), and once I have acknowledged myself as an Other, my own authentic Self can be imagined. This is the basis for Michael King's thesis of schismatic Pakeha identity in *Being Pakeha* (1985) and his other writings. But this new confessional mode can never be freed of the blood of history, and every quest backward to the national origins or outward to the Other eventually leads once more into retreat. The boundaries become tightly drawn around the Self in a defensive posture, a shrinkage, an implosion, and on matters Maori the pilgrim is compelled to make public renunciations or to keep a vow of silence.

This is not to say that history is unusable, merely reduced to being a theory and a method. Historically, the pilgrimage genre grew up with television. Both availed themselves of lighter portable cameras and sound recording equipment which made it possible to shoot outside the studio; for the common man and woman to once again become the fount of wisdom instead of the usual authority figures; and for the Pakeha interviewer to appear in frame as a character within the story. These changes helped encourage the still youthful New Zealand Broadcasting Commission (NZBC), rather than the National Film Unit, to break from the tried and true when it commissioned the first major film series of the pilgrimage genre: *Tangata Whenua* (1974).

TANGATA WHENUA: THE PEOPLE OF THE LAND

The *Tangata Whenua* series was produced by John O'Shea's Pacific Films and directed by Barry Barclay, while the writing, narration, and interviews were by Michael King. According to King, the planned series met with a mixed reception from the Maori: "Some kaumatua (elders), deeply suspicious of both Pakeha and television, wanted nothing to do with us. Others, such as the leaders at Ratana Pa, listened to what we had to say and quietly declined to become involved. Still others debated the proposal with us, rejected us, and then changed their minds."[73] For many of those who did become involved, it was an opportunity for reaching out to alienated young Maori through the medium of television.

The basic strategy of *Tangata Whenua* is to pit Maori culture against New Zealand's (inter-) national history in order to celebrate Maori difference. There were obvious reasons for this in the Seventies: after years of benevolent neglect and negative stereotyping in both the media and post-war social policies, it was worth celebrating "being Maori" as a positive force for cultural revival even if the culture was thought to be in a state of decay. The series tries not to ask, Are the Maori a social problem, or Are they fitting into New Zealand, or What is Maori art and culture? It asks, instead, What does it mean to be Maori? On the whole this strategy is successful. King has written that he and Barclay:

> were determined that we would not make programmes about subjects; we would try instead to persuade people to make programmes about themselves—about their values, their preoccupations, their insights, the things that impelled them to call themselves "Maori" rather than "New Zealanders."

> Our role, we agreed, would be that of facilitators: we would
> encourage them to talk, and we would listen and record
> accurately. There would be no commentary from outside
> "experts," no learned intermediaries, Maori or Pakeha,
> analysing what was said.[74]

Yet this quotation and the series itself are typical of the broad
social preoccupations of New Zealand in the Seventies: the
humanistic anxiety about individual and cultural identity, the
pursuit of historical and psychological authenticity, and the faith
in scientific accuracy. As I have suggested, there was considerable
anxiety at this time about everyone's identity, and not just that of
the Maori. However, Pakeha identities tended to be defined in
terms of individualism and Maori in terms of cultural essence,
even if at this stage both remained secular.

The first question then must be to ask in what ways history
itself was being defined in the early Seventies:

> We wanted to base an entire programme on Maori organiza-
> tion [in the Waikato], using the Kingitanga to demonstrate
> how a large federation of tribes achieved cohesion when
> most others were having to fight disintegration. I hoped to be
> able to explore the *history* and growth of the Maori King
> movement through the recollections of its elders. I also
> hoped they would speak about the phenomena of the *spiri-*
> *tual world* (taniwha, matakite and so on) that confirmed their
> view of life [my emphasis].[75]

The question is, Is it justifiable to analytically separate "history"
from the "spiritual world"? King's approach toward historiography is the knowledge-based kind which historians conventionally
arrange in a narrative studded with a factual insignia of names,
dates, events. This scientific approach, which hopes to step back
from history in order to capture its reflection in narrative, has
never been particularly compatible with Maori beliefs. Even the
Romantic notion of History as a transcendental process of the
human spirit bears only a superficial resemblance to the "spiritual
world" that King and Barclay were hoping to evoke—taniwha,
matakite, and so on. After all, one is a universal system; is the
other geographically specific to Aotearoa?[76] Certainly, many of
the series' informants refer to the "spirits of the past" and to the

ancestors as though this spiritual sense was what they understood by "Maori history."

One way to approach this is that the filmmakers and the Maori informants were talking about different concepts of history. In practice, it eventuates that the filmmakers provide for most of the factual history in the voice-over narration while the elders evoke the Maori spiritual world in to-camera interviews. Thus the former tends to be identified as "history" and the latter with "culture," maintaining the familiar distinction, and *Tangata Whenua* never resolves this conflict—not even its fundamental semantics. Only in the pilot episode of this six-part series, and perhaps in the last episode, does the conflict remain satisfyingly ambiguous. Such is not the case in the intervening four episodes, where the battle between history and culture is won mostly by history.[77]

The Spirits and the Times Will Teach is the first, and in my view, the finest of the series. It comprises three evocatively titled sequences, the first and second being quite short. "In Those Times" is "a conversation about early memories" between King, Waikato elder Te Uira Manihera, and an elderly kuia, Ngaka-hikatea Wirihana. King writes that it was intended "to evoke a feeling of antiquity and a view of life that had originated in the nineteenth century."[78] Consequently, there are many intimate medium close-ups which are expressive of the power of the kuia's face, and as she speaks of her memories (translated simultaneously in English-language voice-over), there is a tremulous shake in the voice and a karakia of loss and death in the background: "The ties that bind us now are torn by death." The audio-visual style recalls Charles Goldie's portraits, with all the ambivalences attendant upon invoking that name (*c.f. Into Antiquity: A Memory of the Maori Moko, q.v.*).

The second sequence, "Moko," is "a discussion among Maori elders about the significance of chin tattooing": Ngakahikatea describes it in striking visionary language, associated in memory with lizard omens and visions in the clouds of trains passing over Taupiri Mountain well before there were trains. Along with the visuals, this is more than enough to establish a sense of Maori difference. King's narration then casts this in the tragic mode: the last kuia moko will soon be gone and this is cause for regret.

The third (extended) sequence, "Herepo's Place," features Herepo Rongo, the last kuia in her Raglan community to have a moko. It also provides a good portrait of Eva Rickard, whose leadership in the Seventies and Eighties was responsible for the return in 1987 of ancestral land taken by the government during the war for an emergency landing strip and later (illegally) turned into a golf course by the local authorities. For much of this sequence, Herepo's comments are refracted through Rickard while background information is provided in King's narration. Several scenes stand out and they all foreground cultural relativism, though only a few examples can be given here. First, in a lively dinner conversation where all generations are present, one of the family says that in Maori Studies at school the children learn about how the Maoris *lived,* and that use of the past tense is picked up mockingly by others present. Second, the juxtaposition of Pakeha golfers' walk-shorts and long socks with Maori controlled images subtly ironizes Pakeha cultural dress codes (*c.f. Holiday Haunts, q.v.*). This is counter-balanced by the sadness felt by Herepo, Rickard, and others at the loss of the marae, bulldozed down in one night without warning many years ago, and by the on-going desecration of the urupa (cemetery). Desecration as a theme is also examined in the next scene; after vandals break into a tomb in search of greenstone, Herepo leads the people back to reseal the tomb and reimpose the tapu upon it.

The final scenes in the film are among the most powerful I have seen in New Zealand filmmaking. Against a soundtrack of cars rushing past, there is a telephoto shot of Herepo in Raglan township shimmering in a heat haze; the shot evokes the sense of her being out of time. However, in the telephoto reverse shots which follow, a Pakeha man can be seen at work spraying the grass, and another rolling a tractor tire along—almost as if this were Herepo's point of view. The Pakeha men and the tire have been in their turn displaced out of time, a time which is controlled now by Herepo. These clever reversals seem to reflect Barclay's influence upon the film (Barclay in a sense "rediscovered" his Maori identity during the Seventies and has gone on to celebrate it in feature films like *Ngati, q.v.*, in the Eighties).

In conclusion, Eva Rickard states: "[Herepo] acts like a medium between the old spirits and the new. They bring back all the ancestors—the ancestors come here and stand with her. She doesn't stand alone when she calls . . . . The spirits and the times will teach. Not man. Not the books. But the times and the spirits of the past.'' What these words mean for ''history'' as either a teleological narrative or a transcendent process or anything else naturally becomes problematic. For the first time in New Zealand films, it becomes impossible to make an analytic distinction between history and culture. Do Rickard's views as expressed here reflect a ''Maori'' view of time, of history, of the spiritual world? Almost certainly. Can they be in any way reconciled with Western interpretations of these concepts? Probably not, and I am not interested in trying to reconcile them.

The point is not that the Maori are ''outside'' history or that they have a different understanding of time, but that in this film, history, the yardstick for King's inquiry, becomes indistinguishable from culture. History becomes a cultural abstraction, culture a historical one, and when this difference disappears, the film's power to represent ''truth'' becomes extremely ambiguous. It leaves the film, if nowhere else, in the contested middle ground between Maori and Pakeha, and this is the film's strength: its failure to subordinate its Maori informants to the overdetermining narrative of historical decay and revival.

The Great Trees is the second in the series. It covers Maori leadership (the ''great trees'') in the broader context of the survival of Maori culture. The shorter first section deals with the Ngati Awa people and covers their belief in the Ringatu religion, their reverence for Te Kooti, and the spiritual importance of the sacred mountain, Patauaki. Patauaki was bought from the Ngati Awa under false pretences and planted in pines for the nearby mill at Kawerau, and some of the speakers speak of this betrayal via moral allegories. This leads to claims that a cultural revival is underway, especially in the schools, because the elders are looking to the children to ensure the continuity of Maori identity. Overall, the prevailing tone remains in the tragic mode.

The second section deals with the Ngati Porou and Whanau a Apanui people. It opens with some evocative aerial photography of clouds and the mountain of Hikurangi, with distant magical waiata and oratory echoing in the background. The legacy of Sir Apirana Ngata is acknowledged first, followed by some well-shot and affecting scenes of a contemporary tangi (funeral) which dissolve out into clouds with the sound of grief behind them. In the first of two sequences that follow, we meet Eruera Stirling, a distinguished kaumatua living in Auckland for the preceding twenty years, who fulfills Ngata's dictum about being ambidextrous in two languages (''Maori is your right hand, English is your left''). Fulfilling it also are Maori university students who talk of their pride and joy in being Maori. Perhaps this is ''equatable with arrogance,'' says one, ''[but] this is what is going to get us through.'' The second sequence concentrates on a conference near Ruatoria, held to discuss education. The overly long speech extracts that follow mostly attack ''the Pakeha education system,'' and the film punctuates these with cutaways to shots of buildings which presumably represent the oppression of Pakeha mythology. The film concludes by returning to Ngata's words and the elders' hopes for a renewal of Maori leadership, but the final waiata is a sad one, leaving the issue in doubt.

Waikato is the third in the series and, as the title suggests, it deals with the Waikato Maori. Structurally it is a little uneven, though King prefers it as ''probably the most integrated and popular programme of the series.''[79] It opens with cultural and historical background information about the Waikato people's kinship ties along the river, the river's sacred importance, and its use during the wars of the 1860s. For its remaining three-quarters, the film cross-cuts between the events at an annual poukai or loyalty hui at Tauranganui marae near the mouth of the river, and elders at Turangawaewae marae in Ngaruawahia who talk of Te Puea and Kingitanga and the ties that bind Waikato Maori together. The poukai helps demonstrate strong iwi/hapu affiliations; the elders give them a historical perspective.

However, there is a third narrative line inserted periodically into the film which unsettles its momentum. This involves scenes of staff and students at Morrinsville College discussing the fate of Maori culture in schools, along with their own personal recovery of the culture, as well as a class of Maori-language teachers at Waikato University who are being instructed by local elders. While these scenes provide for another perspective, they also introduce the cultural decay/revival narrative into the film, and while this is effective in dramatizing the difficulty of encouraging young Maori to value their culture, it trades off a pessimistic diagnosis against the aroha of the rest of the celebrations shown. King's interviews confirm this: near the end he asks a kuia if she is sad that her old people are gone, and this overwhelms other more optimistic feelings she might have expressed.

Tuhoe Ringatu is the surviving half of an original episode titled *The Prophets*. The other half, *Te Whiti,* has been withdrawn from circulation at the request of some of the Parihaka people because of a dispute which dates back to the events of 1881 and the evictions from Parihaka.[80] *Tuhoe Ringatu* confines itself mostly to description of what the narration calls "the spirit of being Tuhoe" and what its main informant, John Rangihau, calls "Tuhoe-tanga." This involves a deep spiritual belief in Ringatu, the religion derived from the teachings of the prophet Te Kooti, as well as Christianity and traditional Tuhoe prayers and practices. Because of its history of exile and struggle, the church is represented as being strongly apocalyptic ("Let the hills sing for joy, together before the Lord, for he comes to rule the earth") and ritual-based (the Ringatu symbol is the upraised hand).

The film's sequences follow one another smoothly. Te Kooti is introduced as a figure of mystery and terror in some New Zealand mythologies, and then as a figure of reverence and power for the Tuhoe. Various Tuhoe people, including Rangihau, are interviewed about the significance of Te Kooti for them and the importance of Ringatu today, and the camera crew is permitted to record a tekaumarua at Mataatua meeting house in Ruatahuna (the tekaumarua are 24-hour services held on the twelfth of every month). Later, the crew visits the deserted marae of Rua Kenana at Maungapohatu, and there Kenana's story of the "New Jerusa-lem" is related. The film concludes with Rangihau's formal defense of Tuhoetanga as opposed to Maoritanga: "These feel-ings . . . are my Tuhoetanga rather than my Maoritanga. Because my being Maori is utterly dependent on my history as a Tuhoe person . . . . It seems to me there is no such thing as Maoritanga because Maoritanga is an all-inclusive term which embraces all Maoris . . . . I have a faint suspicion [that] it is a term coined by the Pakeha to bring all the tribes together."[81] Overall, the film is slightly romanticized, for example, in the use of cutaways to mist rolling up the hills, but the narration and visual style are respectful and the Maori speakers are highly articulate.

Turangawaewae—A Place to Stand, the fifth of the series, is the only one to belong completely to the social problem genre with its characteristic narrative of decay and revival. It opens in the tragic mode with "the problem": the narration speaks of urban drift and loss of turangawaewae, a place to stand. Many Maori suffer alienation; they lack a feeling of identity and a sense of security, a place to belong to, a place for a past, present and future. After showing the effect on rural areas, the film then examines three solutions.

The first solution is return to the land and the rural marae, an idea much touted in the Seventies. Maori Teachers' College students and Nga Tamatoa activists visit a marae on the East Coast to clean and paint the meeting house and to experience marae life, mostly for the first time. They speak of slowly gaining in confidence and feelings of shame at not knowing their Maoritanga. At this stage, the question of "identity" is still a secular one; there is no attempt to equate it with "spirit" or with Maori concepts, and the pop psychology terminology used falls within the counter-cultural clichés of the Sixties. The tone is nevertheless upbeat; return to the marae is regarded as a solution.

This stance is qualified somewhat in the second section, which begins in urban Porirua, once the undisputed home of the Ngati Toa. Now their land is swallowed up by urban sprawl, there are pollution signs on the beach and cars everywhere, and a kaumatua says, "We're just on-lookers now." The film briefly touches on the complex implications involved in why the City Council now controls the land and what it means to have Maori from other areas move on to Ngati Toa land (*c.f. Marae*), but it passes up the opportunity to criticize Pakeha expropriation of Maori land, instead displacing its interest on to the consequences of this alienation—the problem of identity. For example, the kaumatua says, "To become a good New Zealander in the Western sense of the world I'd have to step right away from my Maori culture, and this is what I have done with my children. They are good New Zealanders but they are not good Maoris."

Instead, the film becomes interested in the other Maori who have moved into the area, for example teachers Mere and Ted Davis, and examines what happens to them when they return home to the Hokianga area for a tangi and family reunions. The camera seems intrusive in these scenes, finding hurt in the voices and in the faces, so although a return to the marae is a partial solution, it is simply insufficient in itself to compensate for the massive social dislocation which Dr. Pat Hohepa attributes (in the film) to a history of Europeanization and unjust social policies: "the Maori people are homeless in their own land."

The third section is somewhat ramshackle. It proposes the establishment of an urban marae, Maraeroa, in Porirua as the best solution to the problem of alienation and loss of turangawaewae. The idea of "Ngati Porirua" newcomers using the existing Ngati Toa marae is rejected (a matter of whakama or "embarrassment"), so a new marae is planned, funded, and finally welcomed on to its new site. Inserted into this micro-narrative are tangential sequences about smaller-scale attempts to foster turangawaewae: Nga Tamatoa's urban legal office, visits to Wellington's prison, weekly Maori language classes, a karate class, and so on. Although all are seen as worthy causes, they are considered finally to be reliant on the need for an urban marae. Turangawaewae then is conceived of in terms of identity rather than land, and while this is valuable, it effectively sidesteps the critical issues raised by speakers within the film. Of course, it was shot before land issues came to the fore, but it also reflects the individualistic psychological perspective of the filmmakers and Nga Tamatoa with their mutual problem-solving ambitions. The ethos and imaginative power of turangawaewae remains elusive in this genre, sought for but never realized.

The sixth and last of the series, *The Carving Cries,* is also the most complex. The title refers to a carving in a meeting house at Tokomaru Bay which is said to cry when something in Maoridom is lost. On one level, the film is in the form of an inquiry into phenomena like this and the spiritual side of Maoritanga generally. On another level, the film is an inquiry into the complex political relationships between Maori and Pakeha. The two levels, the first inward into the religious intangibles of Maoritanga (culture), and the second outward toward a secular politics of New Zealand (history), never quite mesh smoothly in the film's structure, foretelling the subsequent rift between Barclay and King over the meaning and significance of *Tangata Whenua.*[82]

The first half of the film is devoted mainly to the secular politics of Maoridom. It records Maori Battalion ANZAC services at Tikitiki and Rangitukia on the East Coast and incorporates footage from *Weekly Reviews 112* and *232* to support the claim by Tuhoe leader John Rangihau that war "was the price for total citizenship in New Zealand." The Maori fought to be recognized "not as a Noble Savage" but as "Maori New Zealanders." Effectively, this is an argument for Maori and Pakeha equality (bicultural nationalism), and the Kotahitanga movement is included at this point as another example of the quest for Maori unity and "partnership" with the Pakeha. Novelist Witi Ihimaera, in voice-over, puts it more metaphorically: "There are really two maps to New Zealand; one is a European map and one is a Maori map, and it's got to do with . . .a whole new landscape of ideas and emotions and ways of approaching things, a landscape that has Polynesian roots." According to the film, it has not turned out that way, unfortunately—the great meeting house of Rongopai at Waituhi (*c.f. Te Ohaki O Te Po*) is nearing collapse and Maori people are steadily losing their turangawaewae. Ihimaera (and the film) then identify Pakeha monoculturalism as the reason for the decay of Maori culture: "We still look through the one pair of eyes . . . [and] I think as a country we're the poorer for it." This half of the film aims to work more by impressionism than straightforward narrative, but the somber tone is difficult to miss.

The second half of the film consists mostly of an inquiry into the spiritual side of Maoritanga, presumably as the ground for cultural revival—as long as protocols are observed. The main spokespeople for this are Ngoi Pewhairangi and Rangihau. In key interview sequences, Rangihau talks of the "life force, aura, mystique, ethos [which is] bound up in the spirituality of the Maori world." Later, he switches to Maori terminology— "mauri" and "tapu"—and other speakers talk of "mana" and "tapu." This is the only time in the *Tangata Whenua* series when some attempt is made to formalize what Maoritanga is with Maori words and with appropriate acknowledgment of the complex web of affiliations and restrictions which come with it. Maoritanga is a "world," a "landscape," which must be entered with respect; it is not something that can be casually picked up. As traditionalists, they view the renewed interest in Maoritanga among the young with some ambivalence; cultural revival is fine but it must observe the laws and protocols of tapu.

The film concludes with a speech by Rangihau that comes as close to Maori separatist aspirations as the entire *Tangata Whenua* series ever comes:

> The number of people who know better than I do how I am to be a Maori just amazes me. I could never be audacious enough to suggest to Pakehas that I know better than they do

how they are to live as Pakeha. But I wouldn't do that anyway . . . . All we're saying is that it is about time we were allowed to think for ourselves and to say which things we want, and to say why we want them . . . . The Maori is content to stand right where he is and be himself in his own country and not be a foreigner.

Unfortunately, the preceding and succeeding scenes cast this essentially affirmative speech in the tragic mode. The film is unwilling to commit itself to unbridled optimism and the most it can manage is a dissolve from a modern painting of reclining Pakeha women (bland, decadent, female) to a Maori tekoteko carved figure (dark, powerful, male), reversing the apocryphal Maori proverb, ''Behind the tattooed face stands a stranger. He will inherit this land. He is untattooed. He is white.''

To summarize then, the hopes held out by the *Tangata Whenua* series for the revival of Maori culture are tentative at best. While most episodes make some attempt at romanticization—clouds rolling over majestic mountainsides, the beauty of the river and the fields, the startling visions and prophecies—they remain somewhat aloof and distanced from the people whose spiritual beliefs they are meant to evoke. Contextualized within a narrative of desolation and loss, a powerful nostalgia consumes most of the optimism, joyfulness and spontaneity. Arguably too, there are shots at the poukai, the tekaumarua, and the family reunion in which the camera and lights seem either intrusive or completely remote, demonstrating the limitations of film technology in evoking subjective states through objective recording. *Tangata Whenua* is a feast of striking images and a landmark in Maori/ Pakeha representations, but the historical context in which it was made determined that it would remain spellbound but sad, an elegy for a racially harmonious New Zealand rather than an anthem or fanfare for the coming of Aotearoa.

BEYOND TANGATA WHENUA

Te Matakite O Aotearoa (1975) is an interesting complement to the *Tangata Whenua* series in that although the Pakeha filmmaker retains control of the technology and the narrative quest, it is a Maori pilgrimage that takes center stage—the Land March of 1975. The film was directed by Geoff Steven in co-production with Television Two. For the first time it is the land, not identity, which is the narrative focus, and it begins where the Land March begins, at Spirits Bay in the far north, where in legend the Maori step off on their way to Hawaiiki. In a sense, the month-long march to Parliament in Wellington is a reversal of that pilgrimage to Hawaiiki in that it leads south toward rebirth.

The initial voice-over and interviews lay out a Maori spiritual and metaphysical link with the land: "Man comes and goes; the land is permanent." The Maori identify with their whenua: "the placenta within the mother that feeds the child before birth," states Eva Rickard. Thus every Maori should know her papaka-inga, his piece of land. In this inversion of so-called Pakeha values, a Maori spiritual reality becomes morally and existentially superior to a Pakeha material reality. This moral superiority then justifies and sustains the Land March as "a protest against the continuing alienation of their land." In the process, Maori people will, as one speaker puts it, regain their "identity as the tangata whenua of Aotearoa." The Land March, then, is a classic reformulation of the desire for Maori unity.

The next few sequences mostly sketch in the practicalities of a land march, from organizing convoy vehicles to massaging sore feet, to who carries the pouwhenua or carved totem of the March leader. In the second half, a series of marae are visited (all but two support the March), a Memorial of Rights is signed in a latter-day echo of the Treaty of Waitangi, and several speakers are interviewed on the actual practicalities of retaining the land: from the Maori names on the map, to capitalism and regional development, to town and country planning and the Public Works Act, to encouragement for the young. As the March reaches Wellington, there is a widening of this perspective to a more international plane: Third World struggles, Aboriginal struggles, "ethnic groups striking back," and so on. Finally, outside Parliament, the Memorial of Rights is read aloud in front of the huge crowd. It calls for legislation "to amend and adjust all laws which inflict injustice and hardship upon the Maori people," and it should protect the "indigenous people of New Zealand," and set up a national referendum on the question of Maori land alienation. The film ends on this high note, seconding the call for legislative solutions.

The future of this particular variation of the pilgrimage genre has always been assured because it concerned itself less with establishing a Pakeha identity than with maintaining liberal-left sympathies for an oppressed Maori identity. However, it is also a variation which has been annexed increasingly by Maori filmmakers, notably Merata Mita who has shot films with Leon Narbey, Gerd Pohlmann, and other Pakeha directors and cinematographers. There have also been a number of similar films—like *Wildcat* (early 1980s) and *The Bridge* (1982)—that are concerned not with Maori and Pakeha identity *per se,* but with a working class identity (joining Maori and Pakeha) against capitalism. Their theoretical impetus has generally been Marxist internationalism, and the practical politics mostly trade union.[83]

Since *Tangata Whenua* and *Te Matakite O Aotearoa* there have been two viable options for the pilgrimage genre: either to tell of a Pakeha pilgrim as he/she becomes increasingly self-conscious, or to tell of a Maori pilgrim in search of his/her Maoritanga. Television New Zealand's *Denny* (1979) and the Australian Broadcasting Commission's *The Importance of Being Maori* (1984) afford examples of the latter.

Denny is written and narrated by Ian Johnstone. It uses a problem-solving method, the problem being the loss of Maori identity within the Pakeha education system. It is basically a portrait of a young secondary school student named Denny who is part-Maori, but he cannot speak the language (his parents are fluent) and nor does he feel Maori: "I can't really call myself a Maori . . . . As far as identity goes, I'm a nil." However, he is seeking to recover his identity through Maori culture classes and visiting Ruatoki primary school where Maori is the first language. Denny himself is quite engaging, but the unctuous and authoritative Pakeha narration incessantly makes comments like "Shouldn't we all be pleased with Denny's progress, for it's our system that has persuaded him, like most youngsters with Maori blood that European history is more important than whakapapa, that essay writing will serve him better than whaikorero, that technical drawing will be more useful than Maori language." This argument (presumably addressed to Pakeha viewers) may well have its truth, but the guilt complex narration explains away all of

Denny's own ideas and actually constructs him as a narrative
function in its own attack on the education system, a somewhat
hypocritical stance for a television documentary to take in 1979.
The film finally promotes a dubious racial essentialism: Maori
should be Maori and not "stuck between two cultures." Perhaps it
is not surprising that this trajectory of the Maori pilgrim has been
adopted more by Maori filmmakers than by Pakeha (this became
the very raison d'être of the *Waka Huia* series in 1987).

As far as the Pakeha pilgrim is concerned, there have been
regular television programs committed to discovering an authentic self formed in response to an encounter with Maoritanga.
These include *Letter from a Marae* (1981), in which Pakeha
school children design Maori murals on a marae (*c.f. Visit to
Motiti, q.v.*), and *The Beginners' Guide to Visiting the Marae*
(1984), which lays out the formal procedures of marae kawa
(protocol). Similarly, the social problem documentary, to which it
is closely related, has survived little changed except that when a
social problem is identified, race lines are rarely drawn. For
example, in Television New Zealand's *Give Me a Love* (1986), in
which the problem of alienation among young urban Maori is
portrayed, the social costs are no longer confined simply to the
young Maori; they ripple right back to undermine the spirits of the
Pakeha social welfare workers. The fracture lines here are social
and economic rather than racial.[84]

Social, economic, and racial fracture is the rationale of Television New Zealand's *South Auckland: Two Cities* (1982). Written
and narrated by Neil Roberts and produced by Alan Thurston,
the film uses a problem-solving method to examine the contrasts
between predominantly working class Maori and Polynesian
Otara, and predominantly upper middle class Pakeha and English
Howick-Pakuranga. The film has a social geographer's perspective: it sketches the historical background to urban migration
patterns, the industrial and social policies of the Sixties and
Seventies, and the cultural factors which have led each city to
think of itself as a unity. Otara, according to the narration,
once "a byword for social disintegration . . . may well be the
least understood place in New Zealand." Experts, both Maori
and Pakeha, are called upon to utter prognoses of hope or gloom.
Howick-Pakuranga is very ambiguously represented; because it
follows Otara in the narrative, the parade of polo matches,

spa pools and boat marinas is made to look thoroughly culture-bound.

The last section of the film begins with the premise that the two cities have separately achieved a sense of community, and the "problem" is not simply that one is rich and one is poor but that there is no communication between them. Snappy cross-cutting between a polo match and parlor video games represents the potential conflict visually, and the narration declares, "Brown and white, rich and poor, and they have very little to do with each other." The film is above all a tale of fracture in the New Zealand body politic and the Integration Myth in the wake of the 1981 Springbok Tour, and it ends ambivalently as if unsure whether this is not really such a bad thing: "It's a story of vitality and energy, and communities that are beginning to find themselves. But it is also a tale of two cities."

A NEW DAWN OR A RACE AGAINST TIME?

Maori: the New Dawn (1984) was an episode in the BBC's *The World About Us* series. It is a classic liberal documentary in that like *South Auckland: Two Cities* it acknowledges the deep fracture lines in the unity of New Zealand, but it retains the liberal tradition of having the Pakeha reporter-interviewer-narrator on pilgrimage to the various authorities within Maoridom. Instead of allowing those authorities to speak directly to-camera or to an off-camera interviewer as in its contemporary *Race Against Time,* the reporter (expatriate New Zealander Michael Dean) remains in-frame often enough to serve as rational center of inquiry, his narration serving as a form of damage control.

The film opens with a karakia and shots of desolate beaches, while Dean's narration provides a revisionist history of New Zealand: Captain Cook who casts "a covetous eye," the Waitangi Treaty which was "never honored," "the 'Maori Wars' as they were called," so many sheep. New Zealand is described as an "English dream of suburbia in the southern seas," a "sanatorium of sun and butter," but "the white foreigner—the Pakeha" severely abused the trust of the Maori. Extracts from *Utu* and *Bastion Point: Day 507 (q.q.v.)* are used to illustrate scenes from this history: "There had been 140 years of Pakeha propaganda, sometimes called 'history,' so, wasn't it high time we had a little Maori propaganda?" Dean later wrote.[85]

The rest of the film showcases various Maori personalities, activists and intellectuals, mostly already well-known on New Zealand television: Eva Rickard attacking the legal system as a Pakeha means of getting and keeping the land ("a Mickey Mouse outfit"); Pat Hohepa stating that New Zealand has "an illegal regime" with "the best propaganda machine outside of South Africa"; Api Mahuika declaring that Maori people are better adjusted to life in New Zealand because they are bicultural and bilingual; and Donna Awatere claiming that "white people" are thing crazy—their obsession with technological power and destructiveness endangers the entire Pacific. The narrative intention here is to enforce differences between Maori and Pakeha. It catalogues Maori virtues and Pakeha vices in an ironic reversal of what Pakeha discourses have done historically in defining the Maori. At times these run into contradiction—Pakeha New Zealand exercises power through its legal system (Rickard) but is itself illegal (Hohepa); and while the main theme is renunciation of Pakeha ways—"we abandoned the seeking for white power, for white knowledge," says Awatere—this is addressed to an agency of white technological power and knowledge, the BBC, and its Pakeha representative, Michael Dean.

After a commercial break, Dean interviews Hone Kaa, who predicts "an explosive mixture" in New Zealand as a "militant proletariat" buys weaponry; violent extracts from *Patu* (*q.v.*) follow and Merata Mita talks about her film; Derek Fox traces the failure of the Integration Myth and discrimination in the media; and Pita Sharples talks about urban, inter-tribal marae and the exciting Maori "cultural renaissance," though he is suspicious of that media cliché. Dean has no such doubts; he calls it a "new dawn." The narrative resolution is only partial then: on the one hand it is cast in the tragic mode wherein New Zealand national unity appears to be a sorry illusion when based on a history of covetousness and dishonor from the Pakeha end, and on the other, it describes a Maori New Dawn wherein Maori nationalism asserts itself.

Where these narratives of Maori Utopia and Pakeha Fall actually leave the Pakeha New Zealander is unclear. Dean is able to avail himself of an expatriate's outsider perspective—he was able to shoot the film because he was thought to be English—and because it was intended for British audiences, so there is no contradiction about where he stands. An uncharitable view could have it that Dean's perspective is a form of morally respectable imperialism, untainted by the difficulties of actively seeking narrative solutions to the social-moral problems his film poses. By analogy, his film invites the conclusion that expatriation or repatriation (return to one's roots) would be one morally acceptable solution for Pakeha viewers to consider. A charitable view could have it that Dean represses analysis of those moral dilemmas facing Pakeha viewers because his first intention is to challenge and unsettle imperial and national value systems. In 1984 this may have been an understandable strategy—possible only by an outsider—but in 1985, when the program went to air on New Zealand television, it had already become passé. It would be *Race Against Time,* screened two years earlier with a lot less publicity, that would signal the limits of what could be said on television, by Pakeha and about Maori.

Race Against Time (1983) is a documentary funded by various government departments and produced by independent filmmakers Stewart Main and Tony Thomson. As the title suggests, it fits the social problem genre: the Maori race is in a race against time and against the effects of racism in contemporary New Zealand. The outlook is apparently bleak. For one thing, the film goes as far as possible to efface the traditional authoritative Pakeha narrational perspective and cede the screen to Maori speakers. An interviewer is heard briefly near the film's beginning but is otherwise absent, and the "talking heads" effect is extremely intense, in that there are no cutaways to relieve the build-up of tension that this necessarily creates. The (mostly) Maori speakers diagnose the state of the "problem," particularly the alienation felt by young Maori, and the failure of the education and social welfare systems. The tone moves from anger and aggression (Apirana Taylor: "My name is Tu the freezing worker, Ngati DB is my tribe, the pub is my marae, my fist is my taiaha, jail is my home, Tihe Mauriora . . . "), to bitterness and tears (Hilda Halkyard: "I'm afraid for the future . . . I've made a commitment . . . to ensure that we survive . . . with dignity. Being Maori is something no one can take away from you"). Of the various speakers in between, only one (Hone Kaa) also appears in *Maori: the New Dawn*. Altogether, there are fewer media personalities and most are involved in some way with the education and social welfare systems, which represents a conscious intention by the filmmakers to get away from the expert witness testimony usually seen on television news programs.

There are of course many complex issues raised and never satisfactorily developed. Early on, for example, speakers identify young Maori and the gangs as "floating" between the Pakeha and Maori worlds, and this is evidently regarded as a problem. However, a return to a traditional and essentialist definition of identity and culture is never articulated directly by any of the speakers, and it may be a measure of their (and the film's) urban perspective which recognizes that the back-to-the-marae message of the Seventies is not the "right" way to go. But none of the speakers offers an alternative; their concern instead is to call on the Pakeha—through the agency of television—to listen to what Maori people are saying, to accord them some self-determination, and to come to terms with their own (Pakeha) "racism." In that sense, the film is first and foremost a polemical attack on Pakeha value systems, not simply in the content of what is being said but also in its form, whereby (unusual for New Zealand television) a succession of orators hectors an implied Pakeha viewer. The film is anti-Pakeha rather than pro-Maori, carving out a definition of "Maori" defined as non-Pakeha. For the speakers, it is the price to pay for entering the double bind proclaiming one's people victims; for the filmmakers, it produces the paradox of repeating the message, "The Maori are oppressed," and simultaneously oppressing them with it.

There is a further contradiction: the film's inclusion of young Polynesians among the speakers. Their first interest is, almost without exception, in criticizing institutionalized racism. But by ignoring Maori-Polynesian differences, the film obviously does not wish to address itself to the knotty question of whether on some issues Polynesians would be better included with the immigrant Pakeha rather than with the tangata whenua. In other words, does the film subscribe to biculturalism or to multiculturalism? Consequently, the complexities of land and language raised by some of the Maori speakers are elided, the film's narrative drive becomes conflicted, and the filmmakers' social-cultural perspective—as outsiders to Maori culture—makes itself apparent.

It must be said in defence of *Race Against Time* that it takes the social problem genre and the narrative of cultural decay to their logical conclusion: Pakeha silence and Maori control of the screen. The producers have attempted to remove all traces of authorial control, but the existence of the film itself is testament to the fact that this cannot be effected completely. Earlier I identified the social problem genre with the analytic strategy of annexation; it asked the question, Were the Maori fitting in with New Zealand? In *Race Against Time,* this strategy of annexation has come full circle to produce an exclusion, not of the Maori but of the Pakeha authorial voice, which becomes an empty space in the film, the voiceless whisper of Tithonus after the body disappears. Maori voices take control, annexing both genre and narrative for themselves, and the logical outcome of this annexation has been seen in the late Eighties in ''Maori'' television programming—frequently in *Koha,* but par excellence in *Nga Take Maori* (and later *Te Kupenga*) hosted by Hone Kaa, a bilingual program in which a panel of Maori experts discussed a different contemporary ''Maori problem'' each week.

The other analytic strategy discussed earlier was segregation or exclusion, which I associated particularly with the mystical and spiritualized films of the National Film Unit. In their documentaries, ''Maori culture'' came increasingly to be defined along essentialist lines, as not only different from ''Pakeha culture'' but superior as well—closer in harmony with nature, more spiritual, and so on. I suggested that as the National Film Unit's own institutional hegemony was undermined by television, so its films on the Maori became more introspective and religious in outlook. As its filmmakers sought to become more cognizant of Maori values, it became difficult to distinguish whether their films were about the Maori or implicit counter-critiques of Pakeha culture. The effect, in an inverse relationship to the television documentaries, has been that as their own hegemony collapsed, the National Film Unit documentaries progressively annexed the space they set aside for Maori culture, seeking to become at one with it, and I identified this with atavism and the Fall.

In short, the two analytic strategies have produced each other, but in ironic and malevolent reverse: each other's Other. The annexation genre of social problems has been taken over by Maori programming as "the Pakeha problem": are they fitting in with us?—so as to exclude the Pakeha. Annexation has produced self-exclusion. The exclusionary genre of cultural essences has been redefined by Pakeha filmmakers in such a way that they now themselves think in terms of a Maori cultural essence in which they too annex a mana and a turangawaewae and wear a bone manaia carving around the neck. Exclusion has produced self-annexation.

At such a time it is no longer possible to conceive of New Zealand in the image of Man and Woman Alone, as the unitary psychological subject of history which the liberal historians constructed in the post-war period. For better or worse, New Zealand in the late Eighties became a centrifugal national mythology which is following the American model of mass-mediated pluralism and fragmentation into artificial differences. Nowadays packaged entertainments like the America's Cup yachting, World Cup rugby, and a Nuclear Free Zone are traded on the international image market, and New Zealand is identified with a plurality of corporations and constituencies of which the government is but one. Similarly there is a centrifugal expansion of Maori identity and the mythology of Aotearoa taking place. While it is no longer politically acceptable to use a totalizing term like "Maori" without also being duly attentive to iwi affiliations, in fact this only conceals the greater uniformity of which it is a symptom. The irony is that differences are usually celebrated when they have already been lost—when (Pakeha) New Zealanders and/or Maori have become a more homogeneous mixture. The museum is not the internal confinement of exotic images of past New Zealand culture and history, or the art gallery the return home from the world of living taonga. New Zealand itself has become the museum, the art gallery, the nostalgia for a disappearing difference between Maori and Pakeha.

PART THREE
AOTEAROA

CHAPTER 8: THE POLITICS OF SILENCE

In 1984, Maori activist Donna Awatere published a series of controversial essays titled *Maori Sovereignty,* in which she called for Maori political representation in the land of Aotearoa, not New Zealand.[86] She described at great length her opposition to a Pakeha system whose values were, she argued, completely at odds with the Maori. She set up an essential and irreconcilable difference between Pakeha New Zealand and Maori Aotearoa that took the separatist impulse within Maori culture as far as possible without shifting completely into the Maori language and thus losing Pakeha readers. The question for many of us who read the book that year was, what was this Aotearoa she wrote off: was it simply the land itself, or was it the whole country? Was it just a cultural thing or was it the nation-state itself?

MAORI SOVEREIGNTY

First, Awatere identifies Aotearoa with the land (pp. 87, 13, 74), always a cornerstone of Maori grievances, for obvious reasons. New Zealand is therefore something that "sits on top of our land" (p.66), like the Pakeha sits on top of the Maori. "This country is Aotearoa. It is ours. White people of *any* generation have no business being in this country" (p.66; also see pp. 45–49). I interpret this to mean that the land's true name is Aotearoa, and whatever "New Zealand" is, it is not the land. Of course, Awatere produces what seems like a contradiction—"New Zealand is Maori land" (p.10)—but Awatere's intention everywhere else is to identify New Zealand with an invading nation and culture, rather than with the land. This first thesis poses a double bind for the Pakeha intellectual who wishes to accept her argument that the true or authentic name for the nation is Aotearoa, not because that

Donna Awatere's book *Maori Sovereignty* (1984) created instant controversy, which was of course its intention. One of its effects was to induce an identity crisis among Pakeha liberals.

would be incorrect, but because to do so would be a denial of one's own right to existence as a New Zealander since she has condemned that name. She further implies that it is a matter of honesty for Pakeha to acknowledge that they belong to the New Zealand superstructure and not to the more fundamental Maori Aotearoa. For Pakeha, this logic leads to the choice between being colonized within Maori Aotearoa (atavism) or going into exile (expatriation).

Second, Awatere identifies New Zealand and Aotearoa with different cultures. Initially, this involves claiming that the Maori have been offering "biculturalism" to the Pakeha all along (p.56), and that this is "the very least" they will now accept (pp. 10, 29). In other words, Pakeha New Zealand and the Maori could co-exist in Aotearoa as two different cultures (p.13), and this is what I understand by bicultural nationalism. The problem, Awatere argues, is that Pakeha New Zealand is a nation which refuses to see that it is also a culture: "Because of blindness to their own culture, they cannot 'see' us from a cultural point of view. To them it is simply a racial matter" (pp. 8–9; also see p.59). Consequently, Awatere rejects biculturalism as insufficient: "The Maori must no longer seek a bicultural sovereignty with the white nation. In such a society the Maori would come once more closely to mirror the psychopathic undercurrent of the white nation" (p.59; also see pp.56, 94). "All efforts at biculturalism have only resulted in integration and assimilation, bitterness and tears. No more" (pp.59–60).

Third, the logical alternative for Awatere is to switch to the term nation. There are strategic reasons for this since nation has been associated historically with the land (demarcating frontiers and regulating land ownership), whereas culture can be diffused anywhere and is no use when the intention is confrontation. Therefore, Awatere poses the "Maori nation" in opposition to the "white New Zealand nation" (pp.8, 26–7, 49), and she adopts the historical romance in order to promote it. Maori nationalism is founded then on the differences she catalogs between Maori and Pakeha cultures (pp.60–93) (*c.f.* her comments in *Maori: The New Dawn, q.v.*). Awatere names this thesis "Maori sovereignty," though there is little difference between nationalism and sovereignty—both terms are separatist-inclined. When she writes elsewhere of "independence" (p.79), "withdrawal" (pp.9, 92), and "self-determination" (p.92), this is evidently a matter of degree rather than an absolute decree—"Withdrawal is a state of mind" (p.103). Sovereignty is, of course, simply a throwback to an earlier European monarchical system, but the reason for adopting it can be found in the critical wording of the Treaty of Waitangi. Nationalism, on the other hand, poses a special problem for Awatere in that it may reproduce the system of domination she ascribes to the Pakeha nation-state, especially since this system requires annexing all the disparate iwi Maori into an artificial unity. In that sense her thesis remains steadfastly utopian, and it may be the reason a number of other commentators have opted for Maori terms instead.

Finally, where does this leave the Pakeha New Zealander? Awatere makes few concessions to cultural rapprochement, and reading the following, one could almost imagine the boot was on the other foot and the Maori were oppressing the Pakeha:

> The Maori people offer the Pakeha an opportunity to become part of that hegemonic consciousness, to establish an identity as New Zealanders which must be forged not in *opposition* to us, but with and for us. A new identity based on Maoritanga *must* be forged. The Pakeha future in achieving a national identity can only be done with the Maori. It is the British way or the Maori way. These are your choices (pp.29, 32).

> The aim is to redesign this country's institutions from a Maori point of view. The aim is to reclaim all land and work it from a Maori point of view. The aim is to enter the Pacific arena from a Maori point of view. To forge a distinctive New Zealand identity from a Maori point of view (p.32).

With this kind of argument, Awatere annihilates cultural difference ("opposition") in the name of a "new identity" defined by the Maori, and then re-establishes this difference (as "choices"), running into exactly the same double bind that confronts the Pakeha mythologist: annexation or exclusion. She offers the Pakeha integration with the Maori, but she means annexation by the Maori. The effect is, ironically, to bring New Zealand's integration process to completion, but from the Other (Maori) point of view.

Awatere's thesis works best, in my view, as an ironic counter-critique to the Myth of Integration. In that sense, what it offers the Pakeha is the *inverse* of what has been offered the Maori over the last hundred and fifty years. This is also consistent with Awatere's derision for Pakeha social policies which profess integration while practicing ''separate development'' (pp.8, 14–15), and her simultaneously calling for Maori separatism and withdrawal. In short, Awatere has produced a parody.

I believe that the most logical Pakeha response to Awatere's thesis is silence. In the next chapter I deal with those who have tried to take it one step further into the politics of self-blame and guilty recriminations. Yet such a step is not necessary and John O'Shea's career at Pacific Films affords an illustration of why. The rest of this chapter is given over to discussion of the four films he made prior to the watershed year of 1981, and his attempt to find a viable imaginative geography for New Zealanders. At times during the Fifties and Sixties, Pacific Films was the only production company making fiction features, and its trajectory is therefore all the more instructive.

The first of John O'Shea's films is *Broken Barrier* (1952), an ambiguous endorsement of the Integration Myth climaxing with a Fall into Maori culture. Then came Pakeha suicide in *Runaway* (1964), and the exuberant celebration of Maori and international popular culture in *Don't Let It Get You* (1966). The final film, *Pictures* (1981), ends in stunned silence. Discussion of *Among the Cinders* (1983) is deferred until chapter 10, and discussion of *Ngati* (1987), the first self-proclaimed ''Maori feature film,'' is deferred until chapter 12. The central thesis of this chapter is that the four pre-1981 films reflect an increasing reluctance to exercise the power of representation if this be involved in inflicting models of identity and behavior upon the Maori, and in ending in self-exclusion and silence this parallels the fate of the pilgrimage genre (chapter 7). The sentiments are honorable, the challenge enormous, but the pay-off not so very rewarding, and Pacific Films (John O'Shea and Barry Barclay) have come out the other side of the Fall and appear to be committed now to support of Maori nationalism.

BROKEN BARRIER: MAKING INTEGRATION WORK

Broken Barrier (1952) is written by John O'Shea and directed by Roger Mirams and O'Shea. As the title suggests, the film is a complex working out of the Integration Myth, structured literally across the barriers of racial prejudice standing between Maori and Pakeha. What cannot be united or integrated at a national level (New Zealand is divided into Maori and Pakeha) *can* be united at a personal level *by* the narrative, if not actually within it. By the film's end, the racial barrier will be broken down by the romantic love between a young Pakeha man, Tom Sullivan, and a young Maori woman, Rawi, who appears to have no last name!

The narrative structure is simple: the first half is set in Rawi's community on the East Coast where, under the watchful eye of Kiri, Rawi's mother, the lovers meet and begin their relationship; the third quarter is set in Wellington where the relationship deepens and is abruptly severed; the fourth quarter is set in the North Island's forest country where Tom learns—through the self-sacrifice of a Maori workmate (Johnny)—what genuine love and aroha mean, and the lovers are reunited at the end. The film contains no sync dialogue, only voice-over narration—a dated device perhaps, but due largely to the expense of sync sound recording in the early Fifties.

The film's exposition begins with shots of Maori fetching kaimoana (seafood), over which a soft-spoken, paternal, and invisible narrator provides an introduction:

> These people are Maoris. For them, as for all Polynesians, the boundary of their world has been the Pacific Ocean. Their ancestors . . . crossed it six centuries ago to discover this rugged land far to the south. Then about 150 years ago, the white man came and called the land "New Zealand." Today many of the Maoris still lead a simple life tilling the soil, and searching for shellfish along the rocky coast. For better and worse, the white man brought with him "civilization." Though the Maoris live in peace with the Europeans, many of them try to keep up with the pace of the modern world. They are stranded, caught like fish out of water. All of them face barriers of misunderstanding and prejudice. Whenever two races live side by side, there are problems.

> Here is the story of some Maoris and Europeans, and this is
> what they think about it all.

This introduction closely resembles its contemporaries, the documentary films of the National Film Unit, where the Maori were
still being annexed into the New Zealand historical romance.
There is a trace of the Noble Savage in the references to the simple
life and the fish out of water, and even a slight ambivalence hinted
at in the seeming inevitability with which the Maoris are being
brought into civilization and modernity. A Pakeha audience is
addressed here; it is expected to show empathy and understanding, especially when the film immediately shifts its narrative point
of view (through narration and POV shots) to the Maori characters, and Kiri in particular.

When Tom Sullivan arrives on the beach, he is represented as
the outsider, the stranger in town. Kiri remarks: ''We don't often

Broken Barrier (1952) explores the barrier of racial prejudice that stands
between Maori and Pakeha. In this scene, Rawi visits Tom's family, where
the conversation is all about ''bad blood.''

see white people round these parts . . . . Something has always told
me that one day Rawi would meet a young white boy . . . . This one
certainly noticed her.'' Tom's outsider status is maintained for
most of the first half of the film. Ironically, it is he who is the ''fish
out of water'' and his arrogance and petulance are distancing:
''Better not tell them I'm a journalist. I bet they wouldn't give me
much of a reception if they knew that I wrote colorful stories about
the Maoris . . . .''

The paternal narrator is initially a stronger presence than Tom,
who has spotted Rawi by now. The narrator provides the bodiless
voice of humanitarian liberalism, of history and rationality,
sketching in the factual information and the film's moral overview: ''Yes, [the Maori] are a kind and friendly people''; ''Rawi
was becoming sensitive about her race—too sensitive''; ''Brown
skin or white, it makes no difference. There's no barrier here'' (at
the rugby). Significantly, most of the narrator's comments are
about Rawi, and they fill the empty space where Tom's moral
code and subjectivity ought to be but are not, and which the film
makes it its duty to provide. The narrator seems to be the
filmmakers' surrogate, steering Tom toward an enlightened relationship with Rawi while retaining for itself the power to intervene in the narrative, and also repressing its own desire for Rawi
through a displacement on to Tom. Although Tom is himself the
major reason for the existence of the ''barrier,'' the film seeks to
break it down much as it breaks down its own desire for Rawi.

Through his articles on the Maori, Tom embodies the quest for
knowledge and the power of representation; Rawi is that knowledge and the representation that he desires. Tom is yet another to
belong to the already substantial tradition of Man Alone—unable
to secure an authentic self-identity in the new land of New
Zealand. Although he is optimistic that he can secure it, the
burden of proof is such that it can only be achieved through
constant redefinition of the Maori. Rawi herself is authenticity
personified, all friendliness and aroha. Appropriately, she is a
nurse (a nurturing figure) and she takes an interest in the local
school with its Maori teacher (the state as nurturer). Much of the
first half of the film is redolent with the anxieties of the
post-World War II liberal democratic tradition, familiar from the
interplay and engagement between the Hollywood genres of film
noir and the western. Film noir serves as a dark rupture in the

sunny optimism of the western: double basses and horns and dark lighting envelop and undercut the soft voices and bright land-scapes in which Tom and Rawi first kiss. To summarize, Rawi's world of nature is invaded by Tom's dark powers of representation.

For Tom stands for more than just covert journalistic exploitation; he strongly resents Rawi's Maori identity and affiliations, and when Kiri tests Tom by inviting him to a "tribal gathering," his voice-over responses are: "I don't frighten that easily . . ."; "They seem to get a great kick out of this tribal business"; "Rawi's happy with the Maoris, well, let her be. I'm not going to wait around here any longer." So the first half of the film ends with the Pakeha rejecting the Maori because they do not match his representation of them. The Maori are therefore split into the exotica of Maoriland within his articles, and the reality of Maori

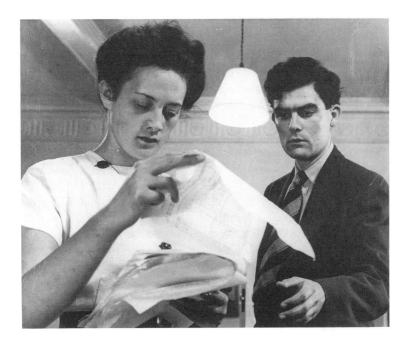

Broken Barrier: Rawi discovers that Tom has been writing about Maori Noble Savages. Liberal guilt sets in.

New Zealand that he experiences personally, and he is unable and unwilling to reconcile them. The relationship is left on an ambiguous note as Rawi leaves for Wellington for another year (Kiri: "I've always wanted her to have the best of two worlds"). These Maori are bicultural, and the Pakeha are monocultural but fascinated.

At the halfway point in the story, the narrative point of view shifts away from Kiri toward Tom, with Rawi as the figure contested between them. Kiri's narration is replaced by the paternal Pakeha narration heard at the beginning, and instead of making Tom the passive and somewhat racist object of scrutiny viewed through Kiri's "Maori" subjectivity, Tom the Pakeha is now the active subjective point of reference, and Rawi becomes the passive object of his scrutiny. It is almost as if there is a Maori first half and a Pakeha second half in this film. This switch helps consolidate the conventional identification process between film spectator and male hero, and it also aligns Tom with the paternal narrator and Rawi with Kiri—a process of doubling along the axes of masculine/feminine:

1. Voice-over narration: paternal narrator & maternal Kiri.
2. Character: Pakeha hero & Maori heroine.
3. Setting: Pakeha Wellington & Maori East Coast.

The second half of the film begins with Tom following Rawi to Wellington because he is irritated that she has not replied to his letters. As the relationship resumes, Rawi discovers that racial prejudice is the price one pays for integration. After a disturbing visit to Tom's family (his father talks of "bad blood" in the family), Rawi thinks: "There's no place for me here . . . . All they ever see of my people are the ones outside the pubs, and the men who do the hard work in the city streets." This Maori rejects engagement with the Pakeha world, though the paternal narrator seeks to de-emphasize this rejection. Fortunately for the story, Tom is learning the same price, and guilt erodes his racism: "I can't go on writing this drivel . . . making them look like primitive savages, just to give overseas readers a taste of romantic Polynesian color. This is the last story I'll turn in. Finish." But Rawi discovers this last article—it is about "cannibalism" and "primitive customs"—and she slaps him and walks out. Rawi's rejection of the Pakeha world is almost complete, her sense of betrayal strong. The film is clearly critical of the post-World War II interest in archaeology and the old-time Maori. The narrative drive is constantly toward a modern, racially integrated nation when the racism of the Pakeha and the simple life of the Maori have passed away through intermarriage. Therefore the crisis reached at this point in the film is directly caused by Maori rejection of the Pakeha world. When Rawi leaves Wellington and returns to the East Coast to foster the ''security and certainty'' of her people, this threatens to torpedo the narrative of integration.

Tom's guilt drives him into the ''clear air'' of the forest areas. He thinks Maoris are too sensitive and there are too many of them around, but with what seems like a fatal attraction, he ends up with a Maori workmate: ''Johnny's a good bloke.'' There the savage

Broken Barrier: Johnny is the film's embodiment of the Maori masculine ideal, yet it sacrifices him to a forest fire in order that the Pakeha hero can learn humility.

breast is soothed and the paternal narrator comments: "This time it is the white man learning from the brown." In keeping with the film's doubling pattern, Tom enjoys working with Johnny and trusts him; isolationism and individualism are not acceptable, but mateship apparently is. Above all, Tom learns humility from Johnny on a visit to Whakarewarewa:

> This is all that too many Europeans ever see of the Maori people: Maoris in the showcase. No wonder they keep on treating most of them as if they should still be wearing grass skirts and making chisels out of shark bones . . . .

Unfortunately, there seems to be very little sense of hypocrisy in Tom's ideas, given that he had been contributing so many articles on Maoris in the showcase. Consequently, the following sequence, in which Johnny sacrifices his life in order that Tom may live (to marry Rawi), is the most awkwardly contrived of the film. It could be argued that the film sacrifices Johnny—male Maoridom—to the forest fire in order that cross-racial integration may be achieved. It is only Johnny's crucial message that survives the fire, heard again (literally) in Tom's memory: "He loves her, he should go to her. The light and the dark can always be together." This formally states the film's theme but, crucially, it is a Maori who says it, just as the concluding narration, which articulates much the same thing, comes from Kiri:

> They love one another and they will marry. No one can stop them. No one should try . . . . Together they can help our two races to understand each other. Help them to overcome the barrier of race prejudice that time has placed between them . . . . Like Rawi and Tom, all of us have come a long way . . . . The future lies with them.

Why should the film attribute lines like these to the Maori characters unless it be to legitimize the Integration Myth through their voices? Kiri makes similar pronouncements throughout the film: "It's a white man's world"; "I'm proud. People think of her as a nurse. Not as a Maori girl."

Kiri and Johnny articulate a "feminine" discourse of integration through self-sacrifice, denial of their racial and sexual difference, self-exclusion, and eventually annihilation. No wonder this social experiment exacts its toll upon Rawi, whose voice-over carries the burden of these contradictions, written off by the paternal narrator as if she were "too sensitive." The turning point for her character is when she too seizes the power of representation and rejects the simplicities of Tom, Kiri, and the paternal narrator. She slaps Tom and leaves for home. However, she must pay a price: she drops out of the story. The paternal narrator and Tom articulate the "masculine" discourse of representation, with segregation between subject and object, self and other. This is expressed through assertion of the differences between the two races and sexes ("These people are Maoris . . . ''), and between Rawi and Tom, in order that "she" can be annexed. It is a process of exclusion of the Other through representation, and a movement in narrative to ensure a subsequent capture. *Broken Barrier* does to its Maori characters what Tom does to them: it consigns them to the exclusionary zone of Maoriland and then annexes them into New Zealand.

For Tom, the ethical dilemma requires returning to Rawi's family to apologize and perhaps write a "true" story of her people—foreshadowing the liberal historians of the next thirty years. For *Broken Barrier* itself, it is a question of promoting integration as the means of overcoming the barrier of racism, hence Pacific Films' future commitment to films on Maori themes. O'Shea writes: "When we made the film, it seemed to me only Maori acceptance of integration was making a chance for the country to go ahead. Mainly by inter-marriage . . . . There was little hope for cultural integration . . . from the Pakeha side [and] one was attacked for making a 'dirty movie' because it dealt with miscegenation."[87] Interestingly, Mirams and O'Shea next went on to make *Dances of the South Pacific* (replete with the "romantic Polynesian color" that Tom came to renounce) before Mirams moved to Australia, an expatriate trajectory later duplicated by Michael Dean, Keith Aberdein, and others. O'Shea, on the other hand, remains within the nationalist framework.

Yet the ending of *Broken Barrier* represents a striking ambiguity which is at the heart of the Integration Myth and Pacific Films' perverse endorsement of it. The final reconciliation between Tom and Rawi occurs back on the East Coast. When Tom arrives to embrace Rawi and Kiri's voice-over talks of their future marriage, where does this really leave the relationship? Has Rawi overcome her doubts about Tom's racism because of some personal rapport? Can Tom live in a Maori community when he has already demonstrated hostility toward Maori ways, let alone incompetence at sheep mustering? Logically, there are two possibilities that follow from Johnny's earlier self-sacrifice: either Tom must sacrifice himself to Rawi, or Rawi must sacrifice herself to Tom. Since it would seem that the only place that their integration can succeed is among the Maori and not among the Pakeha, therefore it must be Tom, the Pakeha, who finally sacrifices himself to Maori annexation, confirming the very fear of castration anxiety that was dramatized in the film noir sequences earlier in the film. For Tom this means self-exclusion and silence. The roles are now reversed: the Pakeha must deny the power of representation and cede it to the Maori. In terms of the Integration Myth, the narrative has produced not Maori integration into the Pakeha world, but Pakeha integration into the Maori world! *Broken Barrier* is, finally, an idealistic and utopian statement of atavism—Tom will ''go native'' and drop out of history.

Runaway (1964): David Manning (right) is attracted to Isobel and Joe Wharewera, a young Maori sister and brother who offer redemption and humility, but he rejects them. That is Kiri te Kanawa on the left.

RUNAWAY: THE RESORT TO FLIGHT

Runaway (1964) by Pacific Films, produced and directed by John O'Shea, does not share the optimism and idealism of *Broken Barrier,* nor its hope of forging an integrated nation. Perhaps it examines what might have happened to Tom Sullivan had he not met the bicultural Rawi; perhaps, as one critic argued, it is an allegory upon Pakeha New Zealand's anxiety and alienation from Britain as the latter moved to join the European Economic Community;[88] perhaps also it is an allegory upon High Culture alienation and the spiritual "uncertainty" (self-) diagnosed by poet and editor Charles Brasch in *Landfall* in the late Forties and Fifties. Stylistically, *Runaway* crosses American film noir (for example, Alfred Hitchcock's *Psycho* of 1960) with the European art-house films of alienation and repression (Cocteau, Bergman, Antonioni, Osborne/Richardson), yet with a distinctively New Zealand ambience as well—the motifs of Man Alone, flight in a stolen car, the empty landscape, lonely eccentric gunmen, the oppression of authority, and all the trademarks of what Merata Mita has termed the "Boys' Own genre." *Runaway* is a prototype for the "revival" of the New Zealand film industry after 1976: *Sleeping Dogs, Goodbye Pork Pie, Smash Palace,* and others.

The narrative initially sets up its anti-hero as an angry young man-on-the-run: David Manning has the innocence and good looks of a James Dean or Marlon Brando, and this makes him desirable to men and women. However, women are "bitchy," parents—especially men—are unhelpful, and money short. His flight from Auckland to the Hokianga area (*cf. Arriving Tuesday, q.v.*) symbolizes the Pakeha (and masculine) quest for identity with(in) rural New Zealand and Maori New Zealand. There follows an extended conflict, both sexually and culturally, for David's psyche: he is torn between the vulgarity of adultery with a European-born femme fatale, Laura Kossovich, who satisfies the demands of the flesh, and the gentle dignity of the Maori of the community, in particular a young Maori sister and brother, Isobel and Joe Wharewera. Ignoble Pakeha savage and noble Maori savage; femme fatale and nurturers. *Runaway* offers a sexual and cultural dichotomy similar to *Broken Barrier,* in that Pakehas are active, exploitative, aggressive, masculine; Maoris are passive,

Runaway: the deerstalker Clarrie (played by writer Barry Crump) begins asserting proprietorial rights over Diana.

sacrificial, humble, feminine. Laura Kossovich says to David: "Those stupid Maoris burnt the forest off centuries ago so the sand would guide their canoes in from the sea"; and later, "You're really weak. You must be, the way you hang around those lazy Maoris up here. Why don't you make something out of yourself?" Joe Wharewera to David: "There's no point in worrying."

On the one hand, David is the active and arrogant Pakeha: at the community dance he forces Isobel out of the arms of her Maori partner, and his conversations with Joe carry a certain repressed homosexual tension. On the other hand, he is forced into the role of passive sacrificial partner by Laura's casual vindictiveness and sexual aggression. The oscillation this sets up between his own expectations of masculine and feminine desires becomes impossible for him to control, and so he takes flight once again. What is particularly interesting in this equation is the manner in which the Maori serve as the passive and the feminine in order to assist David's achievement of what Brasch calls "self-discovery, self-possession"—the ideal of psychic self-integration. Brasch's mythology of the egocentric monad tends to rule out integration with an Other outside itself, either sexually or culturally, and its spiritual pessimism is unable to conceive of a double or split self formed in alliance with that Other.[89] In *Runaway,* "the Maori" provides a feminine and atavistic retreat for David, but his fear of the vengeance of the Pakeha Law embodied by Laura (after he has rejected and scorned her) is far stronger. David therefore appears to subscribe unconsciously to Brasch's mythology rather than O'Shea's. Consequently, *Runaway* kills David off.

The second half of the film is a flight from the Pakeha Law. Soon enough, he is indirectly responsible for the fatal heart attack of the authoritarian father figure who gives him a ride, and subsequently his imagination is consumed with oedipal guilt. Born in a rural area, he desires to return to it, tracing the familiar atavistic search for childhood security, purity, no pretensions. Allegorically, this is mixed in with some hilarious cultural atavism: "Driving's like dreaming . . . . I want to lose myself . . . become nothing, vanish in the dead deserted world of Westland . . . . Look, I'm quitting the whole set-up, I'm getting out, going bush . . . . Trying to go native . . . ." These lines are spoken by David to Diana, a young woman he meets who is the feminine complement and conscience for the stable heterosexual (Pakeha) identity he seeks. Masculine sexual identity is affirmed when David later contests and wins proprietorial rights to Diana (over the deer-stalker, Clarrie)—with a gun—and also when she stays with him during the police manhunt which follows.

David Manning is, however, too conscious of the weight of History and Fate. The inevitability with which the narrative plunges him into oblivion and self-exclusion is excessive, to say the least, and even ironized occasionally for being so. For example, when Diana falls for David's mad impetuous nature, she utters New Zealand film's most memorable line, "Let's go mad in your mad wild Westland." The irony and tragedy make for an uneasy mix. These Pakeha do not belong to the land, and their guilt over its expropriation produces only confessions and ultimately suicide. As Clarrie, the deer-stalker, says, "Nothin' belongs to no-one around here." Westland stands in for the desolation of the human heart, and David's suicide signals the end of futile hopes for Pakeha self-integration. *Runaway* coldly and deliberately rejects Brasch's mythology and the schismatic

Pakeha cultural identity which leads to Michael King's *Being Pakeha* (1985). In 1964, that road led to suicide and silence.

DON'T LET IT GET YOU

Don't Let It Get You (1966), directed by John O'Shea and written by Joe Musaphia, is at first sight very different from the other O'Shea films discussed in this chapter. It is one of New Zealand's great underrated classics, perfectly capturing the exuberance and energy of New Zealand's finest hour in pop/rock musical history. Fashioned in the style of Richard Lester's *A Hard Day's Night* (1964) and *Help!* (1965), it is a showcase for the talents of the period—Howard Morrison, Rim D. Paul, Herma and Eliza Keil, Lew Pryme, Eddie Lowe, and others, including the Australian star Normie Rowe, and even Kiri te Kanawa ("Sing for us now, Kiri"). The songs are written mostly by Patrick Flynn in collabo-

Runaway: Diana and David on the ice near the film's climax, running away from responsibility and reason.

ration with either O'Shea or Musaphia, and they are all uniformly excellent. However, the film is also a knockabout romantic comedy: the dialogue non-sequiturs, pratfall gags, and bizarre juxtapositions exhibit a taste for an offbeat sense of irony and blasé manner not unlike that of television in the late Eighties (*Terry and the Gunrunners* and *The Billy T. James Show*, for example). As a nostalgia piece, the film comes as close to capturing the hopes and aspirations of the period as the *Weekly Reviews* do for the Forties and the *Tangata Whenua* series does for the Seventies, and it is perhaps the last film in which the Integration Myth can be seen to be working reasonably well.

Although most of the film is set in Rotorua (the "Maori town" par excellence as far as New Zealand films are concerned), it actually starts out in Sydney. Furthermore, the hero and heroine, Gary Wallace and Judy Beech, are both Australian. Gary wants desperately to play in Howard Morrison's band at a big concert in Rotorua, so he sells his drums to pay for the plane ticket to New Zealand, and Morrison turns out to be on the same flight. Judy, a Marilyn Monroe blonde, is also on that flight, en route to Rotorua with her mother for a holiday. Aside from Gary and Judy and Howard Morrison himself, the fourth major role is filled out by the obligatory villain, William, a rival drummer who has the job Gary seeks, and who also sets off in hot pursuit of Judy's hand. In terms of narrative construction, the romantic leads are Australian, the paternal authority figure in the background (Morrison) is Maori, and the villain is a Pakeha New Zealander, so it is difficult to imagine a more radical upheaval in the conventional hierarchy of power within New Zealand films.

Furthermore, the film's songs are performed by Morrison, Normie Rowe, and mostly Maori entertainers; even Lew Pryme's song sequence ("Come On") has a strongly American flavor. Therefore, generally speaking, *Don't Let It Get You* is an elegant blend of quirky British-style humor, American-style open spaces, sunshine and consumerism, and a distinctly Maori New Zealand ambience. Consequently, Pakeha New Zealand is practically effaced by the narrative construction, a tendency which is consistent with O'Shea's other films. The difference, of course, is that in *Don't Let It Get You*, O'Shea has achieved a stylish synthesis of all three Others, and in this synthesis is a potential Pakeha identity worth celebrating instead of destroying as he had done in *Runaway*.

Don't Let It Get You: singer Howard Morrison, the personification of Maori New Zealand, and Australian drummer extraordinaire Gary Wallace, at a marae.

Aside from the songs, the film's strongest asset is undoubtedly the complete assurance with which Gary Wallace and Howard Morrison act out their roles as aspiring lover/comedian and showbiz giant. (They are both known by their actual names in the film, as are Rowe and Te Kanawa.) Wallace's antics with an errant pair of drumsticks and his drum solos would be enough to convince any viewer of his brilliance, except of course the very people in the film that he needs to impress. Some of his gags are particularly local, for example mustering sheep by bicycle; others cheerfully ironize conventional domestic romance—Judy: "Opportunity only knocks once, Gary"; Gary: "And I haven't even got a front door." Wallace's lugubrious face and sense of comic timing are not equalled in New Zealand film and television until the arrival on the scene of John Clarke's Fred Dagg a decade later. Morrison, on the other hand, is the very model of friendly domesticity and paternal power—the local boy made good. The titles of his songs reflect this: "Don't Let It Get You," "Haere

Don't Let It Get You: Kiri Te Kanawa surrounded by fans - "Sing for us now, Kiri."

Mai Means Welcome,'' and ''I'm Home Now,'' the last of these
being set to visuals of Morrison walking alongside Lake Rotorua,
then at home with his wife and children, and then playing squash,
on horseback, and so on. Aside from performing, his main role in
the film is to frustrate William's dishonorable intentions toward
Judy and to encourage Gary. Morrison in many ways symbolizes
Maori New Zealand, a role he has continued to promote into the
Eighties. His strength and stability in the film is complemented by
the sadder torch ballads of Eddie Lowe (''Why Am I Alone
Now?'') and Herma Keil (''My World Has Gone''), as well as the
lighter touch of Gerry Merito (''Y'Ever'').

Stylistically, the film not only borrows from many sources, but,
like those sources, is intentionally cavalier with the narrative and
genre conventions. Unusual for an O'Shea film, it is anti-realist,
full of crash-cutting and never waiting around for an explanation,
women in bikinis dancing on a garage roof at the drop of a guitar
chord, all manner of technical special effects, unreadable final
credits, and so on. Alone of the four films discussed in this
chapter, *Don't Let It Get You* does not take itself too seriously and
appears to be genuinely relaxed about and sympathetic to biculturalism, since racial issues are otherwise never drawn attention to
whatsoever. Curiously, however, the only way this can be
achieved is via an alliance between the Maori and an international
world of Australian and American popular culture. The Pakeha
New Zealander—William—is effectively excluded from the
equation by being reduced to helpless silence. At the end of the
film, while Gary wins Judy and plays in the concert, William is,
quite literally, marooned on Mokoia Island in the middle of Lake
Rotorua.

PICTURES: THE ROAD TO SILENCE

Pictures (1981/83) once again traces out this narrative trajectory
toward silence. On one level, it is a historical biography of two
brothers, Walter and Alfred Burton, English photographers who
settled in late nineteenth-century New Zealand. On another level,
however, it is an allegory upon the morality of photographic
representation of the Maori. Walter Burton takes photographs of

the "Maori Wars"—including controversial atrocity photo-graphs—and is unable to exhibit them in Dunedin without the colonial administrators destroying them and him out of fear of what their English masters might think. Walter eventually com-mits suicide. Alfred Burton follows in Walter's footsteps but he takes officially acceptable photographs of Maoris—dressed in European clothes and in picturesque settings—which is to say that Alfred compromises his principles while also learning something of Maori culture.

In this dichotomy, the film presents two models for Pakeha responses to being in New Zealand. In Walter, there is the stubborn artist and social critic who for the sake of his principles must tell of Pakeha oppression of the Maori and be damned. He is philosophically a realist ("That was exactly the way it was"), but

In telling the story of two brothers, Alfred and Walter Burton, *Pictures* (1981) explores the alternatives available to Pakeha photographers of the Maori. On the left is Alfred who becomes known for his picturesque tableaux; on the right is Walter who seeks out atrocity photos.

his photographs are disparaged as "disgusting," so he finds solace in his violent memories and in drinking, and finally in suicide. He is no model on which to construct a future national identity, even if he does have a moral sensibility. In Alfred, there is the commercial portrait photographer who is prepared to take photographs of Maoris dressed and posed for the occasion, though not (yet) *their* occasion. He is philosophically an idealist who understands, if only partially, that any photograph is a conjuring trick, and that because subjects have their rights too, then romanticizing the image in their favor is artistically acceptable. Alfred believes in a better future; he serves as a proper basis for a future national identity. The contrast might almost be a repetition of David Manning (*Runaway*) versus Tom Sullivan (*Broken Barrier*).[90]

Curiously, awkwardly, it is Walter who is the narrative center for most of the first half of the film, but when he collapses, drunk and insensible on the studio floor before a photography session with a girls' school, Alfred displaces him. Thereafter, Walter is confined mostly to inserted cutaways which tend only to rupture the main narrative line structured around Alfred. These cutaways maintain the contrast between the two brothers, and they also sustain the contrast between their two wives. Walter's wife, Helen, is a model heroine, stalwart and stoic; Alfred's wife, Lydia (with her English accent), is given to calling Maoris "savages" and "natives" and to absurd pretensions to the genteel life. At the end of the film when Walter dies, Lydia returns to Britain, thus freeing Alfred and Helen to consolidate their relationship, hinted at already throughout the film, as a prototypical Pakeha New Zealand couple.

Other characters are "doubled" as well: Rochfort, the mercenary surveyor for the Railways, of affected airs and lust for Maori women, much hated by the Whanganui Maori; and Ngatai, the ambiguous Maori guide who ends up in a Pakeha jail. They are, respectively, New Zealand's evil British Imperialist and Maori Noble Savage (Ngatai echoes both Johnny of *Broken Barrier* and Joe of *Runaway*). Given this choice, Alfred finds he must rely on the assistance of the former, but if he could, he would throw in his lot with the latter—another prototype for a future national identity, based not on Rochfort's racist imperialism but on Ngatai's quiet and dignified biculturalism.

This shot of Maori prisoners-of-war from *Pictures* typifies the social realist approach taken by Walter Burton. The filmmakers are on his side.

Like Walter's photographs, *Pictures* is a realist film with an aesthetic of "authenticity" which examines the difficulties of sustaining realism as a viable code of representation. Yet *Pictures* itself generates fewer contradictions than its filmmakers' own press statements.[91] For one thing, in interviews, the director Michael Black and the producer John O'Shea tend to identify more with Walter than with Alfred, though the dialogue never makes it clear whether Walter does have a politicized consciousness or whether he is just a dilettante. In terms of screen time, Alfred becomes the filmmakers' main protagonist, yet they disparage him as a photographer of the "tame" and "picturesque." However, their own film, *Pictures,* dramatizes exactly why New Zealand's realist aesthetic is no longer popular at the box office, and why O'Shea and Black have ambivalent feelings about that other contemporary historical epic, *Utu* (*q.v.*), which was a success and which nonchalantly sacrificed "authenticity" in order to get its more ambiguous moral code across.

In *Pictures*, Alfred is the hero because he is the survivor; he understands compromises and the constraints of power, and in pragmatic terms it is he who is the realist. Walter, on the other hand, is the impractical idealist. The film is founded on this contradiction.

The film ends anti-climactically. If it is not quite a tragedy, perhaps it is better described as an elegy upon the suppression of New Zealand's "true" history. Yet the film itself takes great liberties with the historical record: for example, the historical Walter Burton never took atrocity photographs of the wars and he was every bit as interested in the picturesque as Alfred, and probably even more interested in studio portraiture; Walter's death (in 1880) occurred well after the dissolution of the partnership (in 1877) and well before Alfred's excursions into the New Zealand landscape (in the 1880s); there is no reason to assume a relationship between Alfred and Walter's wife Helen (she returned to England upon her husband's suicide); Ngatai is an almost total fiction; and the imperial and racist dialogue is at best no more than imaginative reconstruction of what the filmmakers would have us believe was the norm in polite colonial society.[92]

There is a further area of potential contradiction. The sequences in the film which illustrate Walter's photographs are of a Maoriland destroyed—chained Maori prisoners trudge through black mud amid violent explosions and sad waiata. This is the tragic mode. The sequences in which Alfred's photographs are taken are of a romantic Maoriland preserved high up the Whanganui River. The soft focus photography and exotic scenography evoke a world still relatively uncontaminated by Western influence—one of the "lost worlds" of the Victorian imperial imagination to be found in Rider Haggard, Conan Doyle and H. G. Wells. Obviously, *Pictures*' representation of this may well coincide with Alfred Burton's own imagination as he traveled up-river, except that most of the shots are from the perspective of distant watchers, presumably Maori. This has the effect of ensuring that Alfred Burton is represented in a sympathetic light as a questing hero in the wilds of Maoriland, while also ensuring that Western technology—specifically Rochfort's railway and Burton's photography—appears as a further agency of contamination following in

Rochfort, the racist Railways surveyor, is the villain in *Pictures*.

the wake of the land wars and land confiscation. This is highly ambiguous story-telling; there are no psychological details to convey Alfred's own moral code (*c.f. Broken Barrier*), other than a scene in which he distances himself from the kind of photographic rape which interests Rochfort, and another in which he has a guilt-ridden nightmare before escaping down the river with Ngatai.

The years in which the historical Burton took his photographs of the area were transitional: "A few years earlier the journey would have been impossible or at least suicidal. A few years later the Maori had become sophisticated in front of the camera."[93] But the film is not interested in the uses the Maori would later find for portrait photographs, for example at tangis. Instead it reproduces the mythology of Maoriland and the Noble Savage, which it can mourn as a victim of the ravages of Western technology. The film implies that it will be the jailed Ngatais who will forge the Maori future. What Black and O'Shea might view perhaps as making it up to the Maori through re-enacting a past history of imperialist invasion, can just as easily be read as doing what Alfred Burton did—romanticizing the Maori, dressing them up in exotic costumes and agonizing over their oppression.

CHAPTER 9: THE POLITICS OF BLAME

As the Integration Myth unraveled throughout the Seventies and Eighties, this inevitably undercut the authority of the liberal historians and other intellectuals charged with custody over the myth. Mostly they presided over this unraveling by embracing a fatalistic pessimism toward historical determinism and realist representation. Others sought instead for an oppositional politics—the contributors to certain Marxist, feminist, and Christian magazines, such as *The Republican* and *Illusions, Broadsheet,* and *Accent,* as well as *The Listener, Art New Zealand* and books such as *Proud to be White?*[94] These writers adopted a stance that resembles what Edward Said has called a ''politics of blame,'' turning on the colonizing culture (in this case, one's own Pakeha culture) in order to denounce it for brutal annexation of another culture.[95] Much of their moral authority to do so derived from invoking Awatere's *Maori Sovereignty* essays (*q.v.*), executing that peculiar form of identification or ''transference'' which is characteristic of the Left.[96] Combining Marx and Freud, they diagnosed ''our'' supposed identity crisis in terms of repression of guilt and the return of the repressed, which now challenges the settler regime's legitimacy to hold the land. Humanist metaphors alluding to land tenure—''alienation'' and ''rootlessness''—were the vogue, in an attempt to undermine Pakeha confidence by visiting the sins of the fathers upon the sons and daughters of today, who have nonetheless shown few signs of a guilty conscience. The adopted pose is that of the truth-teller, the dissident voice of a High Culture anti-nationalism.

To establish a politics of blame requires assembling some vast cultural abstraction like Pakeha ideology, patriarchy, the class system, or racism, then essentializing it as a totalizing system, identifying the victim, and then reading off the appropriate oppression. But self-referential paradoxes are quickly generated. For example, when these ''connoisseurs of diversity'' (the expres-

sion is Richard Rorty's) publicly lambast Pakeha "ethnocentrism" (or "Eurocentrism" or "racism") as the root cause of
culture conflict, an implicit dichotomy is being made between
works which are ethnocentric and works which are not, with their
own efforts presumably falling into the latter (virtuous) category.[97] But ethnocentrism is not an either/or by which the virtuous
can position themselves outside what they condemn. Ethnocentrism informs and conditions their own writings as well, placing
them inside what they condemn. As a rhetorical stance, the
politics of blame is inadequate because it bases Pakeha identity on
a negative—as alienated usurper—and because it is delivered
from an impossible outside. It can offer few practical alternatives
for reform, and it continues to reserve the right of the Pakeha to
speak for the Maori. It must collapse finally into oedipal guilt and
narcissism, and endless schizophrenic confusion about where to
stand.

POST-COLONIALISM: THINKING ONESELF AS AN OTHER

One of the most popular High Culture refuges from the collapse of
realism has been post-colonialism, one of the "offshore" mythologies. In as much as there is some consensus about it, post-
colonialism has been described as a historical period or condition
or genre of literature in which a common identity is discovered
between nations which were once colonies. On the one hand, this
common identity takes the form of political organizations like the
British Commonwealth. On the other, it takes the form of a sense
of dislocation and displacement which results from cutting the
umbilical cord with the European and American post-imperial
powers while yet finding that family ties persist in economic,
technological, linguistic and other affiliations which in many
cases perpetuate colonialism. Therefore, by this logic, New
Zealand is found to be a post-colonial nation, and, in a more
specific sense, writers and their texts which describe or evoke the
national condition—for example Keri Hulme's Booker Prize-
winning *The Bone People*—are named as post-colonial.

Post-colonialism, then, can be used to promote nationalism (as

Fanon does), just as it can be used for a "retrospective reflection on colonialism" (as Said suggests); thus we are still with the Waitangi double bind.[98] The options available to Maori writers vary, therefore, in the degree to which the legacy of the imperial power is annexed or excluded, from the "convulsively irate" writing of Awatere to the sweeping quest-narrative of Hulme's *The Bone People*.[99] Arguably, the former is better aligned with Maori nationalism and the latter with biculturalism, but they can both still be claimed for post-colonial purposes since both are written in the English language and draw on international political economy and literary genres.

More to the point, can Pakeha intellectuals and Pakeha culture be made to fit the scenario described above? A status of post-colonial is somewhat dubious in view of the Pakeha's (mainly British) imperial origins. Again the problem here is only semantic. New Zealand's "settler culture" was, in the context of this terminology, both imperial (British) and colonial (not Britain). Therefore, a Pakeha can declare for post-colonial rather than post-imperial, by emphasizing the things that Maori and Pakeha have in common (i.e. bicultural nationalism) as Michael Neill does in "Coming Home: Teaching the Postcolonial Novel" (1985). Neill writes:

> In its tentative way [*The Bone People*] holds out the possibility of a genuine homecoming for all the people of this country. If there is a truth behind Hulme's nervous and profoundly uncertain vision of homecoming then it is a sign that this country could still be . . . somewhere for us all to stand.[100]

Yet Neill demands of this post-colonial novel what he so categorically denies in the novels of Salman Rushdie, V.S. Naipaul and others who sketch a planet of "irretrievable alienation [and] desperate nostalgia for homes to which they can never return."[101] Intentionally or not, it is Neill's own text which accords best with his formulation of post-colonialism. It is a work which tells of Pakeha self-alienation and disintegration inherited from the imperial era, and it seeks to unite Maori and Pakeha in common effort against that dubious inheritance.

Neill tentatively maintains the utopian tradition with which

New Zealand's national identity was forged, but it is dubious if
this identity can still be achieved without also destroying the
original basis of cultural difference. Social integration (''homecoming'') is proportional to increased social homogeneity, and
that automatically produces the felt necessity to assert a difference. Furthermore, post-colonialism has generally been used for
quite the opposite purpose, as the reproof to nationalism, calling
attention to a history of imperialism installed upon the Maori and
other indigenous people.

The double bind arises here because post-colonialism is, first
and foremost, one of the offspring of the reified and anomalous
Historical Myth. It concerns itself with the familiar humanist
problems of self-definition, decay and revival, Utopia and the
Fall. Like any mythology which carries a prefix of ''post-'' (or
''pre-'') in its name, post-colonialism must bring with it inherent
limitations which are temporal, spatial, and rhetorical. First,
post-colonialism automatically carries with it the connotations of
being defined in terms of one's colonial past, and therefore as
being ''younger'' or ''behind'' the post-imperial nations. This too
frequently slides into a form of historical determinism, as, for
example, the title of this anthology indicates: *The Given Condition: Essays in Postcolonial Literatures* (1985).[102] The ''given
condition'' evokes the fall from grace, a baleful negativism to the
utopian aspirations of the liberal historians. Yet nothing is
necessarily given; to assume that it is will certainly make it so and
thus close the deterministic circle. Second, it connotes being an
Other against a Self which is elsewhere. Certainly, the advantage
of post-colonialism lies in its declaration of oppositionality, but it
also carries with it the assumption of one's marginalization and
subordination, precisely because it still acknowledges, however
subtly, that there is a center which is elsewhere. One is usually
defined as an Other regardless of this (''You colonials . . . ''), but
using the term for a critique or defense of nationalism can also
encourage European and American paternalism and one's own
(self-) alienation. Third, it is an enormous totalizing term in that
most of the globe was at some stage colonized by Europe, and the
legacy of a common identity is made to override the legacy of
differences. This strategy can be counter-productive and even
offensive to those who would assert a separatist or divergent
mythology of self-definition.

There are already signs that reflection upon one's colonial past (the nostalgia for noble origins and authenticity) is a fading phenomenon. Mostly, such reflections sought to shift responsibility for present action into the historical past, as if the models for the future lie in past experiences and past mistakes can be set to rights. Now post-colonialism is being relocated offshore so as to identify the common effort in other smaller nations/cultures nearby, so that it becomes a banner for advancing upon the Other in order to annex him and her to anti-nuclear and pan-Pacific programs, to feminist and Marxist historicisms, to the sovereign realm of literature, and to ever more exquisite articulations of existential confusion. While there is nothing inherently wrong in this, it is the inevitable consequence of an institutional impetus directed toward imposing a power/knowledge structure on anyone who seems to encourage a paternal and maternal interest now that the Maori have strongly discouraged it.[103]

THE GOVERNOR: THE LAW & LIBERAL DISINTEGRATION

The most fully developed and influential exercise in the politics of blame and self-alienation was *The Governor* (1977). It was New Zealand's biggest television venture of the Seventies: a $1.4 million co-production between Television One and the National Film Unit, a six-episode (465-minute) historical epic which provoked widespread public debate and bitter controversy in Parliament because of its cost, the public display of nudity, and its scenes of violence. The series was defended as the fulfillment of public television's duty to present the nation's history, but in its full-scale treatment of New Zealand's Foundation Myth—in particular the Waitangi Treaty of 1840, the land wars of the 1860s, and Governor George Grey's instrumentalist approach toward solving political "problems"—it introduced the revisionist historical model into popular debates about the nation's history and its future. What historians had accepted for years was revived as a topic for editorials and letters to the daily newspapers, setting off another round of national introspection which culminated in the Springbok Rugby Tour divisions of 1981. Around the same time,

The Governor (1977): Hone Heke (left) is faced with a foreign enemy who understands the power of Maori concepts such as mana and utu.

television embarked on an ambitious program of domestic histori-cal dramas the like of which has not been seen since, and for which *The Governor* was the flagship.[104]

Dramatically, *The Governor* is constructed as a tragedy of no less than Shakespearean proportions, with Grey as its tragic hero and pride his tragic flaw. But he is no Macbeth who operates outside the Law; he is that Law, the embodiment of parliamentary reform in a New Zealand designed to be the social laboratory of the world. Grey himself, as presented in the series, is an English-man of impeccable liberal and humanitarian principles and be-liefs, but he conceives of New Zealand as his own social and historical experiment, and the price for his ambition and pride is the colonization of both the indigenous Maori and all those around him. Each of the six episodes (written by Keith Aberdein from an original concept by Michael Anthony Noonan) therefore has a binary adversary structure:

    1. The Reverend Traitor: Grey versus the Reverend Henry Williams, Hone Heke, and Te Rauparaha.

2. No Way to Treat a Lady: Grey versus his wife, Lady Eliza Grey.
3. The Mutinous Lieutenant: Grey versus Edward John Eyre.
4. He Iwi Ko Tahi Tatou: Grey versus the Maori people.
5. A Matter of Survival: Grey versus General Sir Duncan Cameron.
6. A Return to the Helm: Grey versus everybody.

In each case, Grey subjugates the Other, except in the last episode where his power has declined, his visions are fading in a haze of laudanum, and he retains very little self-respect. This confirms the view that the series is in fact a tragedy, lest there be any doubts about the Faustian bargain this Governor Grey struck with history.

As a preliminary thesis, it will suffice for now that *The Governor* examines its characters critically in the hope of finding a viable identity for New Zealand, past, present, and future. The eventual failure of this inquiry (especially in the case of Grey himself) is a reflection of the filmmakers' pessimism about New Zealand at a time when competing and conflicting identities gave the lie to the promise of the Integration Myth. *The Governor* presides over its disintegration, and it is a crucial text in the nation's film and television history. But the series also presides over the disintegration of the liberal humanist consensus which promoted that myth from Grey until the present, along with its power to persuade ''New Zealanders'' that indeed ''Now we are one people.'' The filmmakers themselves belong to this consensus, and *The Governor* is therefore also an allegory upon liberal hubris and tragic self-doubt. Critical analyses of episodes 1 and 4 follow; both were directed by Tony Isaacs.

The Reverend Traitor, episode 1, opens with a prologue on the signing of the Treaty of Waitangi in 1840. To this viewer it seems stagy, a succession of fiery Maori close-ups and cool rational British mid-shots, a little too brightly lit and costumed, lacking in mystique perhaps, but this may indeed fit the filmmakers' intentions. If Waitangi came increasingly to be recognized by Pakeha intellectuals in the Seventies as a symbol of betrayal (this was slowly reversed in the Eighties, hence the double-edged title of the episode), then the irony of revisionism is appropriate.

Basically, the prologue is concerned to introduce the two major inheritances from the British side: (1) the Integration Myth and (2) the concept of Paternity. The dubious origins of the Integration Myth are attributed to Governor Hobson in an apocryphal line at the ceremonies (''Now we are one people''), plus its subsequent status in myth rather than history. The filmmakers' views are more evident in the series' novelization:

> By any historical terms [Waitangi] is an ill-recorded moment. Given that the events of Thursday, February 6, 1840 are still hailed as the reason for New Zealand's existence it is perhaps better that way. If your existence is based on a deceptive farce, however well-intentioned, maybe it's easier that the truth of that farce remains buried in myth.[105]

The concept of Paternity depends on who is to be the ''father'' of the Maori people, who are child-like for being without Law. As dramatized, the primary conflict over the Maori was between the Church Missionary Society, represented by the Reverend Henry Williams, who was concerned with the state of the Maoris' souls as Christians and heathens, and the British State, represented by Governor Hobson and later by Governor Grey, who were concerned with their rights and responsibilities as British subjects. Such a split between Church and State is/was philosophically and politically irreconcilable, but the conflict is resolved temporarily by Williams: ''You will have two fathers—you will have the Governor and myself.'' This is enough to encourage Hone Heke to sign the Treaty—a gesture of biculturalism perhaps? However, it is around these two issues of Integration and Paternity, the one a horizontal model, the other a vertical one, that the fracture lines appear in episode 1: Maori/Pakeha; Church/State.

The titles and exposition follow, establishing that New Zealand has a problem of ''identity,'' dramatized through flag symbolism. The titles begin with a black and white Union Jack which becomes awash with red, symbolizing the baptism in blood of a nation of blacks and whites. Faces then appear (Maori ariki and Governor Grey), and then Hone Heke, and a flagpole (on which flies the Union Jack) is chopped down at the capital, Kororareka, falling in slow motion. Unity/disunity. The world of Kororareka is fallen too, characterized by its lawlessness, its lack of a stable identity, its lack of paternal authority. Williams' ''missionary tribe'' (as

Heke calls them) still imagines a utopian theocracy in the South
Seas uncontaminated by European civilization. Heke himself
ironically parades an American Stars and Stripes and chops down
another Union Jack. British settlers are drunk and disorderly in the
local taverns. The stage is set for Governor Grey and his wife to
bring the rule of Law (the fusion of Integration and Paternity) to
the Maori, and this is, perhaps, the central thematic preoccupation
of the series. However, the Greys are in South Australia at this
point, and they think of New Zealand as a "savage and miserable
land." Before they arrive, it is the Maori who are called "the New
Zealanders," Williams who is the "traitor" (in the eyes of the
British military), and the British settlers who are without identity.
Grey's arrival will change all this, reversing the hierarchy of
power and legally confirming the paternity of the British State.
Equality will be proclaimed but never practiced; the Integration
Myth begins.

However, to bring law to the lawless necessitates confronting
how the Maori perceived their own co-relative terms: (1) mana,
which is the central concern of the first half of episode 1, and (2)
whenua, which is the central concern of the second half. The series
constructs a dramatic problem out of their definition and translation: mana in this context is defined ambiguously as both
sovereignty and power, whenua as the land.

Hone Heke obviously understands mana; Henry Williams does
not. Heke believes he can do anything he pleases at Kororareka;
Williams warns of British retaliation. When two Maori men fight
each other over utu (best translated here as "justice"), Williams
intervenes, arguing that "It is the old law; it is not God's law,"
presumably excluding mana from God's law and certainly undermining the power of the chiefs to arbitrate in such matters. When
Heke arrives soon afterwards, he criticizes Williams' interference:
"Still you do not understand mana," perhaps implying that he
rejects Williams' God-centered paternal Law if it is irreconcilable
with utu and mana, and perhaps also the Man-centered paternity
of the British State for the same reasons. For Heke, utu and mana
are Maori-centered, which does not mean that they cannot be
taken away. When Grey finally does arrive in New Zealand,
Williams sums up the political situation with, "It's a question of
what the New Zealanders call mana." Grey is quick to grasp what
Williams has not, and the crucial middle of the episode demon-

strates this. It begins with a dinner at the Williams household where Grey expounds his theory of humanitarian liberalism and a utopian future:

> Once we have peace we can achieve anything . . . . I have a vision of a country free from the problems and the bitterness that beset England, and the social inequalities, a country where every man, no matter what the color of his skin, can have a say in his affairs, and not only a say but a say with the benefit of education. This country can be the first true democracy in history.

Immediately afterwards, Grey orders the storming of Heke's impregnable Ruapekapeka pa on a Sunday when the Maori are away at church.

No juxtaposition in New Zealand film and television better points up the fundamental contradiction of the nineteenth-century British liberal democratic theories that New Zealand was founded upon. It foregrounds the alliance between utopian idealism and the ruthless instrumentalism at its heart, whereby the indigenous Maori would be denied the very "rights" they were supposedly entitled to as British subjects. It is this revolution in value-systems that Grey represents—is he the savage and the traitor for waging war on the Lord's Day?—that enables Heke to say, "He understands the meaning of mana." Though Grey stands for the Law, paradoxically he also stands for revolution, and this does not depend simply on whether it is viewed from the British or the Maori perspective—British Law in such contexts was revolutionary in its implications. It overturned the competing Maori and British value-systems and brought lawlessness among them in fulfillment of the Lockeian paradox, the law shall set you free.

The second half of the film concerns the whenua and introduces the warrior chief Te Rauparaha. Speaking of Grey, Te Rauparaha says: "First, he must fix the matter of the land, the whenua. The whenua is being stolen. It is the whenua that men kill for. Understand the whenua, you understand everything." Grey, however, does quite the opposite, by undermining the mana of his three main competitors: he seizes Te Rauparaha and only lets him return to his people in humiliation—no advance warning is sent of his return and Grey deliberately does not dress formally for the occasion. He also ensures through the Church Missionary Society and Bishop Selwyn that Henry Williams forfeits much of his 11,000 acres of land. As Heke observes to Williams, "You, me, Te Rauparaha, we are the same." They are all united in having lost their land (i.e. New Zealand) to Grey. Heke's dying words to Williams are:

HEKE:	Pakeha takes the land piece by piece. Te Wiremu, you are part of it. Was it for this I signed your Treaty?
WILLIAMS:	The Treaty was to protect your people, safeguard the land . . . .
HEKE:	George Grey is now called Sir George. It means he's done well. The Pakeha comes as the Norway rat came and ate up all the native rats . . . . There'll be no more of us left.
WILLIAMS:	Aye, I failed you. I trusted in men. In God only can you trust.

Heke has the small consolation of a last joke about having signed the Treaty twice (in Williams' name no less), but with his death, and Te Rauparaha's humiliation, and Williams' demotion, Maori power in the north and south is effectively broken and the Church is subordinated to the State. In a peculiarly allegorical end-scene—a beach party—Grey gives another formal declaration of principles:

> Now across this land lies a mantle of peace. It has not been achieved without sacrifice, but those sacrifices will be worthwhile for this is my vision. I see a future where for the first time in the history of the world, two peoples of different skins, of conflicting cultures can live and work together in perfect harmony, perfect equality . . . . And in all the world this land shall be unique. A country fit for God himself.

This then is the key formulation of the Integration Myth for God's Own Country (Godzone): peace, harmony, equality, and sacrifice—Maori sacrifice before all others. The ideals are hopelessly compromised by the realities, yet Grey has effectively established a vertical paternal model of national unity, with himself (and the Law) at its summit, and the Maori as sacrificial

Other at its base. It is the model for the Integration Myth as a vertical system for bringing the Maori into, and up to, the level of the civilized British; it is also the model attacked by Awatere in *Maori Sovereignty* as the transparent justification for expropriating Maori land; and it is the model for a century of Pakeha narratives of progress(ion), repression, oppression, atavism, and all the metaphorical paraphernalia of depth psychology which is the concern of this book.

There is at this point in the episode, the intervention of an authorial voice-over narration, a formal acknowledgement of the filmmakers' own paternal interest in the fate of their narrative and the ''sacrifices'' required of their tragic (anti-) hero:

> Henry Williams and Hone Heke Pokai had already seen some of the sacrifices George Grey was prepared to make in order to achieve his vision. Although the Archdeacon was finally reinstated, the missionaries never again exerted the influence they had before the coming of Grey. In time, the Maori would rise to fight the causes that had carried the dead Ngapuhi chief into rebellion, but for the moment the Governor wielded undisputed power. The mana was his.

The Law had conquered mana. But not the whenua. That would be annexed in episodes 4 and 5.

He Iwi Ko Tahi Tatou, episode 4: the title is usually translated prosaically as ''Now We Are One People,'' and the explicit purpose of the episode is to demonstrate the flaw in the national mythology. It does so by asking whether it was in fact the Maori who were ''one people'' when they mobilized against the British invader in order to hold on to the land. An intelligently written and directed episode, its narrative center is temporarily displaced away from Grey by focusing on the psychological and political dilemmas of Wiremu Tamehana, who, as a Christian (bicultural) Maori, occupies a neutral position between his Waikato ariki and the British authorities. It must be said that although Tamehana does not suffer any tragic flaw and is thus denied the tragic grandeur of Grey, it is interesting that the filmmakers choose to focus the narrative line (i.e. history) around the psychology of a Maori hero, in the formula (new at the time) of Maori Alone.

In the prologue to this episode, the issues raised in episode 1 are recalled as the young Tamehana refuses a chance to kill for utu. His Christian principles require loyalty to God's Law, though whether to Man's Law as well is not clear. Tamehana practices biculturalism: biologically a Maori of rangatira (chiefly) rank, he has mana; culturally he is also a Christian. Within him is replayed the original conflict for Heke's soul between Williams and Grey, and again it will be Grey who will win by destroying Tamehana's faith in a (British) God-centered Law, forcing Tamehana into taking up arms and putting his Maori side first. This makes Grey the essentialist, not Tamehana, though Grey speaks of unity and harmony. Initially, Grey only seeks to purchase Maori land by legal means through his representative, Donald McLean, while on a personal level he takes up with Maori mistresses. There are strong analogies here between land and women, whether annexed or bought, but in an inverse relationship: as long as Grey takes an interest in Maori women, he does not annex the land.

In the early expository sequences, Maori leaders of the central North Island are divided between passive and active resistance. Rewi Maniapoto speaks for the latter: "Some day you will have no land left to dig. The Pakeha will have stolen it all, because men like you wouldn't fight." Wiremu Tamehana takes the alternative view, calling for peace between Maori and Maori, Maori and Pakeha. Their differences are neatly underscored by Tamehana speaking in English, Maniapoto in Maori. Others are equally divided, for example the chiefs Tamati Waka Nene and Te Wherowhero, whose scenes are shot entirely in Maori, with English sub-titles. Generally speaking, the two strategic positions can be reformulated in contemporary terms as biculturalism versus Maori nationalism/sovereignty. Tamehana's (or Nene's) biculturalism involves understanding the British strategy, of having many children ("That's the only way to keep the Pakeha in check"), and teaching them the English language.

Tensions soon reach a critical level within Maoridom as the news of Wiremu Kingi's struggle to retain the Waitara and Te Rauparaha's death reaches the Waikato chiefs. They ponder whether like the giant moa they too now face extinction. At his home, Tamehana tries to reason with Grey over the loss of land:

GREY: But tell me, do you truly feel that land
                 which is unoccupied, land which is serv-
                 ing nobody, should be withheld from the
                 settlers?
TAMEHANA: You ask a man to sell his immortal soul.
GREY: If he's not using it, probably.
TAMEHANA: What would happen if I went to Queen
                 Victoria and said to her, I have come to
                 buy your Tower of London? She would
                 laugh at me, perhaps chop off my head,
                 and it would make no difference if I said to
                 her, But you do not use it anymore.

Tamehana argues for two Governors, for a Maori Parliament, for
someone to bring Law to the tribes—a dual paternity. Grey instead quotes the apocryphal Maori proverb, "Behind the tattooed
face a stranger stands: he who inherits the earth and he is white,"
which amounts to a declaration of intention to practice cultural
genocide. Tamehana cleverly ripostes with an alternative translation: "He who inherits the earth, and he is without tattoo." This
cultural relativism argument is not lost on the Governor, but
Maori land is the chief stumbling block in Grey's vision of utopia. Conflict is for the time being postponed as Grey leaves for
England, just as the King Movement (Kingitanga) is being formally
established. Grey remarks patronizingly as he leaves, "Imitation
is the sincerest form of flattery . . . . I consider it a manifesta-
tion of how well the New Zealanders have embraced the gift of
civilization." The stage is set for conflicting essentialisms,
Maori and British, and this brings the first half of the episode to a
close.

The narrative line in the second half of the episode follows
Wiremu Tamehana almost exclusively: his gradual radicalization,
his role in the formation of the Kingitanga, and the drift toward
war. Initially, there is a new Governor, Gore-Browne, to deal with,
and a swift succession of scenes conveys the impression that
lawlessness has returned to the land: patronizing British aristoc-
racy, drunken settlers, a sailor who calls Tamehana a "nigger,"
plus a scene in which Tamehana is called upon to decide utu in a
Maori adultery case, a direct challenge to his adopted Christian
law. Tamehana returns to the Waikato, and in the structural climax
of the episode, amid a chaos of voices in his head, he forges an

alliance with his former enemy, Te Wherowhero, and is dubbed "the Kingmaker":

> TE WHEROWHERO: We are Waikato.
> TAMEHANA: We are Maori.

Governor Gore-Browne, who is present at this historic occasion, calls it treason (echoing episode 1), but in the film's regime he plays the pompous imperial fool, and the subsequent montage of waiata and splendid visuals clearly identifies the film's support for the Waikato Maori and their resurgent sovereignty. Again echoing episode 1, a flag flies the new theme of deliverance from Egypt and into Canaan. In subsequent scenes, the Waitara is lost and Maori unity affirmed more strongly—"We are all Maori now," asserts Rewi Maniapoto and he calls for war in the Taranaki. Only Tamehana still cautions peaceful resistance, but alone in the dark with his wife, he mourns, "We will never be one people." The war begins, as it must, and Tamehana confronts McLean and the military: "I have told my people to trust the law. I cannot hold them much longer . . . . If you bleed I bleed too. Do you understand the meaning of life? If you do not prevent war, then you must want it."

Tamehana's radicalization and disillusion with the Law is completed with the return of a much changed Governor Grey. Gone is the desire within him for Maori women; now he is consumed with desire for the land.

> GREY: There can be but one Governor.
> TAMEHANA: You're just another blind Pakeha.

Over another impressive montage sequence reminiscent of Polanski's *Macbeth,* the onset of war is evoked, and the bicultural middle ground collapses in the tug between the competing Maori and British essentialisms. The external narration once again intervenes:

> Wiremu Tamehana was forced to face the *inevitability* of conflict and to take up arms. On July 12, 1863, British troops crossed the Maungataupiri stream and occupied the territory of the King. Three days after that *fateful* invasion, the Maoris received the Governor's final offer of compromise. But the

delay in offering peace terms had already led to disaster. The
Pakeha Wars were begun. [My emphasis].

Thus history is arbitrated by the filmmakers in terms of inevitability and fate, blame apportioned to the Pakeha and sympathy to
the Maori. Victory/defeat; Pakeha/Maori; irreconcilable differences.

The Governor did not leave many options available for filmmakers and truth-tellers generally. Once the full implications of
its thematic structure and moral regime are absorbed, what
options are there but atavism, suicide, silence, repression, or
exile/expatriation? Unlike the films discussed in chapter 8, *The
Governor* produces a Maori Alone in the filmmakers' own liberal
image and radicalizes him as an implacable Other. The politics of
(self-) blame produces radical Maori essentialism. Scriptwriter
Aberdein attempted later to rework the tragic scenario of episode
4 into *Utu* and came up with a similarly tragic conclusion; he
subsequently moved to Australia in fulfillment of the exile
trajectory. Michael Anthony Noonan, in *Legacy* (1987), variously
embraced both multicultural nationalism (the series consists of six
episodes, each one dealing with different ethnic minorities), and
Maori essentialism (in episode 6, he surrenders narrational control
to Selwyn Muru's Maori spirituality thesis—producing his own
atavistic self-exclusion). Three other films, all shot in 1985–86,
are included here because they demonstrate where the politics of
(self-) blame has eventually led: *Just Passing Through, The Quiet
Earth,* and *Mark II.*

JUST PASSING THROUGH: LESBIAN ESSENTIALISM

Just Passing Through (1985) is by a feminist film production
company and it represents one of the most self-righteous forms of
cultural annexation. Its inspirational starting point is the Maori
legend of Hine-titama, the Dawn Maid who broke with her father,
Tane, over his incest with her to become Hine-nui-te-po, the
goddess of death. The film chooses to adapt the legend in terms of
contemporary lesbian essentialism: faced with the totalitarian
image of sexism and male power it constructs for itself, it is

unable to evade it and consequently implodes into mysticism and a vaguely conceived "Maori" utopianism. Two young documentary filmmakers, Fran (who is Australian) and Emma (who is Maori but living in Australia) come to New Zealand to make a documentary on Maori myths and legends. The filmmakers are apparently important enough to warrant a press phalanx as they arrive at the airport in a scene which clearly sets in place the strategies of difference the film subscribes to: male/female, New Zealand/Aotearoa, official news media/independent documentary filmmakers, whereby the former in each case oppresses the latter, and the film soon adds a fourth analogy, Pakeha/Maori. There is considerable irony in the fact that the film's heroines are themselves claiming the right to representation of an Other (for an Australian television company no less), and in the fact that the structured inequalities of society they so resent are reinforced in their own dialogue. Such literal-mindedness precludes alternative radical breakouts from the vicious circle of theoretical masochism analyzed by feminist theorists in the Seventies.[106]

The characters not only feel considerable hatred for their perceived oppressors (Pakeha men) but also strong self-hatred, both biologically and culturally. Emma's identity exists on the conflicted edge of the dichotomies of Pakeha/Maori ("Auckland half-caste") and male/female (dyke), even if she appears to desire to be a Taitokerau and a woman to Fran. On Emma's conflicted psyche, the film rather brutally exercises its own identity crisis, unresolvable even for Fran, whose desire for "communication" and rational explanation provides her with the masculine power of representation vis-à-vis Emma and Maori myths and legends. The film finally resolves the ambiguous sexual and racial tension with a rock slide that kills its two heroines, denying their bicultural union.

From this moment on, their shades are able to see, and be greeted by, Riha, a mysterious Maori woman who is the film's literal embodiment of Hine-nui-te-po. Emma's fall out of history and into the world of Riha represents nothing less than the atavistic desire for relief from the dissonances and conflicts of contemporary New Zealand. When exile in Australia is insufficient, the death-wish makes for a compelling fantasy, and the compensation—as in many utopias—is an anti-world or spirit world co-existent with the "real" world. It is the film's

Rarohenga underworld, supposedly submerged under New Zealand like Awatere's Aotearoa, but recuperated through a feminist act of faith, self-denial, and self-sacrifice.

The ethics of Pakeha filmmakers proclaiming a submerged Rarohenga/Aotearoa invisible within New Zealand are dubious to say the least, but it is rendered even more dubious by the number of Pakeha apparently inhabiting this Utopia; overall it resembles a cross between zombie films, ancient Rome, and the ohu commune movements of the Seventies (its inhabitants say things like "Much is possible. Have courage today."). As far as Fran is concerned, her desire for rational explanations occupies the last section of the film after Emma has dropped out of it, but Fran also appears to surrender to the atavistic desire for oblivion, her motivation apparently being her desire for sexual union with Emma. (Before they part, Emma places her finger on Fran's lips and says, "All you have to do is want to.")

Just Passing Through displays enormous disgust for contemporary New Zealand, a disgust which annexes the Maori as a convenient Other and into which it withdraws for solace, even as it moralizes against others for doing so! It resembles the pilgrimage genre and Tom Sullivan's atavism in *Broken Barrier,* except that the mythology of Hine-nui-te-po as original incest victim, with its discourse of separation, shame, and broken trust, is particularly suited to aspirations of lesbian separatism (as is Maui's death, crushed between her thighs). Naturally, the film Emma and Fran intend to make never gets made, thus precluding the awkward moment when one's ideals are put into practice and the public can scrutinize them. *Just Passing Through* is evidence that lesbian essentialism's realist aesthetic is sliding into the same religious-inspired mysticism as afflicted the National Film Unit. It offers only Utopia, silence, and death.

THE QUIET EARTH: ADAM ALONE IN AOTEAROA

Another film to dramatize the politics of blame is *The Quiet Earth* (1985), directed by Geoff Murphy and produced by Sam Pillsbury and Don Reynolds, and based on the Craig Harrison novel of the same name. Like the other films in this chapter, it plays out a

The Quiet Earth (1985): Man Alone, Zac Hobson, in a desolate world of his own making.

scenario of Pakeha guilt and escapes at the end into transcendence and death. Zac Hobson is a scientist who has worked on an American-designed global security system code-named Operation Flashlight. In an imaginative construction which recalls Kubrick's *2001: A Space Odyssey,* at the precise moment when the apocalypse arrives (it is called ''The Effect''), only those who are at that moment dying survive into the post-apocalyptic world. As one advertising slogan for the film put it, ''The end of the world is just the beginning . . . .'' This is linked subtly and ironically to the stunning opening shot of a golden sun rising out of the sea, specifically evoking nuclear holocaust and New Zealand's controversial official policy of a nuclear-free zone.

Zac (his name evokes Zac Wallace, star of Murphy's earlier film, *Utu*) finds himself alone in this brave new world he has helped to create. This is to carry the Man Alone mythology to its literal and logically absurd conclusion! The first half of the film is dedicated to an examination of Zac's sense of guilt, once repressed and now out in the open, but to what purpose? The penitent requires a confessor and there is none. Zac slides into atavistic fantasy, imagining himself by turns President of the World, a woman, Christ, God, and so on. His first formal

The Quiet Earth: the essential triangle of players in Eighties racial politics: Maori activist, Pakeha feminist, and Pakeha reactionary, temporarily united in the necessity for survival.

confession is a public address to an imaginary audience: ''How easy to believe in the common good when that belief is rewarded with status, wealth, and power . . . . That awesome power that I helped to create has been put in the hands of madmen . . . . Is it not fitting, then, that I be President of this . . . quiet . . . earth? I've been condemned to live.'' To transcend one's fellow human beings, to be the new Creation, is also to be condemned to live alone. So Zac considers suicide (*c.f. Runaway, Pictures*) but the crisis passes. Instead, he sets himself a task: to find out whether The Effect will repeat in a few days. He discovers that it will, and so the scenario for the film becomes Revelations rather than Genesis. Zac intones into his tape recorder, ''I get the feeling we're either dead or we're in a different universe . . . [and] the fabric of the universe has not only altered, but is profoundly unstable.''

In the next sequences, Zac meets two other survivors: a young Pakeha woman named Joanne and a young Maori man named Api. A triangle is established which generates sexual and racial tensions. Zac is a dissembler, a Pakeha technocrat with only enough sense of moral responsibility to think of committing suicide. His egocentrism controls him even when near the end of the film he says to Joanne: "Sometimes I feel as if you and Api have known each other a long long time, as though I am the victim of some huge conspiracy, and you and Api have been sent to be my guardians." Zac retains the moral center of the film only because he seeks to forestall a second Effect and thus save other life on the planet. Api, however, is one of the most diabolical Maori figures yet seen in New Zealand films, an Ignoble Savage to set against the noble Johnny, Joe, and Ngatai of earlier films. Like Zac he has apparently killed another person (this turns out to be untrue). Therefore, the question of killing is a matter of scale: the entire planet in Zac's case, and a friend's wife in Api's case. Joanne is identified with "feminine" nurturing qualities, as the stable center on which the two men ("masculine" science and passion, respectively) will contest her possession. She sleeps with each man once, and in a sense she could stand in for the body of New Zealand, torn between the two essentialisms, Pakeha and Maori.

Api intimidates with his military clothing and automatic weapons, and his aggressive racial arguments: "First, honky, haven't you noticed? Things have changed around here. The white boss grilled with the rest of them. There's just you and me now." He imagines all manner of personal slights and, as reason's Other, he serves to obstruct the path of scientific knowledge. This is meant to be consistent too with his belief in the traditional spiritual values associated with the marae: "For a while there I didn't know what I was, and when I found I was alone in this world, I thought I was a ghost . . . . I reckoned if I was here and alive, I thought I'd better head north and look for survivors, and if I was a spirit I thought I'd better head for Cape Reinga. Either way I was heading in the right direction." Zac demands scientific knowledge, to know how The Effect occurred; Api is an "artist" (says Joanne), who is defined as everything that Zac is not.

Effectively, the Maori/Pakeha divide is as wide here as it can be: Aotearoa has erupted into the landscape of New Zealand. Joanne offers a tentative solution (as Pakeha feminism sought to do in the Eighties), but her choices are forced into an either/or: Zac or Api. She initially tries to persuade Zac, "I'm thinking of the three of us now. Not just you and not just me.'' However, before long, she growls, ''I'm not going to live with two of you at each other's throats trying to prove which one of you is God.'' An allegorical problem like this demands nothing less than a *deus ex machina* solution: The Effect recurs. It does so with a perfect ironic symmetry: Zac, the only original suicide in the group, again destroys himself and yet again crosses the warp Effect from death into life; Joanne and Api make love (Creation) and yet cross in the reverse direction into death. Science therefore produces its own antidote in order to preserve natural life on the planet, but at the expense of every human being but one. The self of science has become all, alone in the wonders of its own creation: Adam, the scientist.

The ending of *The Quiet Earth* returns to the moment Zac first found himself alone following a suicide attempt, almost as if the scenario were endlessly circular. He stands alone ''on the beach'' in an extraordinarily beautiful and cryptic final shot which reminded critics of the ending of *2001: A Space Odyssey*. This time it does not really matter if Zac commits suicide or not—there is no one else left to care. Adam alone cannot repopulate the planet. Analogically, Pakeha masculine essentialism is all that survives the racial and sexual battles of the film. The guilt of history is atoned for (in as much as it can be) but at the price of destroying everything worthwhile in New Zealand/Aotearoa.

MARK II: THE MAORI PAKEHA

The final film discussed under the politics of blame is *Mark II* (1986), written by Mike Walker and Mitchell Manuel, and directed by John Anderson for Television New Zealand. Superficially, it is the story of three teenage Maori: Eddie, who has just saved up enough money to buy a red Mark II Zephyr; Matthew, his somewhat younger friend; and Kingi, an acquaintance who is in trouble with both the police and local drug dealers. The three friends go ''on the road'' to find their ''freedom,'' as the title song calls it, in an adventure which ends up with Kingi in jail and Eddie gaining a criminal record. In between, there is an episodic structure which is in keeping with the film's free-wheeling spirit.

Mark II (1986): Maori beefcake on display in a TV movie that revitalizes the old tradition of sexualizing the Maori figure, but this time it is masculine.

Although the film was much praised, there are several aspects which position it within the politics of (self-) blame: a homoerotic identification with its young heroes; an identification with their getting into trouble with the law; a narrative trajectory which leads its heroes directly into the double bind of oppression; and an indictment of troubled Pakeha liberals.

Mark II represents more than just New Zealand's first television movie; it also demonstrates what happens when the politics of self-blame comes out the other side of death and transcendence and annexes a new Maori self. As with *Just Passing Through*, the National Film Unit's religious-inspired films, and the pilgrimage genre generally, the narrational self of *Mark II* has already imploded and assumed an atavistic identification with its young Maori heroes. For example, in an interesting scene which brings up the half-way point in the film, the three friends go swimming in a forest pond. The full-frontal male nudity, the jokes about masculinity, and the fact that Kingi saves Eddie from drowning all affirm a strong male bonding. It is the happiest moment in the film, and Matthew says, "You guys are like a family to me." The scene evokes Maoriland except that where there once would have been naiads and Hinemoas, now it is young Maori beefcake on display. In the following sequence, Kingi drives a farmer's tractor wildly all over the farm before ditching it in a pond. Shot for visual excitement, the scene invites questions about why there is no sense of responsibility attached to actions like these, when later in the film the full force of an oppressive and racist Pakeha legal system is brought down upon Eddie to convict him for something he did not do.

As in *Just Passing Through*, the film constructs a totalitarian image of power on which to crucify its heroes. Can this be reconciled with the fact that it is directed and produced by Pakeha who are doubtless not oppressed? Is there a dividing line between romantic glamorization and exploitation? One answer can be found in the film's scathing characterization of Pakeha liberals, in particular a young woman named Judy, a university student of wealthy background who desires Eddie. Her awkward initiatives toward friendship with him are designed to be patronizing in the extreme. The same applies to the lawyer she hires to defend Eddie. Then there is Judy's boyfriend, the archetypal racist with whom Eddie is forced to fight. These ignoble Pakeha are the diabolical images of Pakeha filmmakers who seek to think themselves Other, imagining the worst for a political characterization they have supposedly abandoned for themselves.

The moral integrity of the film is summed up in a lengthy speech addressed to Eddie by a radical Maori acquaintance, Rangi, after Eddie has been convicted and discharged in court for assault. Effectively, it is the film's manifesto, directed toward alienated young Maori in the hope of getting them off glue-sniffing and petty crime and into the "war" with the Pakeha System: "Face the facts, man . . . . You're young, you've got a brown face, and the odds are you'll end up in court. Now that's how it works. . . ." Rangi persuades him that anger is not the solution: "You can be angry, man, you've got every right . . . . But there's too much to do . . . . We need the warriors. Not locked away behind bars." At this point, Judy has flown out to the United States to finish her university degree and Eddie and Matthew return home. Whether the downbeat ending atones sufficiently for the levity and anarchy celebrated in the first two-thirds of the film is debatable. It is certainly the case that unlike *Kingpin,* a much better film, the options are progressively closed down for *Mark II*'s heroes, snaring them within the double bind of oppression. Crime and punishment are completely misaligned in order to achieve a simplistic message that the Pakeha system is racist and that smashing it is the best solution.

CHAPTER 10: THE POLITICS OF REPRESSION

The politics of repression occurs when the power to define the Maori Other is stubbornly retained even as definitions of "Maori" and "Pakeha" become more and more ambiguous. The history of New Zealand literary nationalism contains many examples of this politics and one of its central problems, it would seem, is deciding whether or not the Maori have written their own "literature," "poetry," and "history," and on what grounds it ought to be included in national anthologies.[107] This problem is not as simple as it may appear since it requires that semantic distinctions be made—does Maori oral storytelling constitute "history" and can whaikorero be considered "poetry"? To argue affirmatively or negatively immediately falls into the trap of the double bind; logically it makes more sense to question the categories themselves—history, poetry, and so on.

THE QUESTION OF NATIONAL ANTHOLOGIES

Back in 1945, in an introduction to his first anthology of New Zealand poetry, Allen Curnow excluded Maori poetry on the grounds that "their history is not available to us, except as we may enter it by some identity of vision."[108] This policy of exclusion has been continued by later anthologists including the Oxford trilogy of Chapman and Bennett (1956), O'Sullivan (1970), and Adcock (1982).[109] However, by 1960, Curnow himself had changed his mind and in his Penguin anthology of that year, Maori and Pakeha had both become New Zealanders together, with the "Maori poems" translated into English.[110] In the recent *Penguin Book of New Zealand Verse* (1985), one of its editors, Ian Wedde, may have been alert to the dangers of annexing "foreign" texts in this way (his word), but he did so anyway, and all in the interests of the national mythology. I must confess to not really understanding why anyone would want to assemble such an anthology, but Wedde adopted the novel idea of printing the Maori poems in both Maori and English! He raised the vexed question of "translation" (from Maori into English) but only as if it were a simple matter of degree, of "transposition . . . from one context to another."[111]

The main problem here is that the Maori poems were selected by Wedde with the help of two other Pakeha, and, rightly, they were taken to task for it by Carl Stead: "I predict [the Wedde anthology] will be the only one in which the editors offer poetry in a language they don't know! . . . How can I or Wedde or anyone not competent in the language put any sort of value on what is offered in Maori? . . . To represent Maori poetry as part of a lively New Zealand literary scene is simply dishonest."[112] Stead is right to argue that Maori culture has had little to do with the "New Zealand literary scene," but he is wilfully ambiguous in that the "New Zealand literary scene" can be interpreted differently depending upon whether one wants to emphasize "literature" or "New Zealand." Stead obviously intends to stress literature and Wedde New Zealand. For Stead, Maori culture is different from New Zealand culture; for Wedde (as for Curnow) it is justifiable to include Maori poetry as literature produced in New Zealand. It is simply a question of boundaries. Stead's argument defends the virtue of international modernism; it allows for Maori "difference" while not assisting it in any way whatsoever. Wedde's is frankly nationalist but also something of a gimmick; it may seem to be doing the Maori a favor by including them in the anthology while reprimanding previous anthologists for excluding them, but it also amounts to annexation since it continues to assume the Pakeha right to represent the Maori.

This is the same classic double bind which afflicted the national historians: there is no way to deal with Maori culture without totally annexing it or excluding it. This situation has been aggravated by prevailing literary assumptions which have rigidly confined debate to the objective level of the text in its relationship with the world, as if this could (or should) ever be separated from the subjective activity of the New Zealand anthologist who selects them.[113]

There were partial solutions available to the editors if they could only have seen their way clear to abandoning the claim to

the right to speak for others. It was a Maori critic, Sidney Moko
Mead, who pointed out that the Maori poems could at least have
been selected by Maori and thus a "bicultural" work might have
resulted.[114] While I agree with this, it nevertheless remains
ambiguous as to whether the anthology would indeed be bicultural in view of its title. As Awatere puts it, Can biculturalism ever
be compatible with nationalism?

Around the same time the Wedde anthology was published,
there was a related debate about the "Maoriness" of *The Bone
People* and its author Keri Hulme, again as if some vital issue
were at stake! In the *London Review of Books,* Carl Stead objected
to the way the Mobil Pegasus Award was to be given to "a novel
or autobiography by a Maori, written in the past decade, in
English or in Maori . . . . The works entered had thus to be
considered 'Maori' not in language, or in form, but by virtue of the
racial antecedents of the authors."[115] Here Stead is again enforc-
ing Maori difference, requiring that Maoriness be consistent both
in the author's bloodlines, and in the use of language and form.
Where the Pegasus Award (arguably) acknowledges biculturalism
and Hulme's "mongrel" muse (her word), Stead prefers to reify
cultural essences and deny any kind of cross-cultural influence or
technology transfer.[116]

Simon During has made a similar case for *The Bone People*'s
"modernism": "Against its own wishes, the text provides precisely the final seal in the destruction of [Maori] culture. For its
own structure and presuppositions are borrowed from modernity."[117] Indeed the novel does "borrow," but is there any reason
why it should be centered in one culture from which it can
"destroy" the other? Furthermore, why should this be equivalent
to "appropriation of the precolonial," as During suggests it is?
This too is essentialist thinking, which denies Maori culture a
present tense, which consigns taha Maori to the dubious function
of perpetuating a "precolonial" inheritance as if there had been
no on-going dynamic between past and present in the meantime. It
may as easily be asserted that it is modernity itself rather than
Maori culture which has reified cultural practices and discourses
within an imaginary past. Maori intellectuals are obliged to speak
constantly of their taonga and korero being "alive."

Constructing Otherness in order to mourn for it, repress it, or
recuperate it satisfies a desire to see Maori culture as "opposi-

tional'' or ''marginal'' in relation to one's own. If an intellectual fears losing his/her own oppositional politics, what could be better than touristing among those who are already defined as oppositional and adopting them as one's legal brief? Yet, unlike official histories or poetry anthologies, novels (like authors and half-castes) can occupy median positions between cultures such that they throw into question any essentialist labels assigned to them far more successfully and enjoyably than High Culture intellectuals can ever do. *The Bone People* does not belong to an identifiable constituency; it resists it. It does not perpetuate the double bind; this is its strength.

The strategy of annexation pursued by Curnow and Wedde resembles, as it must, the historical romances of the national historians. The films discussed in chapters 8 and 9 attempted to reconcile the Pakeha right to representation of a resurgent Aotearoa; they do not repress the Maori so much as implode upon themselves. The essentialist and exclusionary strategy pursued by Stead and During, on the other hand, belongs to a lineage associated with the repression and subsequent eruption of Maoriland/Aotearoa. The five films discussed in this chapter—*Sylvia* (1985), *Among the Cinders* (1984), *Other Halves* (1984), *Arriving Tuesday* (1986), and *The Lost Tribe* (1983/85)—all deal in some way with this eruption. They are reluctant to abandon their Pakeha liberal status and so opt instead for a conservative backlash which reprimands the Maori for their presumption and attempts to reinstate a High Culture rule of Law.

SYLVIA: PAKEHA SAVAGES IN THE BACKBLOCKS

Sylvia (1985), by Michael Firth, opens with a sub-title proclaiming the film ''A true story.'' Nominally a historical biography of New Zealand educator and writer, Sylvia Ashton-Warner, it deals with only a small part of her life during the Second World War when she had many of the formative experiences that would power her later books.[118] In that sense, the film is a feminist tribute to a New Zealand heroine, a Woman Alone who struggled, suffered, and survived against the suffocating paternalism of the New Zealand education system and the hostility of rural Maori.

Sylvia (1985): a male tribute to a feminist heroine. This shot shows Sylvia and her family in the backblocks in happier days.

The film's nearest kin are *Constance, Trespasses, Pioneer Women, Nga Wa O te Tau* (aka *The Seasons*), *Arriving Tuesday,* and others which appeared in the mid-Eighties as the Man Alone mythology broke apart into Woman Alone and Maori Alone. Significantly, almost all of these films were produced and directed by liberal men, which invites the conclusion that some form of guilt complex prompted the filmmakers to celebrate female heroines while simultaneously oppressing them by the end of their films. Essentially, *Sylvia* is a realist tragedy: its narrative describes the mythology of alienation and repression, but in faithfully "reflecting" that mythology in its own story, it also faithfully reproduces those conditions of alienation and repression. *Sylvia* tames Sylvia Ashton-Warner as she must never have been in her own volatile life.

Sylvia's narrative involves solving two related problems, the one with the other. Publicly, Ashton-Warner's reputation is deservedly based on her innovative educational methods, in which she encouraged "illiterate" rural Maori children to seize and possess the vocabulary of the English language by weaving it into their own personal/cultural experiences, many of which were fraught with violence and fear. Privately and personally, Ashton-Warner's life was a battle for self-integration and identity in a world which seemed to shut down her professional and sexual options. The film explores this tension: in both public and private worlds, Sylvia seeks to stave off the effects of "cultural imperialism," as she calls it, and avert the vertical descent into the "monster of madness" referred to by the "real" Ashton-Warner in a black-and-white prologue to the film. The monster of madness is thus an analog of Maori illiteracy and violence. In both public and private worlds the solution proposed is the rise into language, into language-as-power. The children must learn to control words, and Ashton-Warner will go on to write best-sellers.

Sylvia's liberal politics require the familiar scenario of imperial oppression and reification: an education system divided between embattled liberals like Sylvia, her husband Keith Henderson, a sympathetic school inspector Aidan Morris, and a local district nurse Opal Saunders, set against caricatures of totalitarian Wellington bureaucrats. The bureaucrats evidently draw their support from the local Pakeha, the publican for example, who greets one Maori customer with, "And what's this ragbag member of your race ever done for Mother England?" In the film's climax, Sylvia is unable to unleash the repressed Maori Other upon the System, so she tries sweet reason: "If we force an alien culture on them right from the start, they rebel. The violence in them erupts. That's war. We can stop war." The Chief Inspector retorts by invoking Churchill, Sylvia's methods are rejected, and before long she is evicted by her landlord. Symbolically, the feminist/liberal breakout from repression results only in rape, and at this point, Sylvia begins to become a ghost like her husband, friends and children.

As so often happens in the Woman Alone genre, it is the private world which must serve to release the tensions of the public life, and so Sylvia becomes ambiguously engaged in amorous games with both Aidan and Opal. Sequences with Aidan objectify Sylvia's femininity as object of masculine desire while others place her in the masculine role as objectifier of Opal (much as she is toward her own submissive and feminized husband). There is something in the sexual posturing of these scenes that is reminis-

Sylvia: the quest for self-alienation. This shot shows Sylvia with Aidan Morris, the friendly school inspector—Pakeha savages fixated on themselves.

cent of soap operas—of egocentric Pakeha savages who do not belong in the landscape because they are fixated upon themselves.

Sylvia's alienation and repression stems not simply from her own "war" with the imperial system and her identity problems, but also from the Maori world she has entered as knight-errant to spread the word and world of light. Maoriland (Aotearoa?) is repressed into service as the dark and diabolical Other, and the town is even endowed with the allegorical name of Te Whenua. The repressed violence and horror Sylvia finds in the children's lives and its exorcism through oral story-telling, writing, painting and music are linked to the (unexplained) mysteries of the tekoteko (carving) which is reclaimed from the Bush and given pride of place over the entrance to the school. The repressed violence is also linked to the ever-present threat from young Maori men and to the meshing of tapu, death, and loss of the land.

Surprisingly perhaps, there is nothing in common between these Maori and Pakeha; even World War II which might have brought them together is all but absent.

Is there any irony in Sylvia's talk of missing "civilization" during her "years in the wilderness"? Like most New Zealanders, Ashton-Warner believed in racial integration as the solution to the nation's problems, whether the Maori liked it or not. When at one stage Sylvia says, "presumably it's the authority and discipline I represent" which generates the children's hostility, she has correctly identified the problem that liberal education is in itself inherently ethnocentric with its own tendency toward oppression, but that it can hardly be otherwise appears to have passed the filmmakers by.

AMONG THE CINDERS: REPRESSED HOMOSEXUAL DESIRE

Among the Cinders (1983), by Pacific Films and N.D.R. Hamburg, is produced by John O'Shea, directed by Rolf Haedrich (who is German), and based on the novel of the same name by Maurice Shadbolt.[119] The setting is small-town New Zealand during the Sixties, and the story tells of how young teenager Nick Flinders passes through a rite of passage into adulthood. The themes are woven through cross-currents of inter-generational conflict and sexual and racial ambiguity, and they threaten to cripple him with guilt and emasculation.

Early in the story, Nick is indirectly responsible for the accidental death of his young Maori friend, Sam Waikai, because of a violation of tapu, and so the stain of Original Sin hangs over Nick's achievement of a stable self-identity. Later, while he is convalescing, there are allegations of homosexuality from Nick's older brother (who himself would appear to be homosexual). Nick flees from all this by "going bush" with his elderly grandfather who, on an allegorical level, epitomizes the Man Alone Pioneer Tradition before it became emasculated by women and the Law (or so the mythology goes).

The most peculiar aspect of *Among the Cinders* is the way the "Maori" problem (Nick's guilt/racial oppression) vanishes, to be

Among the Cinders (1984): the film's young hero, Nick Flinders looks forward into male sexual adulthood, but the way is fraught with temptation and panic flight.

displaced on to the "sexual" problem (Nick's sexual identity crisis/repressed homosexuality) with surprisingly little to show for it. Although both are clearly tracked in the Shadbolt novel, the film version accentuates the homosexual aspect far more, suggesting a certain tension between the film's two main producers—thus there is an O'Shea problem and a Haedrich problem. The O'Shea problem concerns the Original Sin of conquest with which New Zealand was founded—the destruction of the Maori way of life and Pakeha anxiety in the new land; the Haedrich problem concerns an individualistic and Europeanized obsession with repressed male homosexuality.

To begin at the beginning, Nick's initial voice-over narration states: "Dad's always saying that we should treat the Maoris better. They were here first, with their own language and all. The only friend I had was a Maori kid I once saved from drowning— Sam Waikai." Paternal advice suggests that the Pakeha owes a debt to the Maori; personal experience (saving Sam's life many years earlier) suggests the reverse. Scenarios which dramatize political generalities in personal terms frequently produce such contradictions, and in this case they become intolerable to Nick.

He desires Sam's friendship yet he is constantly aware that their common legacy involves either a burden of guilt or a burden of unequal obligations. Nick's desire to force the contradiction ends up resulting in Sam's death. The O'Shea problem is explored retrospectively, reaching out to the past through flashbacks of Sam's accidental death but quite unable to reverse time and resolve it. Perhaps as compensation, the film is populated by many incidental Maori characters, from the Waikai family to rural Noble Savages, to a completely Pakeha-oriented fashion model.

The Haedrich problem looks forward into male sexual adulthood achieved through loss of virginity (to a Rhine maiden no less!) before regretting and repressing it. Nick's grandfather in particular articulates this view: "This used to be a man's country," implying that New Zealand is now a woman's country where the feminizing influence of the Law has tamed and civilized the original virgin maleness of the old-time pioneers and the old-time Maori where it was only the land itself that was feminine (shades of Leni Riefenstahl?). The effect of such feminizing is that Nick

Among the Cinders offers its hero a choice between the masculine Pioneer Tradition (left) before it was emasculated by women, and female sexuality (right). Between the two there is a place for male homosexuality.

has a mother who is the stereotypical castrator and a father who is emasculated, and though the Maori hold out some hope of a homecoming (Nick is attracted to the warmth, the singing and the kissing of the Waikais), Sam's death puts an end to it.

Unable to resolve the knot of contradictions any other way, Nick adopts an excessive posture of self-denial and a felt need for atonement. When no one else will accept this (just as the Pakeha general public is not interested in liberal guilt), he represses it and seeks out a stable sexual identity instead. The only way this can be achieved is under the paternal guidance of his grandfather; the alternative would appear to be homosexuality. Several scenes testify to the initial fear of and flirtation with homosexual desire, including Nick's fascination with quoting Oscar Wilde's "Each man kills the thing he loves" upon the death of Sam, and his subsequent panic flight from the frank advances of a girl from his school. Nick faces his second crisis when he must choose to put the pre-sexual mateship of men behind him and enter sexual engagement with women. When at the end of the film he is on his own again, his virginity gone, a strangely ambiguous nostalgia comes over him: "Why couldn't things have stayed the way they were?"—implying some measure of regret at the turn of events. This does not rule out the possibility of a future homosexual identity, setting "things" on the right path again, and drawing on a fantasy held in memory of a repressed homosexual liaison with the now lost-for-ever Sam.

The central Maori/Pakeha relationship of *Among the Cinders* is of repressed homosexual desire. Its first crisis derives from anxiety at intimacy between the two cultures; it results in death (manslaughter?). This effectively eliminates the bicultural option homosexuality could have offered and leaves the Pakeha hero alone with his memories. The Maori does not survive except in memory as a repressed Other.

OTHER HALVES: THE TUG OF RACIAL DESIRE

Other Halves (1984), produced by Tom Finlayson and Dean Hill and directed by John Laing, is a free adaptation of Sue Mc-Cauley's best-selling autobiographical novel of the same name.[120] The novel is New Zealand's second most successful best-seller

Other Halves (1985) revolves around classic binarisms of gender, race, age, class, and identity: new wrinkles in the Integration Myth.

after *The Bone People* and a reason for their success must surely have something to do with the idea of romantically welding a Maori and a Pakeha together, allegorically working out the Integration Myth and biculturalism.

Unlike the other films of the Eighties dealt with in this chapter, *Other Halves* involves a successful relationship, and the relative success of both novel and film was certainly influenced by public knowledge of McCauley's real-life successful relationship with a much younger Maori man, and this was in some part duplicated by the much publicized casting of well known actress Lisa Harrow with an "authentic" (albeit Niuean) "street kid," Mark Pilisi, as the two leads. The film presents audiences with the challenge of an unorthodox social model: here is a romance which bridges the triple antitheses of race, age, and gender and actually succeeds— hence the film's publicity slogan, "A Dangerous Love Story." The analysis which follows examines those antitheses and how they are represented through different strategies:

Liz Harvey	*Tug*
Pakeha	Maori
Female	Male
32 years old	16 years old
upper middle class	urban street culture
suburban/homely	homeless

These antitheses are sketched in at the beginning of the film—
Liz's world in the pre-titles sequence, Tug's post-titles. The first
half of the film is designed to bring the two together sexually; the
second half is to test and rationalize why the romance has formed
and what its future will be. This cross-racial romance draws its
dramatic tension from the same source as *The Governor, Sylvia,
Among the Cinders* and others—the ambiguity as to whether the
relationship is one of ''equality'' or ''maternity''; i.e. whether
those ''other halves'' are in a horizontal or vertical relationship.

Pakeha culture in *Other Halves* receives a highly negative
representation, which is the reason that Liz's atavistic Fall
through an attempted suicide and psychiatric therapy into a
relationship with a young Maori ''rebel'' is possible in the first
place. Her young son, Michael, is identified with an anti-human
technology of home video games and a toy electronic tank; her
businessman husband, Ken, is simply Michael's adult equivalent.
At the psychiatric hospital, Liz comments that Ken has said she is
''repressed,'' and she says he is ''progressive,'' but the film goes
on to suggest that the exact reverse is true. The Pakeha male
culture of Michael and Ken is terribly repressed but able to
displace its anxiety on to Pakeha women, in the process destroying the maternal, the feminine, and the sexual. This is an
essentialist argument commonly heard within New Zealand feminism: Pakeha male culture is supposedly paternalist, joyless and
sexless, and obsessed with the mythology of power and conquest.
This is also represented in the film by the intimidating and
patronizing employees of the Welfare State—hospital psychia-
trists, nurses and receptionists, the police, and so on.

Pakeha female culture survives the humiliation and trauma of
the nuclear family breakdown (after eleven years of marriage) as
Woman Alone. Its desire is then displaced onto an erotic/exotic
Other: young Maori and Polynesian men. This is another Fall of a
kind, but it is also ''progressive'' when measured against the

Other Halves: Tug is the erotic-exotic object of Liz's desire, right down to the headband, earrings and necklace.

climate of pervasive cultural decay represented by Pakeha male culture. It also suggests that a certain equality is possible between the two protagonists. What other alternatives are there for Liz? In hospital she shares a ward with a drug addict who has no inhibitions about sleeping with Maori men, but the drugs she desires are a displacement of her own repressed needs; later, Liz is befriended by an embittered single woman whose vulgarized feminism the film satirizes ("Us single people are more real. Have you noticed?"). On leaving the hospital for a "loft," Liz evidently desires sexual release, and her first "experiment" is with an art gallery owner, Jim, who at one point remarks, "I've never really known a Polynesian," yet he also wears greenstone pendants. The irony in all these scenes approaches caricature, its sole purpose seemingly being to legitimize Liz's desire for Tug.

Most significant of all is the fact that liberal Pakeha culture has language (words, theories, explanations in abundance) and it has history (a sense of tradition, protocol, the fixed order of ideas and things); however, urban Maori and Polynesian street culture is its exact antithesis. It is linguistically inarticulate and finds expressiveness through challenging the law (drugs, theft, extortion) and through physical exertion (chase scenes, music, sex). Tug and his friends live very much in the present moment—almost timeless, as it were—and their bricolage clothing styles—shark tooth necklaces, patchwork colors—are a form of ironic mimicry of Pakeha-controlled consumerism and primitivism. This urban street culture simultaneously threatens Pakeha culture with the face of a camouflaged identity, the undecidability of what such clothing means other than rebellion itself. As artistic expression, it offers a warm and vibrant contrast with the cold neons of Jim's art gallery and the dead "primitive" objects on the mantelpiece of Liz's loft. Tug is exotic and glamorous, he has the energy and vitality that Ken, Michael, and Jim lack. This is clearly the basis of Liz's attraction to Tug and the narrative coincidence of their first sexual encounter occurring immediately after Tug returns from a burglary (erotic desire/crime) is probably apt.

The relationship is basically equalized at this point—equal halves—but as it becomes increasingly domesticated, the power begins to slide toward Liz and the maternal hierarchy she represents. Liz is clever enough to realize that Tug does not come to her encumbered by a consciousness of history, language and cultural determinism (even if he does have a criminal record), that it is she herself who does, and that their successful future together depends on her losing some of it and Tug gaining it. Tug must learn when and where to draw the line against "friends" and define an individual identity against collective loyalties; Liz must learn to open herself to Tug's world so that the relationship exists pre-eminently in the present tense. Tug must develop a personal strength; Liz must break down her own liberal egocentrism and her stake in Pakeha institutions and power without losing her identity in the process. Part of Liz's problem is the cluster of self-conscious recognitions that Tug is also part of her own repressed emotional life. At one point she tells him, "When I was at school I used to draw these faces . . . Maori faces I suppose . . . could've been your face." In allowing this recognition to surface in dialogue, she is also theorizing her desire in a way Tug would never do, but it enables her to objectify herself. Tug completes almost the reverse trajectory, learning to think of Liz as an individual rather than a "honky," but he does not suffer from a repressed Other as she does.

A major problem with the film which is not there in the more expansive novel is that neither Liz nor Tug changes significantly. For example, in the novel Liz marks her severance from middle-class values by shoplifting; in the film she resigns from a demeaning job. The lack of character development is only a problem in as much as conventional film narrative expectations require some crisis/resolution at film's end. The inclusion of a violent fight between Liz and Tug at this point, followed by a montage sequence and eventual reconciliation in bed, largely evades this requirement. Relying upon sexual solutions to racial problems has a certain logic to it, but the ending is at best only tentatively optimistic.

This opens up, finally, the question that motivates audience interest: what else do they see in each other if racially they are as close to violence as to love? The key here is the ambiguous oscillation of tension between them, literally the "tug" of desire. Is Tug the son she desires instead of Michael; in her words, is he the toad she can turn into a prince? Tug is quick to sense any civilizing mission initiatives, and Liz intelligently calls his bluff whenever he asserts his rebelliousness. Is Liz the maternal figure he desires, providing the sympathetic refuge from Pakeha institutional racism? Liz is deeply hurt by his barbed comments about her age, although actress Lisa Harrow's persona behind the character implies an enormous strength and resourcefulness. The film is at its most interesting when it examines these complex interchanges. Two examples will suffice:

1. LIZ: I thought you were just going to screw me and leave.
   TUG: You're disgusting.
2. TUG: You [Pakeha] are all the same you know. You think you're all so fucking civilized. Some day you're gonna have to answer for it.
   LIZ: I am?
   TUG: You're one of them, aren't you? Honky.
             (Liz simply takes his hand instead and in silence. The tension passes.)

Finally, the main appeal of *Other Halves* is not simply its racial antithesis but also its age and class antitheses. After the "balanced" romances of *Broken Barrier, To Love a Maori, Sons for the Return Home,* and the repressed homosexual/lesbian romances of *Among the Cinders* and *Just Passing Through, Other Halves* introduces a new wrinkle to the Integration Myth formulas. In matching an older Pakeha woman with a younger Maori man, its nearest equivalent perhaps is *The Makutu on Mrs. Jones* (*q.v.*), which matches a younger Pakeha woman with an older Maori man, although the narrative point of view is centered on a third person. The only variant as yet not dramatized would match an older Maori woman with a younger Pakeha man. Unfortunately, *Other Halves* belongs to the politics of repression because the central romance is still structured around Liz's point of view, not Tug's, and it celebrates her journey toward liberation from social constraints rather than his. In fact, it domesticates Tug as a narrative convenience, repressing him within Liz's dream of order. If the film is initially Liz's Fall out of the social world and into Tug's, by the end she has fairly well succeeded in rehabilitating him back into the social.

ARRIVING TUESDAY: INNOCENTS ABROAD IN AOTEAROA

Arriving Tuesday (1986), directed by Richard Riddiford, presents a contradictory thesis on the confrontation between the Pakeha liberal tradition and Maori essentialism, a thesis which is finally unable to see its way clear to a compromise consistent with biculturalism.

Nick and Monica are a young Pakeha couple in their late twenties. Their preeminent concern, which provides momentum for the narrative, is the desire for some form of personal psychological unity and identity, both with each other and within themselves. Nick is a sculptor of metal and a part-time inventor who appears to be "at home" in New Zealand. His life in a rural farmhouse has all the ambience of the Sixties counter-culture now withdrawn from political engagement and protected by a hermetic art school aesthetics. This matches the Man Alone literary myth well enough, which in the middle Eighties had become thoroughly

Arriving Tuesday (1986): Pakeha savages, Monica and Nick, lost in the land of Aotearoa.

eccentric. All Nick's happiness requires, apparently, is Monica's commitment to him, but it is this very desire for stasis and stability which is most dissatisfying to Monica (she calls him a "slug"). As the film opens, she is returning to New Zealand (and Nick) after ten months abroad, bringing with her the failure to find her "roots" in Britain. Evidently, she does not share Nick's sense of having grown into the land in New Zealand and she is not optimistic about discovering it through Nick. After their reconciliation, it is Monica's initiative which leads to their traveling north, in a quest designed to satisfy her restlessness and alienation. Man and Woman Alone, innocents abroad in Aotearoa.

The film takes more than half an hour to set this up, and the drift in both the central relationship and the film's narrative is quite apparent by this point. Nick and Monica are both so relentlessly stubborn in their individualism that their conversational sparring recalls the familiar mis-matched couples of other New Zealand films (notably *Smash Palace*). The film is a reworking of Seventies cultural politics: Nick is the egocentric male hero who centers so many of these films, and Monica is his egocentric female equivalent who has moved into his space in order to decenter it. Her personal quest (to being "spiritually uplifted" or "running naked if we want to'') increasingly comes to dominate the narrative, bringing it into line with a liberal feminist position (*c.f. Other Halves*). There follows an abrupt turn into Eighties cultural politics as the narrative moves into the more highly charged territory of Maori/Pakeha culture conflict.

The vignettes that follow are designed to negatively stereotype (rural) New Zealand Pakeha culture: a hotel harridan in wet and empty Dargaville, a farmer driving by who stops to grab a dead opossum off the road (''dog tucker'') without offering Monica a ride, and a dangerously threatening farmer with a shotgun. Given this loading, it becomes possible to establish Maori culture—as embodied by Ricky, a poet and artist—as warm, friendly, natural, spontaneous, and unburdened by Pakeha oppressions. As in *Runaway* (*q.v.*), a film it often resembles, Maori culture serves as a possible solution held out to liberal Pakeha pilgrims in search of a ''spiritual'' (cultural) identity. Ricky first appears in the film singing in a hotel bar which Nick and Monica visit. From his opening ''Kia ora'' he drives a wedge between the other two, exploiting Monica's liberal guilt. She is sexually attracted to Ricky (''a randy she-goat,'' says Nick), but given the lack of frank dialogue, it is difficult to say whether the basis of her attraction is Ricky's romantic bohemian air or his Maoriness. Probably both: the line between the personal and the cultural remains highly charged and highly ambiguous. If on a personal level Monica tries to remain suspended between her desire for Ricky and her love for Nick, then on an allegorical level she is the conflicted Pakeha liberal who desires to share in the excitement of Maori radicalism without alienating the Pakeha community she belongs to.

There is an exchange earlier in the film which foreshadows this, on the subject of Pakeha learning Maori:

> MONICA: You know Carol is having Tui learn Maori?
>
> NICK: (laughs) Oh, that's typical. Exactly the sort of thing Carol would do.
>
> MONICA: Oh, I don't know. I think learning Maori would be a good thing.
>
> NICK: She's just trying to be fashionable. Using her children to ease her own guilt. Look, you can't change the color of your skin; you

Arriving Tuesday: Ricky, Maori poet and artist, represents a sexual and cultural solution to Monica's spiritual problem, but she rejects it.

	certainly can't ingratiate yourself into another culture.
MONICA:	God, you'll be the first one up against the wall.

This stakes out the positions fairly clearly: Monica is the film's "progressive" character but she is earnestly naive about what this might entail. Nick disparages this as "ingratiation" and thus espouses Pakeha essentialism and repression. Consequently, on their meeting Ricky, the dramatic tension derives on the personal level from the psycho-sexual triangle, and on the cultural level from the conflict of two essentialisms (Maori versus Pakeha) for the body and soul of the liberal feminist middle ground (biculturalism?). For example, Monica's dancing with Ricky to a diner jukebox explicitly dramatizes (via reaction shots of Nick and his retreat from the scene) a familiar jealousy scene (*c.f. Smash Palace, Sleeping Dogs*), with the added twist of a cultural mix (*c.f. The Quiet Earth*). Monica herself becomes a whirling blur in the film's center, singing "I'm in love with you, honey" as if it were meant for Ricky, while Nick fades away as if destined to become a Pakeha ghost in the new land of Aotearoa.

In the scenes following, Monica and Nick are introduced to friends of Ricky's—a mini-hikoi (trek) of urban Maori—in another scene which seems designed to convey (for Pakeha audiences) the warmth of the Maori in the face of oppression: lots of Kia oras and hongis as temporary respite in dragging a huge rock, Sisyphus-style, back home to the marae. That night, it remains completely ambiguous as to whether Ricky and Monica have slept together, and the inevitable crisis with Nick comes the next day in the car when Ricky's anti-Pakeha animus breaks out into the open:

RICKY:	Imagine, eh? Aotearoa was covered in bush like this from the coast right to the mountaintops. Along comes the Pakeha . . . chop chop chop . . . all gone. They've got heaps to answer for, I reckon.
NICK:	Well, I heard that one third of the forest was already destroyed before the Europeans got here.

In *Runaway,* there was an almost identical conversation between two Pakeha; in *Arriving Tuesday* the battle lines have been drawn between Maori and Pakeha essentialist positions. However, the situation is now entirely personal, no longer veiled under the superficial politics, and there are fracture lines between all three: Ricky disappears, Monica goes north to find him (and return his dog) and Nick returns home. The domestic tragedy of these scenes slides perceptibly into tragicomedy and the absurd, and if it were not for the realist mode in which these scenes are bracketed, the film could have slid completely into self-parody, a consequence of its inability to distance itself adequately from the spectacle of Pakeha liberals making fools of themselves. A shot in which Monica plays the Last Post on a trumpet for Ricky's expired dog signals a slide into Antonioni-esque existential confusion, and it is shot apparently without a trace of irony.

The narrative now stays mainly with Monica: having rejected the Pakeha essentialist option (Nick), she arrives at Ricky's marae at the same time as the hikoi. Watching the karanga from a distance, Monica faces up to her own cultural identity as a Pakeha with the full implications of being unable to cross the cultural divide. Monica retreats from Ricky in much the same way Nick had retreated from her desire for Ricky (ironically, this confirms Nick's earlier stand on "ingratiation"). In this narrative version of the double bind, the liberal imagination can conceive of no middle ground between cultures if its terms of reference are personal relationships and individual identity.

RICKY:	Shoulda just come and joined in.
MONICA:	I felt wrong
RICKY:	Yeh. Course it's gonna feel wrong.
MONICA:	It just wasn't comfortable.
RICKY:	That's dumb. The marae is the most comfortable place in the world.
MONICA:	For you . . .
RICKY:	Why don't you stay? Stay up here. You might figure a few things out.
MONICA:	I can't.
RICKY:	Well, it's better than scooting back to England and pretending you fit in there . . . . It's time you got yourself together, Monica.

In this dialogue, which commences the film's denouement, Ricky appears to offer Monica biculturalism: she would learn about Maori culture by visiting a marae in the fashion of the pilgrimage genre of the Seventies and early Eighties. However, Ricky remains ambiguous about his own sexual interest in her, and wilfully naive about the threat that a marae means for a troubled Pakeha liberal. Perhaps Monica rejects his offer because she senses the double bind Ricky is in turn forcing upon her. Yet in deciding to return to Nick, she also rejects biculturalism. What is so threatening about visiting a marae, and must the cultural difference between Ricky and Monica overwhelm their sexual identity?

Arriving Tuesday recalls the failed cross-racial romances of Rudall Hayward's films from the Twenties in that it overturns the logical progression of its middle sequences and reinstalls the racial divide. Though the final reconciliation between Nick and Monica is completely consistent logically with the lack of imagination these characters possess, it is also tantamount to a retreat back into the oppressive bourgeois domestic politics that opened the film. Its message is, finally, Stay with your own kind, and the "Maori" sequences which dominate the film's narrative interest read as a temporarily disruptive Other in the jerky momentum toward resolving the personal problems of two egocentric Pakeha.

Why then does *Arriving Tuesday* center its narrative interest in the psychological dilemmas of its female protagonist if only to have her return to the very situation that had become intolerable to her? Because the film satisfactorily resolves neither Monica's relationship with Nick nor her relationship with Ricky, it is completely unable to resolve its own internal contradictions in relation to feminism and Maori radicalism, and it ends up promoting a reactionary discourse on bourgeois romance and a Pakeha essentialism divested of biculturalism.

THE LOST TRIBE: THE END OF BICULTURALISM

The "darkest" film of the politics of repression is *The Lost Tribe* (1983/85), written and directed by John Laing. It is a horror film and an allegory upon the transformation of the earnest liberal

Pakeha (Edward Scarry) into the darker doppelgänger of the "Pakeha backlash" (Max Scarry). Edward Scarry is a journalist searching for his identical twin brother, the anthropologist Max Scarry, who has gone missing in Fiordland while searching for the lost Hawea tribe. The narrative then, like the characters, involves a doubling of the one quest over the latter, but it is Edward's quest for Max's Pakeha heart of darkness which is the concern of the narrative, not Max's quest for a Maori heart. Edward finds that darkness at the end of the film, only to be killed by Max, who has become psychopathic, having earlier murdered a woman back in "civilization" and now doubling it with his brother's murder. In the darkly ironic conclusion it is Max who returns to civilization, protected by the safe identity of his brother's name.

Nominally, *The Lost Tribe* is a Cain and Abel story complete with the distinctive visual imagery of New Zealand Catholicism—a cross between the primeval Bush, light and fire, apocalypticism and Manichean values. It is also clearly derivative of Stanley Kubrick's *The Shining* with its psychic child, domestic violence, and electronic soundtrack, and perhaps too of Peter

The Lost Tribe (1983): the Pakeha self fades into the mist in this atavistic fantasy of fratricide.

Weir's *The Last Wave,* which uses Aboriginal symbolism and motifs to project a horror in the Australian heart. But *The Lost Tribe* is not about Maori revenge via tapu and makutu, or even about the lost tribe that Max went to find; it is about the "lost tribe" of the Pakeha, spiritually bankrupt in the new land and turning increasingly to a diabolical form of mysticism, and in this it resembles Vincent Ward's *Vigil. The Lost Tribe* is populated by lonely and repressed Pakeha men and women at the edge of civilization, presided over by a Maori policeman who seems to be the sole figure of trust. It might well be asked why Edward had to pursue his quest so single-mindedly when it would lead to his death; evidently his fractured identity could only be healed by knowledge of his darker side, represented by Max, and yet it destroys him.

In other words, *The Lost Tribe* plays out an atavistic scenario but it takes place completely within the Pakeha heart of darkness; there is no fall into Maoriland or Aotearoa, though Max uses its motifs to terrify Edward. What the Maori policeman thinks of a Pakeha diabolism reborn can only be speculated upon, but Max is an infinitely more terrifying threat to Maori sovereignty than Edward. As an anthropologist he has secret knowledge and the power to abuse it; *The Lost Tribe* destroys the principle of brotherhood and augurs a dark future for biculturalism.

CHAPTER 11: THE POLITICS OF IRONY

BICULTURALISM, MULTICULTURALISM OR POSTMODERNISM?

In 1982, one year after the bitter divisions of the South African Springbok Rugby Tour, Race Relations Conciliator Hiwi Tauroa produced a report named *Race Against Time* in which he argued that biculturalism must be the "first step" toward multiculturalism, since Maori and Pakeha represent the "two cultural foundations of New Zealand society."[121] It would seem that what Tauroa and others have been calling for is what I have been referring to as bicultural nationalism. Its particular appeal must be that although it splits the one (nation) into two (cultures), it still offers to consolidate the center against further internal dissolution (e.g. Maori nationalism or multiculturalism) for the time being. In that sense bicultural nationalism is a conservative and integrating social ideal even if superficially it appears to drive a wedge into the national body politic.

Logically, the next question must be, Can biculturalism be sustained in the face of a corrosive post-modern irony and skepticism? Personally, I doubt it, because I think multiculturalism will probably prevail in the long run. Post-modernism, with which it is associated, has been theorized variously as a historical process associated with capitalism; as an international cultural condition eroding value systems and decentering discourse and the psychological subject or self; and as a genre of self-parodic literature, to name but a few.[122] Whatever explanation one adopts and whatever name one chooses to give it, there has been a tendency within recent New Zealand films toward using irony, parody, and pastiche, as well as toward overtly allegorical (non-realist) narratives. Does this confirm that we are no longer living in the same New Zealand I identified with nationalism?

For the time being, however, let us return to biculturalism via the concept of Aotearoa. This name has always had a certain blunt effectiveness in irritating conservatives, just as many Maori resent its expropriation by Pakeha, but it has gained a certain currency as an alternative name for New Zealand. Yet the linguistic and legal protocols of the double bind insist there be only one name for the nation, so its future is not assured. Indeed, some formulations invite the same fate as Maoriland, which began as a synonym for New Zealand and ended up as a ghostly whisper.[123] The bicultural nationalist model is a compromise: it recognizes the advantages to be had from belonging to Pakeha-controlled New Zealand (one nation, two peoples, two cultures), but it rejects the Pakeha annexation of Aotearoa implied by the Integration Myth while not going so far as Maori nationalism. It posits a split self whereby both Maori and Pakeha cultures can share the same space. (See figure 3)

Perhaps, then, it is all just a simple matter of translation: Aotearoa as the Maori name for New Zealand? What then if Aotearoa were not defined so exclusively through nationalist paradigms? The land has been the lynchpin in both the Maori and New Zealand nationalism arguments, but raising the land question always keys into nineteenth-century nationalist paradigms and potentially endless debates about Waitangi, 1840, and Original Sin. During the Eighties, as Maori arguments turned more to ''mauri'' and ''wairua,'' there were relatively traditional alternatives available. For example, in the book accompanying the *Te Maori* exhibition, Sid Mead wrote: ''Although economic factors have helped to scatter the Maori people from their homelands, a majority of them see themselves as belonging to a tribe whose turangawaewae (place for the feet to stand) and whose ahi kaa (burning fire) are located at specific regions (see maps 2 & 3). . . . The concept of tangata whenua (people of the land) remains intact despite the alienation of the land.''[124] The maps Mead is referring to turn out to be in the book's appendix and they show the ''homelands'' and ''regions'' with no overarching names other than ''South Island'' and ''North Island.'' I would argue that his maps are best thought of as maps of Aotearoa. They are defined according to iwi/hapu regions—whakapapa rather than the categories of social geography, and cultural identity rather than national identity. Could the bicultural relationship between New Zealand and Aotearoa be defined in this way?

Figure 3:
Models for New Zealand nationalism and biculturalism.

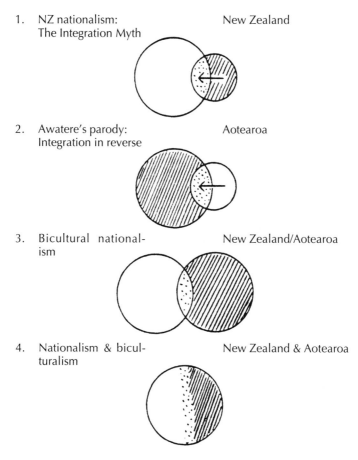

1. NZ nationalism: New Zealand
   The Integration Myth

2. Awatere's parody: Aotearoa
   Integration in reverse

3. Bicultural national-   New Zealand/Aotearoa
   ism

4. Nationalism & bicul-   New Zealand & Aotearoa
   turalism

For one thing, Sid Mead generally uses the double term
"Aotearoa (New Zealand)."[125] He writes: "While the Maori
people use their art to identify themselves ethnically and hence
nationally as well, the Pakeha population tends to use it as a
national marker, and then only the portions that appeal to
them."[126] In other words, many Maori can have a separate cultural
identity such that they are actually bicultural: they are New

Zealand nationals, but they are also privy to the cultural heritage of Aotearoa. For Pakeha, this heritage of Aotearoa is not directly accessible to them. If New Zealand and the Maori are bicultural, then the Pakeha is not, and the program for Mead (as indeed for others) must be to make the monocultural Pakeha bicultural to the degree that they can accept and appreciate cultural differences within Aotearoa/New Zealand. Hence taha Maori and kohanga reo in schools, *Koha* and *Nga Take Maori* on television, and so on.

Yet another approach might be to ask why biculturalism must be subordinated to nationalism at all. It can provide for something much more imaginative if its Maoritanga is not bent to fit a legal system of power and control derived from a European heritage. The legal paradigm is after all associated with the Pakeha rather than the Maori. The incorporation of Maori values into New Zealand law is a necessary step, but Aotearoa can also help to shift thinking away from the legal paradigm toward ''culture'' in its more general sense, as the awareness of different ways of doing things, of different and competing realities. Then it may be defined according to different language systems: New Zealand as an English-language system defined by laws and anchored in history, and Aotearoa as the Maori-language system of Maoritanga anchored in land, mana, iwi affiliations and wairua. Indeed, this was the original conflict at Waitangi in 1840—the Law versus Mana. In this way, just as culture can be seen to be a national historical construction when viewed from a New Zealand perspective, so the whole apparatus of nation and history can be seen to be a cultural construction when viewed from the perspective of Maori culture. The films discussed in this chapter attempt to negotiate that problem.

''New Zealand'' offers at best an integration model which ends up privileging the Pakeha over the Maori, and it also endorses a multicultural pluralism in which Pacific Islanders too will claim their turangawaewae. ''Aotearoa'' will most likely remain as a Maori version of the national historical romance along with its narratives of Utopia and the Fall. However, Aotearoa does still reverse the New Zealand mythology by allowing the two cultures to occupy different spaces within the same land, and the Maori are privileged over the Pakeha as the host (tangata whenua) to the guests (manuhiri). In theory and practice there can be then a New Zealand and an Aotearoa, a national mythology and a bicultural mythology which relativizes it. Each other's Other. New Zealand/ Aotearoa.

UTU: EXPLODING THE DOUBLE BIND

This chapter examines three films produced by the New Zealand Film Commission and it asks why there has been increased skepticism toward the national myth. *Utu* (1983) is only the most recent of the historical epics to deal with it, and it has also been the most willing to explore a "Maori" interpretation of last century's events. Directed by Geoff Murphy and co-written by Murphy and Keith Aberdein, the New Zealand version (there is a shorter U.S. version) is over two hours long, cost millions to make, and is shot through with all the ambiguities and complexities of New Zealand's racial and cultural history.[127]

The choice of title for the film is a useful place to begin. As with its companion piece, the film *Patu, Utu* is named after a Maori word and concept, and the filmmakers and subsequent reviewers have gone to great lengths to find a suitable translation into English. To do so has clearly been considered important because with the resurgence of interest in national history and the politics of self-blame that much of this has entailed since the 1981 Springbok Tour, a concept such as "utu" can be very useful in identifying issues for national and cultural agendas. But utu for whom and from whom and for what reasons? For the Maori from the Pakeha because of one hundred years of land dispossession? For the Pakeha from the Maori for violation of the Law? In a publicity release for the film, Murphy has translated utu variously as "reciprocation," "balance," "revenge," "compensation," "payment," to which reviewers have added "retribution," "atonement," "honor" and "justice." The blizzard of terminology is as potent a symptom of present-day inter-cultural ambiguities as the concept itself.

The central figure around whom the question of utu turns is Te Wheke, a Maori warrior and rebel, and a tragic figure of no less than Shakespearean proportions who is given to ironic quotations from *Macbeth* on appropriate occasions. That great play has a certain aptness for New Zealand given that its driving themes are

Utu (1983): Maori "friendlies" drumming the imperial theme at a British army encampment.

regicide and usurpation of power—essentially the themes diagnosed by New Zealand's theorists of the politics of blame. Certain similarities with *The Governor* are also immediately apparent: both scenarios are nominally tragedies, and Te Wheke stands alone in implacable defiance against British and Pakeha power just as Grey stood in defiance against his rivals for a dream of Utopia in the South Seas.

If Te Wheke is not exactly Maori Alone, vintage 1870, then he is quite obviously a Maori anti-hero, and the narrative resolution must depend upon either his repression or his execution. Indeed he represents, almost from the beginning, the very phenomenon that *The Governor* ended up producing: Maori nationalism and Aotearoa in eruption. *The Governor* concluded with a formal declaration that consigned the Maori/Pakeha conflicts over whenua and mana to the vicissitudes of historical inevitability and fate, and in one of its many translations utu can indeed mean fate, but the series also diagnosed a legacy of Maori anger and resistance—utu. The film *Utu* may be interpreted as an attempt to come to terms with this legacy as well as with the complexity of this Maori word and concept, and to extend the range of translations in dramatic terms so as to explode the monocultural double bind produced by the earlier television series.

Echoing *The Governor,* the narrative construction allows initially for several Maori/Pakeha oppositions to be established around and against Te Wheke:

> Te Wheke versus   1. Williamson
> 2. Lieutenant Scott
> 3. Colonel Elliot

Williamson is a Pakeha settler who initially may have been sympathetic toward the Maori, but he turns to revenge when his wife is killed by Te Wheke; Lieutenant Scott is a young army officer born in New Zealand who is given the charge of hunting Te Wheke and dispensing justice; Colonel Elliot is the racist commanding officer of the British Army whose campaign for retribution is responsible for Te Wheke's campaign for utu in the first place. There are also several Maori/Maori oppositions established later in the film:

> Te Wheke versus   1. Kura
> 2. Matu
> 3. Wiremu

Kura is a young Maori woman whose notion of utu allows her to save Lieutenant Scott's life in return for his saving hers, but Te Wheke interprets it as betrayal; Matu is an aunt to Kura, and also a cousin to one of Te Wheke's comrades (executed by Te Wheke when his wounds slow down the rebel party); Corporal Wiremu is a kupapa (''friendly'') fighting on the British side in the wars, and his notion of utu has more in common with a sense of balance or equity. For the sake of simplicity, I have divided the narrative of this complex film into seven sections: introduction, Maori village, the church, the siege of the Williamson house, bush warfare, the siege of the town and subsequent pursuit, and the trial.

Utu: Kura and Lieutenant Scott decide whether to sleep together or shoot each other. Another metaphor for early New Zealand?

The film opens with a swelling imperial theme—oboe and slow drumbeat, and a Union Jack flying atop a British military fort. John Charles's fine musical score evokes a richness of texture in keeping with the film's highly mobile and elusive moral textures. The scene then shifts to a (by contrast) peaceful Maori village in the forest. The British Army attacks the village, technology invades nature, and there is widespread destruction and death as a consequence. The scene is apparently based on the notorious massacre of Rangiaowhia in the Waikato, which directly triggered Kereopa's killing of the Reverend Volkner at Opotiki in 1865. In the film, the village is Te Wheke's own, and he switches from kupapa to Maori warrior and rebel, taking on the image most usually associated with Te Kooti Rikirangi whose name Te Wheke evokes to some degree (*c.f. The Te Kooti Trail*).

In its narrowest sense, Te Wheke seeks utu from Colonel Elliot for ordering the massacre. In a wider sense, Te Wheke demands utu from all Pakeha; thus he is aligned with contemporary Maori nationalism as the threatening Other that imperialism fears and yet desires to fear. Te Wheke's actions are easily justified of course, both from a cultural relativistic perspective and from within their own cultural context, and *Utu* in fact turns this problem to its advantage throughout the film. For example, when Lieutenant Scott is talking to a Maori soldier about a trick the Maori rebels played on the British—adding human meat to a barrel of pickled pork—the Maori soldier laughs uproariously while Scott remains puzzled. This throws the issue of cannibalism into an ironic light, in that cannibalism is only horrible if you identify with the victim.

More to the point, Te Wheke's reasons for utu are formally articulated in the following Maori-language oration (with English sub-titles): ''I must kill the white man [Pakeha] to avenge what he has done. The spirits of my people command me. I cannot live this life.'' This indeed is the film's driving theme. So what are Pakeha to make of this allegory, this morality tale? How else should a warrior respond? Should utu mean more than revenge? How should one recognize barbarism and savagery? The film opens up these questions rather than closes them down. These sequences are punctuated throughout by the film's titles, and at this point the ''Utu'' title appears—three short metallic letters on fire, like iron out of the furnace. By the time they have cooled, Te Wheke has

Utu: what is a warrior to do when his people have been senselessly massacred by the invader? Requesting a full-face moko (tattoo) signals Te Wheke's declaration of war on the Pakeha.

received a full face moko and the tragedy has begun to run its inevitable course.

Following the titles and lasting until intermission, there are two lengthy set-pieces designed to establish Te Wheke as a renegade in British eyes and to demonstrate his considerable style and flair. The sequences are Te Wheke's killing of the Reverend Johns (i.e. Volkner) in his church, and Te Wheke's warriors attacking the home of a settler couple, Williamson and his wife Emily. The latter especially is reminiscent of Te Kooti's raids during the late 1860s. The Reverend Johns' sermon is, conveniently, from St. Matthew 26: 51–2: "For all they that take the sword shall perish with the sword," which is accompanied by dire predictions that the "messengers of Satan are loose in the land." The sequence has a splendidly surreal quality to it, and it closes with the first of the film's three formal articulations of the central theme (which are all spoken by Maori characters) when Te Wheke addresses the church congregation:

> A fire lit by the white man's lust for our land and fanned by the breath of the Pakeha's words of God. Is this the Lord's plan? Perhaps the vicar has other masters than God? What other choice does the Lord offer a warrior? Imagine . . . imagine if you put aside your swords, your weapons, but not too far aside. Imagine if you took up the plough, took on the guise of farmers, traders, but were always ready. Could we put 10,000 warriors on the streets of Auckland for just a few hours? Wait, be ready.

The historical revisionism of this speech is perfectly obvious, a feature which incensed many local reviewers who argued a naive case for historical authenticity and realism. Cavalier about such scruples as the film obviously intends to be, it begins at this point to transcend the politics of blame inherited from *The Governor*.

The next sequence—the siege of the Williamson house—begins the cross-hatching of the utu theme whereby others will in their turn claim utu from Te Wheke. Williamson himself is another character in the Man Alone tradition (as indeed is the actor, Bruno Lawrence, who specializes in this kind of role). He possesses the traditional moral sensibility of the Fool ("Are we obliged to import all our worst habits to this new land? Why are we here? Are we here to build monuments to civilization or to tear them down?'') while also being given to a grandiose eccentricity which accelerates after his wife's death. Visually, the sequence is the most exciting in the film, mixing in explosive special effects, crisp reverse shot and angle cutting, and casual black humor—door handles do not work at critical moments for either side, and Williamson finds himself holed up in a shed with barrels of dynamite. Best of all, there is a wealth of cross-cultural allusions, for example:

> WILLIAMSON: Get off my land or I'll shoot you down.
> TE WHEKE: (laughs) He says it's his land.

In addition, there is a bone manaia or lizard pendant which circulates as a portent of death, and Te Wheke's warriors treat the Williamson crockery and grand piano (icons of Pakeha status) with less than the proper respect. As David Chute remarked in the *Los Angeles Herald-Examiner*: "Te Wheke . . . doesn't just want to kill the British, but to rock the foundations of their sense of order, to induce in them a sense of moral vertigo like his."[128] The Williamsons' house is at length totally destroyed and Emily (somewhat inadvertently) killed. The screen reddens and this brings up the film's intermission.

From the intermission onwards, the vertigo is in abeyance as the conflict becomes as racially polarized as it was in *The Governor*. At one extreme is British imperialism represented by Colonel Elliot and the Law: "We did not take this country in order to abandon it to the rule of the mob. Law and order, Mr. Scott, that is the issue." Lower-rank British soldiers are given to comments on how to identify Maoris: "That's simple. They're the brown ones lying on the ground, they're not moving, and they've got the flies around them." On the other (Maori) extreme stands Te Wheke. Williamson is to be aligned with neither: he is an eccentric maverick with loyalties to no one, an ironic version of the Man Alone prototype for a future New Zealand identity (the real prototypes are Lieutenant Scott and Wiremu). Williamson is the irrational dark side to Elliot's law and order, but by the end of the film his irrationality has proved more attractive than Elliot's rationality: "Sometimes I'm mad . . . Sometimes I'm not."

Spiraling underneath the main narrative conflict, however, are the softening influences of a politics of biculturalism which moves the film well beyond the imaginative vision of *The Governor*. As the film moves to the bush, it occasionally cuts for light relief to Williamson perfecting his extravagant weaponry. In other sequences, Lieutenant Scott and Wiremu discuss the war, and their dialogue seems designed to weaken the polarization by use of humor and ambiguous political alignment. For example, Scott remarks to a Maori soldier, "You Maoris have a strange sense of humor. I was over at the Arawa encampment the other night and they were celebrating the fact that Te Wheke seems to be on the run." He cannot easily understand that the Maori are just as divided in their loyalties as the British/Pakeha. Wiremu, meanwhile, is more controlled, more knowing:

> WILLIAMSON: How can you tell they're not [Te Wheke's] men?
> WIREMU: I can tell.
> WILLIAMSON: How can we tell you're not one of them?
> WIREMU: You can't.

To know what is really going on, one has to be Maori, though Scott is making the right gestures. Throughout these sequences the irony is pervasive. There are wild haka chants, bizarre improvised drum rolls, tiger skins nailed to back walls, and the beginnings of a gentle romance between Henare, a young Maori soldier in the British Army, and Kura, whom he meets in the bush. On returning to his detachment, Henare delivers the film's second formal thematic speech:

> HENARE: Why do we fight, tribe against tribe? Thirty years ago they dug a Maori bullet from my grandfather's leg. On and on it goes and always the Pakeha sides with those who best advance his cause. Will we still face each other across battle lines in one hundred years?
> WIREMU: (in Maori) Then stop!
> HENARE: (in Maori) Tomorrow.

Henare's comments prompt Lieutenant Scott to ask which side Henare is on:

WIREMU: Sir, will these [rifles] help to make a better
              world?
SCOTT: (in Maori) I doubt it.
WIREMU: Then does it matter which side we're on?

As if to punctuate this bicultural thesis, there is a sudden attack on their encampment and Henare is killed. Curiously, Scott attends Henare's tangi, a historically improbable turn of events in that Scott is hunting Te Wheke's people, but it is in keeping with the bicultural revisionism the film attempts to establish. Other subplots, meanwhile, explore the emotional cost to Maori of this biculturalism: does it not amount to collaboration, to "exterminating our people"? Though Wiremu survives, Kura, who later has a brief romantic liaison with Scott, does not. She is executed by Te Wheke.

The longest section of the film involves the siege of the small town where Colonel Elliot's soldiers are stationed. Mostly, this is a sustained effort at maintaining the suspense, the humor, and the ambiguous political alignments. For example, when Kura escapes from captivity, Scott remarks: "I think my ambition escaped with the prisoner." Later he asks, "Which side are you on, Wiremu?" and Wiremu replies with a laugh, "Same side as you. I was born here too." Meanwhile, out in the scrub nearby, one of Te Wheke's warriors dips his face in flour and states, "Hold it, I'm a Pakeha." It is not well received, so he observes, "I've only been a Pakeha for one minute and already I hate you Maoris." Numerous other surreal discussions and parodic echoes of *Macbeth* follow, even a Birnam Wood ("You're burnin' your own wood") which creeps toward the town as cover for Te Wheke's warriors. However, the attack is driven off (largely due to Williamson), and the final pursuit comes to an end with a shootout in which Te Wheke is captured and Wiremu secretly shoots Colonel Elliot. One of the racial extremes is therefore eliminated.

The final trial of Te Wheke is a very rapid and rather complex sequence of events in which various people claim utu, justice, or whatever, from Te Wheke. Of the six challengers identified earlier, Kura and Elliot are dead, and Wiremu is able to reject the claims of the other three. He can reject Matu because she is a woman and is from a different tribe, and allowing her utu would create new conflict. He can reject Williamson because William-

Utu: it is Wiremu, Te Wheke's brother, whose utu is the most just because he understands that Maori and Pakeha must live together in a commitment to biculturalism.

son rejected military protection and because his individualism has no moral status in a general racial conflict. And he can reject Scott because he is not without prejudice, and, "Besides, I think Pakehas have killed enough Maori and Maori have killed enough Pakeha." Wiremu then gives the third formal speech of the film:

> I am a corporal in the militia, I have standing in this court,
> and my mana is of this earth . . . . I have no desire for utu, no
> ledger to balance . . . . I am without prejudice . . . . My name
> is Wiremu, Te Wheke. This is my brother.

With this startling revelation, Wiremu places a whakamana (an empowering spirit) on the gun and on the bullet of execution. He hongis with his brother and the end comes. Appropriately, the final shot is of Wiremu, there is a waiata in the background, and the screen fades this time to black.

It may be asked whether the strategic narrative changes in *Utu,* as compared with *The Governor,* somehow reflect the emotional fall-out in the wake of the events of 1981: the South African Springboks' tour of New Zealand and the subsequent Waitangi protests? Certainly, one of the film's publicity slogans was: "*Utu.* One hundred years ago is today. The past is the present. And the future is now.'' In my view, the film implicitly accepts that the national division experienced in 1981 was also the final crisis of New Zealand realism, and it is something which is directly foretold in *The Governor. Utu* holds out the hope of healing the national division by allegorically eliminating the two extremes of Maori and Pakeha essentialism, but it does so by means of willful abandonment, indeed outright parody, of the traditional realist aesthetics to which New Zealand film reviewers subscribed. This attack on realism seems to me to be far more important than the issues raised by those reviewers at the time of *Utu*'s release. They mostly devoted their arguments to cataloging the supposed ''flaws'' and ''contradictions'' and ''confusions'' they found in the film—in particular *Utu*'s cavalier (i.e. allegorical) approach to history and its unrealistic (i.e. parodic) film style. This suggests instead that it is those reviewers who worked themselves into a critical impasse derived from reading the film off against an outmoded historical narrative and an illusory ideal film of their own devising. Subjecting *Utu* to a critique of historical authenticity amounts to a futile strategy for distancing oneself temporally from the film's political implications.

Significantly, overseas reviewers were much quicker to grasp all this. For example, in her review for the *New Yorker,* Pauline Kael noted the parody (she refers to the acts of ''travesty'' and ''mimicry'') and the allegorical approach:

No doubt Murphy was conscious of taking a balanced, nonjudgmental position, but you feel that the material itself—and his own instincts—dictated it. He couldn't have made this movie any other way, because it's a comedy about the characters' racial expectations of each other, which come out of the tragedy of their history—a history too grotesque for tears.[129]

If one accepts Kael's argument, as I do, that *Utu* is a comedy derived from the tragedy of history (she also refers to it as a "horror comedy of colonialism"), this throws into doubt whether the resolution offers anything tangible or hopeful. In my view it does. Allegorically, the film achieves a greater moral complexity than *The Governor* because it does not strive to eliminate the bicultural options along the way; it moves virtually in the opposite direction and eliminates both British imperialism and Maori nationalism instead! Certainly *Utu* explores the territory of the double bind of the Treaty of Waitangi and in a sense rewrites it. On the one hand, it is about the necessity and propriety of utu—even Te Wheke's. By the end of the film, Te Wheke (as well as Colonel Elliot) has been executed for his transgressions against Maori and Pakeha, so for Te Wheke (and Elliot) *Utu* is a tragedy. On the other hand, when utu is resolved properly, it is also about the necessity and propriety of Maori and Pakeha living together in the land of New Zealand/Aotearoa. The ending would appear to be a comedic reconciliation wherein the survivors have every intention of honoring a bicultural commitment to each other.

I believe *Utu*'s commitment is to biculturalism (albeit Pakeha-centered) rather than to bicultural nationalism, and there is an important difference. For one thing, Te Wheke's achievement has been substantial: his pursuit of a limited tactical warfare against British imperialism brings dignity of a kind to Maori on both sides of the divide since these Maori did not simply roll over when the invasion came. For another, out of the conflict comes a new fusion of consciousness for both races. Warfare, like marriage and sexual liaisons, can produce unity, even if neither has been particularly successful in the history of New Zealand film. Russell Campbell has argued that such "visions of harmony" are dashed when Kura is executed by Te Wheke.[130] However, this is to confine such

visions to the purely sexual, and to measure them against the kind
of nationalist model utilized by Rudall Hayward. In fact, *Utu*'s
resolution affords a more complex pattern than this. It dramatizes
a traumatic moment for all those involved, such that a blood bond
is sealed between the characters, not necessarily in terms of
national unity, but in terms of a Maori sense of utu which may be
interpreted as a ''higher'' ethical code, if one chooses to think of
it that way. Recent debates over the Treaty of Waitangi tend to
mirror this development, since the ''spirit'' of the Treaty (its
''utu'') is coming to mean much more than the literal meanings
provided by the written word.[131]

In Shakespeare's *Macbeth,* the narrative is resolved by the
death of the tragic protagonist and social order reestablished
around a dramatically uninteresting representative of the Law. In
the western genre, with which *Utu* has also been compared, the
narrative resolution tends to be reliant upon individual heroes to
solve social problems with some gun-play (*c.f. Shane* and *High
Noon*). *Utu,* however, is cross-hatched with competing and conflicting claims to the narrative resolution (''utu''), hence its claim
to the epic genre. In providing Wiremu with the final power of utu,
the film goes one better than either *Macbeth* (ironic resolution) or
most westerns (comedic resolution); it opts for an appropriately
tragic resolution. In keeping with *Macbeth,* Williamson would
have been the appropriate Macduff figure avenging his wife's
killing; in keeping with westerns, Lieutenant Scott would have
been the appropriate agency of rationality and justice (the cavalry?). But in *Utu* the resolution is constructed as a fratricide. This
provides an extraordinary metaphor for the allegorical level of the
film. If the execution of one's own brother is the price to be paid
for national reconciliation, what greater (self-) sacrifice can be
expected of another? This implies a fraternal relationship between
Maori and Pakeha which is sealed in blood, mana and utu, and it
must humble others present who have personal motives of
revenge. Wiremu's gesture is in effect a reduction to silence after
the last shot has been fired. Where *Pictures* ended with a tangle of
unresolved problems—Ngatai in jail and Alfred Burton reduced
to silence—*Utu* ends with the promise of unity, and there is
integrity in that stance.

CAME A HOT FRIDAY: CELEBRATING
BICULTURALISM

Came a Hot Friday (1985), directed by Ian Mune and produced by
Larry Parr (who is of Maori descent), takes the parodic dimension
of *Utu* and exploits it even further. The surface narrative describes
a New Zealand society which is clearly racially mixed, but the
racial problems are repressed to the sub-plot where a "deadly
serious" frontier war acts as a parody of *Utu*'s racial wars.
Allegorically, the film appears to promote biculturalism, but,
unlike *Utu*, this is mostly at an unconscious level and there is no
formal resolution by film's end.

Most of the action takes place in the sleepy little town of
Tainuia—in 1949 a comic historical anachronism which does not
have the feel and flavor of historical small-town New Zealand at
all. Instead it evokes nostalgia for the supposed simplicities of an
earlier time and place when incipient nationalism was the norm,
when a local dance or an ANZAC ceremony rallied the community together, and when New Zealanders were prosperous and
living in racial harmony (*c.f. Footrot Flats*). This is Tainuia's
utopian side and it is represented by two ideal couples: small-town
boy Don Jackson, of big heart and little brain, and Esmeralda, the
upwardly mobile "dusky maiden" who works at the tea rooms;
and Dick and Dinah, the local car salesman and his buxom wife.
Tainuia's fallen side appears later, with the sub-plot.

Into this small town utopia come two small-time con-men—
Wesley Pennington and sidekick Cyril Kidman—and while
Wesley is obviously Pakeha, Cyril could pass for half-caste
Maori. By means of a horse racing scam which recalls *The Sting*
(1974), plus a fancy way with the "ladies," they prey upon small
towns like Tainuia. They are the feckless agents of urban assurance and semi-sophistication, these things being relative. But if
they are in Tainuia to break the law, then the Law itself is barely
present in the film—just one mostly uninterested town policeman.
Consequently the narrative's moral center is displaced toward the
(relatively) criminal end of things where it is occupied by Wes and
Cyril. Clearly Tainuia is repressed; Wes and Cyril are there to

unleash its irrational dark side. This is mostly at the expense of notorious bookie Norm Cray, a Maori who has the town in his grip (legal betting was introduced in the mid-Fifties). For most of the first half of the film, the plot follows their skirmishing, with the comic value deriving from the heroes' big-hearted naiveté which is surpassed only by the locals'. Norm Cray is a fairly likable villain in that he feels genuine regret at having smashed a war veteran's artificial leg while in a rage, and seeing his car plummet into the river before shortly following it himself is more than sufficient punishment for being one of the film's villains.

This all goes to suggest that the central dichotomy of the film's main plot is based not around race, class, or gender, or even around legal/illegal, but around stranger/local. This dichotomy is a horizontal one: out-of-town con-men versus the local con-man. These extremes are then tugged vertically downward by what starts out initially in the sub-plot: the crazy frontier war between the Tainuia Kid (the forces of the irrational) and arch-villain Sel

Came a Hot Friday (1985) sets up a strange alliance between the local eccentric, the Tainuia Kid (played by comedian Billy T. James), and a small out-of-town con-man, Wesley Pennington.

Bishop (pure conniving super-rationality). By the end of the film, the sub-plot has virtually taken control. Where the main plot deals with the interruption of outsiders into the fabric of social life, this sub-plot is a repressed Maori/Pakeha culture conflict which erupts into the main plot. The Kid, of course, comes to side with the heroes, and Bishop sides with Norm Cray, cross-hatching the racial politics with the inevitable result that the forces of comic irrationality are more than a match for unbridled rational criminality.

Historical anachronism can also become the culturally schizophrenic, notably the prospect of Billy T. James as the Tainuia Kid, a Maori who thinks he is a Mexican cowboy. James was undoubtedly the main attraction of the film, which became the third highest grossing New Zealand film after *Footrot Flats* and *Goodbye Pork Pie*. His comic persona creates some memorable moments: a gloved hand reaching into frame to delicately pluck a still smoldering cigar from the ground, the cries of "Aribaaa!" and the hysterical child-like laughter, the toy guns and splendidly gaudy outfit with the Confederate flag on the sleeve, the manic look in the eye and the utter confusion he wreaks all around. "The Maori lunatic" becomes Sel Bishop's obsession and nemesis. Bishop, like many of the film's characters, is not a recognizable human being so much as a recognizable stereotype: a parody of the repressed control freak who runs amok with a gun in Roger Donaldson's films, *Sleeping Dogs* and *Smash Palace,* and also in *Bad Blood* and *Utu*. He would happily kill the other man for purely psychopathic reasons; thus pure rationality circles around and meets the irrational.

Allegorically, Bishop's angry cry of "You're not a Mexican, you're a Maori!" asserts the Pakeha essentialist extreme, which cannot tolerate breakdowns in the fixity of things and which must annihilate them instead. (This may be compared with his treatment of Don Jackson: "I can't stand idiots.") This is for me the most provocative aspect of the film: an entrenched Pakeha essentialism bent upon reducing the "fantastic, disruptive anarchic force" of the Tainuia Kid to logic and law and order, a not unfamiliar trait in stereotypical villains.[132] Bishop fails in his quest, in the film's most radical departure from Ronald Hugh Morrieson's 1964 novel: the Tainuia Kid is struck by momentary

Came a Hot Friday: the Tainuia Kid in full flight.

rationality and is able to turn the tables (quite literally) on Bishop and escape with the money.[133]

In this context, what overt ''Maori'' content there is in the film is associated with Billy T. James as the Tainuia Kid. However, as in much of his radio and television work, James's style is to ironize cultural stereotypes to the degree that it is barely possible to sustain a cultural difference between Maori and Pakeha. His is a skeptical centrifugal force, disintegrating all the constraints of the New Zealand double bind—a form of anti-matter, a postmodern schizophrenia which has much in common with an urban Maori street culture which has rejected the fixed identities of both marae and Pakeha prescription. The effect is a serious challenge to Wes and Cyril as the center of the main plot-line, let alone to Sel Bishop, but this is minimized by introducing the Kid into the film as slowly as possible, as an object of mystery.

The film does at times touch on sensitive areas, particularly with the Tainuia Kid. The Kid does after all let the air out of car tires, cannot count past ten, does not know he is supposed to be a Maori, and appears to be every inch a child, and this does allow the possibility of reading the film in racist terms. However, such a ''realist'' reading was heavily over-determined in the Eighties by audience awareness of the star persona of Billy T. James and the resurgence of Maori activism elsewhere in the Pakeha-controlled media. Consequently, naive "coon humor" or Hori/Maori jokes have all but disappeared in Pakeha discourses, and there are now few precedents available with which to read off the Tainuia Kid as racial buffoon. The "anarchist" reading predominates by default. However, I am unhappy with this term since it tends to connote a Pakeha nationalism-centered fear of what it takes to be irrational-ism. After all, the film can also encourage an ironic or parodic reading which does not subscribe in any way whatsoever to a realist aesthetic.

The stranger/local dichotomy of the main plot-line is returned to at film's end. The dangerous eruption of the Maori/Pakeha culture conflict in the sub-plot has been resolved, so the town can return to some semblance of normality. However, the final shots give the lie to this. They show Wes and Cyril pulling their car to a stop at the local cemetery to observe an ANZAC memorial service at which most of the town is present. In keeping with the fact that none of the comic characters in the film can be relied upon as a stable identity, not much sense of social integration is achieved. The film may have pulled the town together somewhat, but its heroes are leaving it again in search of other small towns to gull, and the Kid has dropped from sight once again. *Came a Hot Friday* is the comic antithesis to *Utu*'s tragedy. Both films are unself-consciously revisionist and parodic, however the differ-ence is that at the end of *Utu,* a bicultural identity is affirmed with the extinction of essentialist extremes. In *Came a Hot Friday,* a New Zealand identity remains fractured between the locals and the strangers, and the normal and the marginalized, even though the racial sub-plot has been healed.

As such, *Came a Hot Friday* presents an unstable nationalism which is insecure in the threat from an international world outside. Nicholas Reid correctly characterizes the film as being "about second-hand culture"—American "cultural colonialism" wherein the "indigenous" is barely able to drive out the "ex-otic."[134] Analogically, the town is as unable to cope with Wes and Cyril as it is with the frontier war from the sub-plot. Both the exotic outsiders and the eruption of the irrational undercut the uneasy identity or center represented by Tainuia and its people. However, Reid's reservations about cultural colonialism identify him with the responses of the townspeople at film's end. Essentialist nationalism always equates the exotic with domination and contamination, whereas it is equally possible, after all, to discuss *Came a Hot Friday* in terms of irreverent piracy, pastiche and parody. Parody cannibalizes meaning, not least of all the notion of an authentic self which constitutes an imaginary "first-hand culture." Is it even possible to maintain a cultural difference between Maori and Pakeha after watching the Tainuia Kid? Taking essentialist identities seriously becomes somewhat pretentious.

The same applies to Maori nationalism: when the river taniwha actually materializes (in a clever piece of set design) before the astonished eyes of the Tainuia Kid, the Kid promptly throws all the money into the river. This scene could be interpreted as a mockery of Maori spiritual values, yet one could just as easily argue that the material and spiritual worlds can be woven together without destroying each other, with the scene being read as a reminder of the constant presence of taniwha and the futility of seeking after material riches. Although it is strongly iconoclastic, *Came a Hot Friday* begins to resemble *Utu* in that it too promotes a Pakeha-centered thesis of biculturalism. At a personal level, the friendship between Wes and Cyril and between Don and Esmerelda are signs that it can succeed.

KINGPIN: WHO NEEDS AN IDENTITY ANYWAY?

Kingpin (1985) was written by Mike Walker and Mitchell Manuel and directed by Walker. It is set in a Social Welfare Boys' Training Center which is part of the frontline in the confrontation between a Pakeha system of power (symbolized by computer print-outs and a compassionate staff armed with humanist theories) and the young Maori who give the system its raison d'être by refusing to own up to a fixed identity as anything in particular. The film's basic dichotomy is not strictly Maori versus Pakeha—there are also Pakeha boys in custody and some Maori on the staff. However, most of the boys are Maori, and the question of who will be "kingpin"—the toughest kid on the block—is strictly a Maori/Maori conflict, played out against a social background in which Pakeha have the power and Maori fight it out for second-class citizenship inside a penal institution. The kingpin is only a king of the dispossessed and identity is only established through opposition.

Kingpin makes it abundantly clear that the social divide or "barrier" is racial rather than cultural, and that it is crossed with a class inflection. In practice, institutional racism is based on physical appearance (race) rather than on language and beliefs (culture).[135] These teenage boys do not speak Maori and in all likelihood their parents do not either, despite one boy's father being given some Maori to say which comes out only when he is drunk. They are from working class backgrounds and the likelihood is that they lack an identifiably "Maori" cultural background. So, instead, they use a street culture language which is Pakeha colloquial if it is anything—"wanker," "bunny," "flunky," "walking like a hard jube," and they identify with the pastiche of American popular culture—breakdancing, jeans, and so on. This pastiche identifies the film's young characters as the romantic heroes, though the film does not make the system monolithically oppressive.

Kingpin (1985): Riki (back to camera) takes on Karl, the resident kingpin, in an unspoken quest for a stable Maori identity.

"Race" is important here because these boys are visibly Maori, and their appearance and movements are both very physical and sexually coded. Walker has remarked on this "extraordinary poetic quality. It's got to do with a sort of grace in their body movement and it also springs from their oral tradition and their marae ceremonies which are full of drama."[136] In other words, race is still a useful critical term so long as difference is defined and understood physically and biologically. It cannot be banished by fiat. Nevertheless, these boys are fiercely resistant to attempts to prescribe them with a fixed identity as Maori or anything else. Only in the hierarchical stability of kingpin and flunkies is there any stability of identity. Their battles with the system and with each other are a bitter parody of Pakeha aspirations toward being upwardly mobile.

But *Kingpin* is not a social problem film. It utilizes the classic western scenario in the manner of *Shane,* where young Joey Starrett worships the wandering gunfighter who rides into his life and makes the valley safe for the ranchers. The narrative trajectory is two-fold, split around its two heroes, Riki Nathan and Willie Hota. The first concerns Riki's refusal and then final acceptance of the burden of power and the role of kingpin which he wins from Karl Stevens. The second concerns Willie's desire for a stable identity defined against a paternal or fatherly figure of strength, which cannot be his absent father, nor Karl (who bullies him), but Riki.[137] These two trajectories are neatly interwoven, with Riki as the stable "masculine" center of the film, and Willie assuming the oscillating "feminine" figure. The homo-erotic qualities inherent in this narrative construction are not exploited the way they are in *Mark II;* nevertheless they are maintained at a repressed level and appear to be proportional to the degree that Riki's arrival has created a hierarchical imbalance within the institution. The repressed surfaces only once, when Willie finds Riki exercising in the gym and confesses to him that girls do not seem to like him. He finishes by giving Riki a hug, and though it does not go any further, Riki is obviously aware of the sexual implications, even if Willie is not.[138]

For most of the film, Riki refuses to assume the role of kingpin, and this could be either because he does not feel ready to do so or because intellectually he rejects the authority and power it represents. Whatever his reasons, it triggers a schizophrenic crisis: Karl is unable to resolve his own conflicts while there is a challenge to his power as kingpin; and Willie is frantic for some consummation in the manner of the romantic lover, with much of his sexual energy being displaced onto a young woman staff member, Alison Eastwood. Psychologically, the weaker characters desire a fixed stable identity defined in opposition to and subservient to a leader, which is not to say that their desired identity is either an individual one or a collective modern tribal one. Quite the reverse: what they desire is a unifying of these two polarities, a sense of balance and belonging, where the necessity for an identity is no longer an issue. *Kingpin* seems to understand the paradox here, that one must gain an identity in order to lose it. Certainly, Walker has remarked: ''I think our society and our culture bring all sorts of pressure to bear on each of us about how we should be behaving—finally a lot of us live lies for the sake of living a life that we think our families approve of.''[139]

The first half of the film is given over to sketching in scenes

Kingpin: Willie Hota takes on the staff, expressing his frustration with father figures in general.

during which the quest for an identity is pursued: Willie pretend-
ing to have a girlfriend, Willie trying to ingratiate himself with
Riki, Karl picking on Willie and trying to force a confrontation
with Riki, Willie trying to regain contact with his father. These
scenes also sketch in the physical background to life in the
Training Center—shoveling coal for the boilers, working on the
farm or in the kitchens. In a sense, *Kingpin* resembles the quest for
identity in *Utu,* except that here it occurs at the level of Maori
versus Maori, and resolution can only occur when one defeats the
other. When Riki accepts the role of kingpin by fighting and
defeating Karl, this consummation arises only because it appears
that Willie has died in a car smash indirectly triggered by Karl's
bullying. Willie later turns out to be alive, so although the
consummation was achieved via a deceit, it returns social order to
the Training Center, and provides all the characters with a
relatively unconflicted sense of self-identity.

What then does *Kingpin* say about the institutions of the Pakeha
state and the creation, or discovery, of a Maori identity within it?
Allegorically, the film celebrates a new unified self-identity but it
belongs with the other films in this chapter in being dubious about
its being "Maori." *Kingpin*'s Training Center offers a social
system of measurable limit, and power is invested in individuals
with names and faces. The battle for power mirrors the battle for
identity, and a new hierarchy at film's end means a new kinship
system, a new social bond. But the film reminds us that "identity"—a consistently ambiguous term in itself—almost certainly
becomes a "problem" when a social system deprives individuals
of the economic, cultural, and political means to define themselves in relation to that social system, and deprives them of the
power to refuse the definitions that it prescribes.

Changing social patterns in New Zealand suggest that it is
becoming multicultural and post-modern in the sense described
by Fredric Jameson and Jean-François Lyotard whereby identities
are constantly being contested and atomized. On the one hand
there are constant incitements to assert one's identity (Maori,
Pakeha, feminist, individualist); on the other, it is constantly
being neutralized by daily experience of life in an enormous and
diffuse social system. For many smaller societies and communities which are outside the capitalist mainstream (including a few
Maori ones) there may be less of a felt need to assert that

individual identity when the social system is small enough to provide each member with a sense of the social whole. After all, it is not as if "identity" is somehow unnecessary in a post-modern world. Race and class, for example, are just as important in defining identities as they ever were. They remain inextricably interwoven in the sense that being Maori is still used as a basis for oppression by the Pakeha, and no amount of post-modern atomization of identities has managed to change that as the 150th anniversary of the Treaty of Waitangi came and went.

Maori identity will continue to be asserted in the attempt to redefine the social whole to suit Maori aspirations. As New Zealand becomes increasingly internationalized, the boundaries of the national self expand to embrace the rest of the world—in a reversal of the imperial era (explosion)—and smaller constituencies redefine it to suit their own agendas (implosion). Consequently, the task for Maori intellectuals who wish to redefine the social whole and the Maori place within it remains just as difficult as it has ever been.

CHAPTER 12: MAORI FILMMAKING IN THE EIGHTIES

It is fitting to conclude a study of Pakeha images of the Maori with a brief discussion of the first films by self-consciously Maori filmmakers. Maori images have always been around, of course, if not exactly in film and television, and I would not wish to imply that the images discussed so far have always been Pakeha since all along they have been shared by the Maori. One way or another, the discussion always ends up caught in the double bind. The arguments in this book are designed to work best at the macro level of "New Zealand," where "Maori" and "Pakeha" are meaningful only as relational terms. Consequently, it assumes that there are now Maori and Pakeha films as there were (and still are) New Zealand films. This is basically just a question of naming, of contested rhetorical positions, and no final authority on the matter.

A NEW MAORI CINEMA?

A number of propositions made earlier in this book may be restated now as the basis for certain conclusions about what Maori filmmaking might be. (1) Maori have always made crucial contributions to New Zealand filmmaking—from scenarios and locales, to costumes and extras, to the "raw material" for fantasies of the erotic/exotic. (2) From the Forties onwards, Maori speakers began to appear in films as hosts and authority figures, a trend which accelerated in the Seventies. (3) As the national (New Zealand) master narrative lost its persuasiveness in the Seventies—i.e. became a reality to be taken for granted—

the mood among Maori intellectuals turned more separatist. Many are now committed to ironic attacks upon Pakeha hegemony and to building a self-consciously Maori cultural production. (4) Initially, most Maori film and television production has been imitative of Pakeha models. Television New Zealand's *Te Karere* was simply the news; *Koha* followed a traditional current affairs format; *Nga Take Maori* and *Te Kupenga* belonged to the social problem genre; *The Natural World of the Maori* recycled the conventions of nineteenth- and twentieth-century Pakeha ethnography. (5) A major consequence of this has been that the historical narrative of cultural decay and revival has in recent years undergone a spiritual transformation such that Maori culture is once more identified with the timeless eternal.

All this raises what seems to be becoming the core problem: how to define a Maori aesthetic or cultural practice—taha or tikanga Maori—as different from the hegemonic Pakeha internationalist style. Whether or not this is necessary is quite another matter, but the arguments in its favor tend to fall into three categories: (a) textual; (b) cultural; (c) consensual. The textual and cultural arguments propose some sort of Maori essence which generates the meanings in the films, meanings which—by inversion—can be interpreted in order to uncover that Maori essence. For example, it might be argued that a film like Barry Barclay's and Tama Poata's *Ngati* (1987) constitutes a Maori film because it is shot partly in the Maori language and with Maori themes; or a film like Merata Mita's *Bastion Point—Day 507* (1980) can be a Maori film because it is shot in a Maori context with a certain spiritual ahi (fire) generated. The third argument—consensus—follows on from the first two but in its simplest sense it means that the people who made the film call themselves Maori, and it is loosely based on racial biological grounds.[140] For example, *Patu* (1983) was directed by Merata Mita. These are, of course, only analytic distinctions so all three arguments can be used to name all three films as "Maori," if one so desires. What then of derivative Maori television or cultural hybrids like *The Makutu on Mrs. Jones* (1983), directed by "part-Maori" Larry Parr, or Keri Hulme's novel *The Bone People*?

THE FILMS OF MERATA MITA

Merata Mita's films, particularly *Bastion Point—Day 507* and *Patu,* have confronted the double bind in challenging ways.[141] Her work displays a sharply polemical documentary style which maintains New Zealand's historical materialist and Marxist tradition but with a distinctively Maori orientation. These, her two best-known documentaries, have already been written about extensively, mostly in terms of their ideological correctness, and coverage of *Patu* has also focused on the police harassment, smuggling the negatives out to safekeeping in Australia, the complicity of the media in allowing images to be used as evidence in the prosecution of demonstrators, and Mita's difficulties in finding completion finance and receptive exhibitors.

Mita's films are interesting above all for their gently mocking irony. In interviews, Mita has stated that she sees herself in the tradition of the oral storyteller who works with whakapapa (genealogy), deliberately refraining from authoritarian commentary. The political analysis is there, of course, reflecting Mita's

Bastion Point: Day 507 (1980): Maori protestors at Bastion Point in Auckland before the eviction.

Bastion Point: Day 507: the police close in for the eviction, in an excessive show of force that is a prelude for the Springbok rugby tour of 1981.

influence by Marxism and critique, but there is also a particular filmic style she has developed which throws cultural differences into sharp relief. This has to do with two things: (1) the relativizing of Pakeha values—subjecting them to an alternative cultural viewpoint such that Pakeha values leach out of every image; and (2) an immediacy and impact which derive from the insights of the insider to Maori culture. By comparison, Geoff Steven's *Te Matakite O Aotearoa* has the distance of an outsider; it lacks humor and a sense of mischief. It is "on" the Land March, whereas Mita's films are "on" Maori/Pakeha collisions.

Bastion Point—Day 507 was directed by Mita, Leon Narbey, and Gerd Pohlmann and, as such, resists claims to being a Maori film, yet in terms of cultural perspective it might as well be. Shot as a news-style documentary of the eviction from Bastion Point of its Ngati Whatua occupants after 507 days, it also contains additional footage and photographs from South Pacific Television, Television One, Radio Hauraki, and *The Auckland Star* (*Patu* was shot without help from the official media). The film's structure is very simple: there is an initial challenge from the State, followed by titles, then the police moving in at dawn and the

Bastion Point: Day 507: the arrests begin, with the media in hot pursuit.

protestors waiting for them, and finally the subsequent evictions. This structure is not unlike a bitter travesty or parody of marae kawa (protocol)—from the opening wero, through the arrival of uninvited guests, the destruction of the marae itself, and the eviction of the tangata whenua. There is no karanga, and for the powhiri there is only sad waiata and an angry display of passive resistance.

In retrospect, the confrontation between the ponderous machinery of the Pakeha State and the irritated Maori protestors has an awful inevitability about it, more so than the confrontation in *Patu*. In *Patu* there is always a greater sense of flux and fluidity, of possibilities opening out in all directions, but at Bastion Point the narrative unfolds naturally toward the eviction. There is clearly an enormous difference in consciousness here between the polarized sides. The State speaks of the law and Crown Land, and uses written signposts and writs; the protestors talk of Maori land and perform hakas. In essence, it is the precise letter of the law versus improvisation and spontaneity, a classic example of the double bind in action, whereby the protestors are ruled out of court (literally) because their ethical/moral argument is not translatable into Pakeha law (this has begun changing with the Waitangi legal judgments of the Eighties). It is a symptom of the same cultural collision diagnosed by *The Governor* and it is implicit in most of Rowley Habib's angry works—*The Protestors* (1982), which is a fictional film based on the Bastion Point evictions, and *The Gathering* (1979). It is also the subject of the last episodes in 1987 of the television series, *Open House*.

The film certainly demonstrates the sheer bathos of excessive police enforcement. The total lack of a sense of humor among the policemen and officials, and the archaic literalness of their interpretations of what they are empowered to do are stiff to the point of being humorous. There is a sense that the "rules" have never been challenged like this before, at least not in this generation, and no one knows quite how to behave. The only cracks in the facade appear on the faces of Maori policemen, for whom the whole exercise appears to be a painful ordeal. White men in orange helmets with large yellow bulldozers flatten the marae, and the parallels with South Africa are obvious (characters remark on this in the dialogue). Emotionally the occasion is enhanced throughout by persistent electronic rumbles on the soundtrack, crash-cuts, and frequent cutaways to an elderly kuia who (along with the Hawke family) serves as the primary focus of identification with the marae. When the film finally subsides into stillness with a shot of young policemen standing, arms folded and with boyish smiles, behind a gate, on it can be read the (by now) ironic inscription, "Bastion Point—Maori land."

The Bastion Point eviction was also one of the first occasions when the police forcefully evicted the media along with the protestors. By the time of *Patu,* although physical violence is threatened toward its camera operators, the ebb and flow of the demonstrations had become such that the cameras were a lower priority for police attention, since there no longer seemed to be a "center" or "sides" for police and demonstrators to align themselves on as each sought to protect the illusion of order.

Patu is New Zealand's most powerful documentary in recent decades. Superficially, it is a film "about" the tour of New Zealand by the Springboks, South Africa's national rugby team, and the psychological civil war that erupted as a result. However, it would be more accurate to describe it as the tale of the anti-Tour movement's confrontation with the police, the government, and the pro-Tour movement. In the first half, the anti-Tour movement prepares itself for a Tour which somehow never got cancelled; in

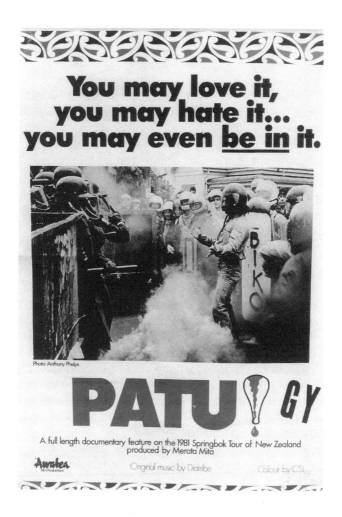

The poster for *Patu* (1983) says it all: the confrontation between police and anti-Springbok Tour demonstrators; a provocative caption; the South African connection (Biko); and the Maori patterns at top and bottom.

the second half the Tour itself unfolds. This emphasis on the broader time frame and the fact that Mita keeps events in chronological order suggest a directorial preference for reading the film historically—as a narrative of how the anti-Tour movement responded to this ideological challenge and progressed from naiveté to something like maturity. *Patu* is not, strictly speaking, a film "about" the Tour, nor need it be. For reasons that were both tactical and inevitable, rugby itself and the pro-Tour arguments are repressed in favor of a portrayal of the various alliances which constituted the anti-Tour movement.

But if the film is the story of the anti-Tour movement's apotheosis, it is equally the story of liberalism's collapse and realism's failure. Unintentionally or not, it is a film which casts an implacable gaze on Pakeha liberals, male and female, and reveals them to be peculiarly culture-bound. Watching the veritable obsession with "organization" (meetings, committees, flyers, speeches), the distinctive cadence and assertiveness of the middle-class Pakeha accent, the taste for slogans and street theater (building a "Bantu shack"!), the demonstrations, and the utter self-absorption of the whole enterprise is to understand something of Pakeha culture and its way of doing things. The sincerity and self-effacement of the pre-Tour phase suggests that liberalism had already reached a stage of paternalistic complacency, and the anger and violence of the actual Tour mark liberalism's rite of passage into the vicarious experience of oppression familiar to black South Africans and many Maori.

In the light of all this, I think it is possible to say that the film ambiguously allows the conclusion that the Pakeha sector of the anti-Tour movement closely resembled its antagonists—the police and the pro-Tour factions—in ways which were not so apparent at the time. What, after all, are the differences between a rugby game and a demonstration when both pit two sides against each other in a gladiatorial context with the national honor at stake? This is not to deny the moral efficacy of the anti-Tour movement but to suggest that the capacity to become morally outraged at a particular political anathema (Apartheid in South Africa) has a peculiarly personal and subjective aspect to it. Did the anti-Tour demonstrators not express their violent fantasy that their hopes and dreams had been repressed for too long by the New Zealand of Prime Minister Muldoon? At what point did their

Filmmaker Merata Mita, seen here acting the part of Matu in *Utu* (1983).

altruism cease and annexation of the black South African cause
into the Pakeha liberal self begin? It is one of the great ironies of
Patu that many liberals criticized Mita for over-emphasizing the
Maori contribution to the anti-Tour movement when the Tour was
supposed to be about racism in the first place.

There is a moment in *Patu* when a young woman protestor
looks up from an injured friend who is lying on the ground and
sees the camera. Her lips mouth the words, ''Why don't you get
involved?'' to the cameraman (who was not recording sync
sound). In that silent enunciation can be read the total absorption
of the anti-Tour movement in the affairs of the moment, and its
loss of an external self-critical perspective. When this happens,
it is reflected in an irritation at the media for what seems like
the luxury of objectivity. It was a similar image which captivated
Pakeha reviewers upon the film's release: it showed an elderly
Maori or Polynesian woman looking out her window at a riot
unfolding in the street below. Her face caught their attention
because it was the face of the objectivity which the anti-Tour
movement had relinquished in its hysterical fixation upon spectacle itself. A more interesting image, in my view, shows another
elderly Maori woman who remarks confidently that Maori people
are not afraid of anything—of the police or of dying—and

this goes a long way toward anchoring the film in a Maori perspective.

Could it be said then that *Bastion Point—Day 507* and *Patu* have a Maori perspective? I think so, on the grounds that they subject Pakeha culture to critique, that many of their authority figures are Maori, and that they emphatically make the connections between racism in South Africa and racism in New Zealand (this of course by no means exhausts what would qualify as Maori filmmaking). However, the films also have a deconstructive perspective which undercuts the security with which bicultural terms like Maori and Pakeha can be made to replace New Zealand as an organizing narrative. On my early viewings of *Patu*—back in 1983—a pervasive undercurrent of menace emerged out of the film and was absorbed by the cinema audience (most of whom were anti-Tour). Mita's striking choice of title (it means ''to strike''), the use of crash-cutting to create an edgy narrative, and the persistent rumble of helicopter rotors off screen made it all but impossible to find a stable point of identification in the events unfolding on screen.

Throughout the film, Mita's use of irony is rather dark, particularly the electronic distortion of the national anthem, ''God Defend New Zealand.'' Curiously, appropriately, there is a noticeable slide into burlesque by the end. Wagner's ''Ride of the Valkyries'' over the final rugby match felt—and still feels—appropriate, because at this point the parallel narratives of the national sport, the Tour itself, and New Zealand national unity have all disintegrated into some sort of crazy chaos. When, earlier, demonstrators at Hamilton chant ''The whole world's watching,'' their skepticism about the national myth is also nearing a crisis of identity. By the time the flour bombs (tossed from a small plane) land on the heads of rugby players during the Auckland game, the spectacle of organized sport, with its rigid distinction between the players and the spectators, has turned into burlesque. It has become the spectacle of the audience watching itself watching.

Mita must also have been tempted to include more images of the national apocalypse: full-blooded riots on the streets of Auckland (*c.f.* the symbolic lines in *Utu*), the armored demonstrators, the paramilitary police force. In much of her writing, Mita refers to the national schizophrenia which developed as New Zealand nationalism unraveled. Yet it is also a measure of Mita's commitment to a constructive politics of reconciliation that the bitterness in *Patu* takes second place to the sense of something new and strange making its appearance on the national scene. In retrospect, this new phenomenon was partly the anxieties and paranoia of liberal guilt (see chapters 9 and 10), but history has also confirmed that it was the first signs of a potentially rich and creative Maori film and television culture. After all, there is more life, exotica, energy, movement, color, and incidental humor in *Patu* than in almost every other New Zealand film before it, and there are signs that it may have inaugurated a new indigenous film style.

Patu was first screened on New Zealand television in 1991, ten years after the fact! The fact that it could have more of an effect when it was not seen—what it represented rather than what it said or did—is also surely significant. This suggests that cultural production is essentially a symbolic activity where what is said may actually matter less than who says it and for whom. If it is true that one can only reveal a phenomenon when it is disappearing, then this may account for the contemporary difficulties in defining a new Maori aesthetic and cultural style. This is as it should be. When this aesthetic resists such easy definition, then it may be said to be still in the process of being developed, its apotheosis not yet achieved, with exciting things yet to come. This is occurring for Maori filmmakers at the same time that options for Pakeha filmmakers are steadily closing down. The latter are faced with either a cannibalistic recycling of exhausted narratives and genres, or a flight into abstraction, or into embracing a post-modern internationalism.

LARRY PARR AND THE MAKUTU ON MRS. JONES

Not all films have been obsessed with their identity as Maori (or Pakeha), or with what others think they are. For example, Larry Parr's *The Makutu on Mrs. Jones,* an adaptation of Witi Ihimaera's short story, demonstrates the truth that being Maori is not necessarily a matter of being defined by others or by oneself. It may be something that one simply accepts as a fact of life in New Zealand that allows one to go on doing exactly what one wants without having to defend it against others.

The story is engagingly simple. Young Tawhai Bennett (through whose point of view events unfold) is employed by Mrs. Jones, a Pakeha widow with a sharp tongue, to help her deliver the groceries by car to their rural neighborhood. Only Mr. Hohepa, a tohunga, proves to be a problem: he insists that she open three gates to make the deliveries when she wants only to leave them at the first one. She resents his patriarchal manner and open war results, with all the bureaucratic machinery and feminist fast talk they can each muster. As she gets "skinnier and skinnier" and people shake their heads knowingly, it appears to Tawhai that Mr. Hohepa has placed a makutu (spell) on Mrs. Jones. One day young Tawhai steals into Mr. Hohepa's house while Mrs. Jones is there and finds his worst suspicions confirmed. When it turns out that Mr. Hohepa and Mrs. Jones are about to get married, Tawhai is mortified: "I suppose it was because I loved her that I was the last to guess." The film closes on a freeze frame of an older and wiser Tawhai.

This scenario suggests a whole range of things: the stubbornness and wiliness of Maori and Pakeha who have lived together

The Makutu on Mrs. Jones (1984): Mr. Hohepa on the verandah of his house, waiting for Mrs. Jones to fall into his clutches.

for generations and who know how to use the system against each other; the provocative liaison between a much older Maori man and a Pakeha woman—a new wrinkle in the national oedipal romance; and the wry sexual banter and verbal abuse. The film (and the short story) also pose the question whether love does in fact involve a form of makutu anyway, since Mrs. Jones definitely does come under Mr. Hohepa's spell (it is just that we do not see him come under her spell). The appeal of this arrangement derives from the strength in playing off Pakeha feminism against Maori patriarchy, two contemporary worlds on a collision course which in this case become the stronger for their having discovered a love for one another.

Perhaps the best thing about *The Makutu on Mrs. Jones* is that it is a witty cautionary tale about the dangers of jumping to conclusions about other people. Because it is told through Tawhai's point of view, it has to end in humility, with his realization that he has totally misunderstood a situation by attempting to read it exclusively in racial and cultural terms. Like *Broken Barrier,* the film reminds us that there are times and places when the personal, the timeless, and the universal provide identities which may be more important in the long run than the divisions and differences. If *The Makutu on Mrs. Jones* is finally a nostalgia piece, a tale of love and temporary misunderstanding, then these may well turn out to be two national ideals definitely worth keeping.

BARRY BARCLAY'S NGATI: THE FIRST MAORI FEATURE FILM

It is with films like Pacific Films' *Ngati,* however—widely regarded as the first Maori film—that the future for a Maori cinema aesthetics probably lies, and as with *The Governor* and *Utu,* there has been a lot riding on its success. This has depended as much on what it has symbolized as on its actual content. *Ngati* is more than simply a story of a community; it is also a symbol of cultural self-determination.

Ngati is set in 1948 in the small town of Kapua (actually Waipiro Bay) on the East Coast, and it seems to have the same

Ngati (1987): Greg Shaw (center) is a racist young Australian who is shocked to discover he is partially of Maori descent. Jenny Bennett (right) is the film's super-liberal character. Both demonstrate the thesis that identity is not a question of skin color.

ambition as the films of the Forties (*East Coast—District Nurse, TB and the Maori People of the Wairoa District, People of the Waikato*) which were located in specific tribal areas but packaged with an appeal to all Maori. Though *Ngati* is a Ngati Porou story, using this title invokes the generic sense of "tribe," and though writer Tama Poata and most of the cast are of Ngati Porou descent (director Barclay is of Ngati Apa), the film's success, both critically and commercially, occurred right across the country. Kapua, which means cloud or a bank of clouds, even evokes Aotearoa (Land of the Long White Cloud).

Ngati's narrative structure explores several interlocking stories: (1) the arrival in town of a somewhat racist young Australian, Greg Shaw, who comes to discover he is actually of Maori descent; (2) the town's struggle—led by Iwi and his daughter, Sally—to save the local freezing works and their communal livelihood; and (3) young Tione coming to terms with the death of his friend Ropata from TB. Allegorically, the first two stories sustain the same dualism as the *Tangata Whenua* series: culture and history respectively. Culture in *Ngati* is identified with personal matters—discovery of one's identity, the ties that bind the community together, romantic entanglements, raising children, attitudes to disease and death, and so on. History in *Ngati* operates at a more macro political-economic level whereby the town symbolizes the resistance of all rural Maori communities to the ruthless instrumentalism of Pakeha industrial and corporate power (*c.f.* Patricia Grace's novel *Potiki*). The third story weaves between the two: the threat to the Maori historically from diseases like TB, leukemia, and poliomyelitis, that is framed not through the usual social problem discourse but through the personalized viewpoint of young Tione. The mysteries of life and death transcend the simple either/or of Pakeha medicine versus Maori tohunga (as in *Aroha*); the solutions remain an open question.

Overall, the first half of the film is concerned with resolving the cultural problem of personal and social identity, and the second half with resolving the historical problem of economic survival. The effect is almost as if the narrative were integrating into itself a sense of community and cultural cohesion in its first half, the better to resist the forces of Pakeha-imposed historical determinism in the second half. Maori communal values and myths (good) come to triumph over their Pakeha antithesis (bad), and superliberal Pakeha characters like Jenny Bennett and her family, whose commitment is to the community, are in effect claimed as Maori. Those Maori who have lived too long in the Pakeha cities (including Sally and an unwitting Greg Shaw) are reintegrated before they lose their Maori ways. On the other (out-) side are the Pakeha businessmen who wish to close the freezing works, and while they are not archetypically evil, they are sufficiently stereotyped to contrast with the quiet dignity and nobility of the people of Kapua. In *Ngati,* being Maori is to understand and accept community, home, whanau . . . ngati. The title is aptly chosen, whatever one may think of it as a political agenda.

Since *Ngati* dissolves Pakeha history into Maori culture, in this sense it is a completely revisionist film. It does not have the tone of a New Zealand film of the Forties and Fifties, like *Aroha, TB and the Maori People* or *Letter from the Teacher,* let alone the darker *Backblock Medical Service,* and Barclay has rightly cautioned against privileging a historical reading. Mostly the revisionism derives from the greater range and richness of tones available in color photography, the excellent theme song, and the

Ngati demonstrates parallel quests. In the top photo, Iwi (right) leads the elders of Kapua in a fight to save the local freezing works from closing. In the bottom photo, Sally (center) is able to retrieve her Maori identity in Kapua after being too long away in the Pakeha cities.

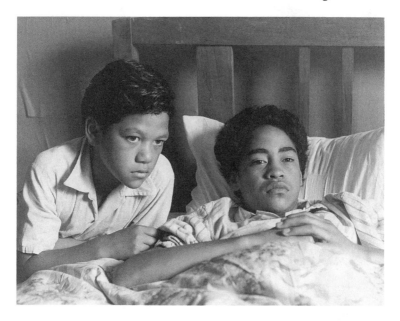

Ngati: Tione (left) and his doomed friend, Ropata, who has TB.

multiple points of view which are a characteristic of fiction story-telling.

Nevertheless, *Ngati* is still a ''historical'' film; it evokes a very contemporary nostalgia for that earlier period of transition between the return of the Maori Battalion from World War II and the onset of urban drift, industrialization, and the erosion of territorial associations with the whenua. It examines the utopian myth that once sustained the Maori New Zealand nation, and, without rejecting it out of hand, adopts Pakeha capitalism and shapes it to its own ends. The town saves its freezing works from closure and binds the community together again. It is this emphasis on community that has most appealed to reviewers, yet this raises the question whether the film can ever transcend a nostalgic reading. Affirmative and dignified though it is, the film refers to a historical period which is now past, and although the problems it portrays persist today, they also need to be addressed in an urban setting where most Maori now live, where identities are spread across multiple points of reference, and where the media institutions are located. *Ngati* does not generate enough momentum to expand all over the new land of Aotearoa, but it does represent a kind of holding pattern, a consolidation of forces, before making the next drive into the future.

In recent years a consistent Maori position has begun to emerge on matters of the media and the right to self-expression. Manifestos from lobby groups such as Te Manu Aute have argued that Maori culture has a right to create images of, for, and by Maori people, and if there is a necessity to represent Maori culture, then it ought to be left to the Maori to do it, not the Pakeha. Such arguments immediately enter the double bind. They may imply that to date Maori culture has not been able to express itself to its own people, which would be true only to the degree that Maori culture has become colonized by the Pakeha media. Such statements may also assume that film and television production is a "good" worth having. Historically, Maori resistance to Pakeha media systems has been based on a perfectly understandable reluctance to embrace the inevitable objectification and commercial imperative with which the media threatens Maori cultural forms like whaikorero and tapu.

What then is this right, this necessity, this compulsion to self-expression and self-determination which now seems to be the brief of Maori filmmakers? It hardly matters if such self-expression is "authentic" if the first problem must be to have it expressed in the first place. Maori self-expression does appear to be a necessity for survival in a historical context when, on the one hand, self-expression is valorized above most other things on the international commodity market—Thou shalt express thyself—and on the other, the power to do so is skilfully restricted. Prescriptions/proscriptions. Double bind.

That Maori film and television production will continue to flourish is now apparent. At time of writing (1988), another Maori feature film, Merata Mita's *Mauri,* has been completed to mixed reviews; more and more Maori programming is appearing on New Zealand radio and television; there has been a gradual increase in the number of Maori willing and able to work on Maori film and television so as to gain production experience; there are sporadic initiatives to launch a Maori television channel and Maori radio stations; hui are convened regularly to discuss media issues and plan future initiatives; and Maori media groups are lobbying

Pakeha-dominated media institutions for an equipment base, for control over Maori archival footage, and for a say in how they are managed. Overall, the future looks most exciting for Maori film and television production, but whether it will render the double bind an irrelevance remains to be seen.

CONCLUSION: NAMING THE OTHER

One of the basic functions of twentieth-century nation-states is to regulate traffic in exiles, refugees, emigrés, and expatriates setting out for home, any home. Consequently, there have been many strange experiments in welding nations together and dragging them apart again like Humpty Dumpty. Each seems to give rise to a compelling mythology of the Other, of how this or that frontier is the symbol for our time: Germany and its Berlin Wall, Vietnam and Korea and their DMZs between North and South. For every Nigeria a Biafra, for every Yankee a Confederate, for every Pakistan a Bangladesh, and, conversely, for every Tibet there is a China. For New Zealand there has also been a Maoriland and an Aotearoa. Binarisms and doubling seem to be endemic, but beyond this it is very difficult to draw any hard and fast conclusions about nationalism, other than that it is a system which works half well and that it is constantly liable to disintegrate into schizophrenia.

Once it could be said that the Maori were divided (among themselves) and conquered (by the British). But the Pakeha now find that the Maori are looking to return the favor and to find their own place in the sun. Utu. This experience differs markedly from other settler cultures—the United States, Canada, Australia, the Latin American nations, where indigenous minorities have stood less chance of placing their political sovereignty on the national agenda, though there have been some encouraging signs in recent years. In New Zealand, the national mythology has always been inherently dualistic, whether it was located on the fracture line between the British Empire and Maoriland or whether it repressed the Maori Other within itself.

In my later chapters I drew attention to the decline of New Zealand's Literary Historical Myth throughout the Sixties and Seventies, and I argued that 1960 may signify a convenient date at which it could be said that the national identity—as a concept—

279

achieved its apotheosis and began its decline. It was in that year that the Hunn Report on the Department of Maori Affairs provided the fullest expression of the Integration Myth, and it was in that year that television came to New Zealand. It was the year that Maoriland returned in popular music and school texts as the ghost of what it once was, and Aotearoa also began to make its appearance as a subterranean eruption.

No sooner does one claim that a national identity is a reality than it is vulnerable to both internal dissolution and external invasion; in short, to a failure of realism. By 1981, the national myth was under attack from all sorts of emergent constituencies, from revisionist historians to feminists to Maori activists, who mostly resented the (self-) construction of the Kiwi New Zealander in the image of the Pakeha middle-class male. Historians loyal to the older model sought to avert this by recourse to more overtly scientific methods and the effect was obvious in *The Oxford History of New Zealand* of 1981.[142] It advertised in most solidly academic fashion that New Zealand had now achieved its own precarious maturity as a nation-state, with its own authentic identity. This maturity can be observed in both the formal organization of the book—its "weight" of detailed scholarship—and the enthusiasm for the local which characterizes some of the chapters. However, the sheer size of the book is daunting. As the national story continues to expand, it threatens to burst the constraints placed on it by the Historical Myth, and like the British imperial histories before them, it becomes unmanageable for the solo historian and unreadable in less than a week.

In the utopian story told by the historians, it is not the nation which achieves an apotheosis but New Zealand historiography itself. During 1981, the Springbok Tour of New Zealand demonstrated that the national myth was disintegrating, and in the following years it became perfectly evident that it was no longer acceptable to relegate the Maori to being an object of the historical imagination identified with somebody's special turf.

The traditional historical model on which New Zealand nationalism is based closely resembles fiction writing. The historian or filmmaker conjures up a representation of what he/she believes to have "actually" happened in the past as the basis for living in the present. However, the past is, by definition, not around for us to confirm the truth of such representations; history therefore has no ultimate authority, and an appeal to some transcendental process only begs the question.[143] The present dilemma is not so much to find a way "beyond" the limits of the current representational model, nor to engage in a frantic scramble for more "data" which would enable the historian or filmmaker to provide a "better" or more reliable representation of our past and present. Neither is it a question of finding a more appropriate arsenal of terminology, or of putting it in plain language for everyone to understand; both carry their own ideological implications.

Nowadays there is a blizzard of terminology, the naming game run riot. Nationalism was once a set of internal and centripetal discourses posed against the external and centrifugal discourses of empire and internationalism. After 1981, many High Culture Pakeha intellectuals opted to go "offshore" to adopt more expansive mythologies such as feminism, post-colonialism, and post-modernism, or they have attempted to rehabilitate humanism, mythologies about which there is little or no agreement. There are others calling for biculturalism, multiculturalism, and Maori nationalism, and still others adopted terms such as Maori culture, Pakeha culture, Pakeha backlash, white nation, honky, and so on. Furthermore, whatever Aotearoa means for Maori people, it has—for better or worse—developed a special appeal for many Pakeha as well, because it is a Maori word and concept with a sense of being the authentic name for the land itself. Currently, it does not represent an exclusively Maori land (whether it should is another matter) since it has been used already by Pakeha advertising agencies, feminists, Marxists, Christians, and environmentalists, quite aside from Maori intellectuals and gang "patches." Perhaps because it has a relatively short genealogy, Aotearoa is a hybrid mythology, an overlapping space between Maori and Pakeha where there is a form of rhetorical warfare going on which repeats the one last century before the 1840 annexation: a battle for the definition of and the right to use the term itself.

Whichever name eventually prevails, the two key terms here would seem to be "nation" and "culture." Nation, nationalism, and national identity, and the analogous terms culture, (bi-/multi-) culturalism, and cultural identity, plus all their other variants, have each come to prominence at different historical moments. Their greatest impetus derives from the European Enlightenment of the seventeenth and eighteenth centuries when, in part, these terms satisfied the need for a new system of naming and ordering, brought on by the collapse of monarchical systems of government and the enormous expansion of European imperialism around the globe. In the genealogies provided by Raymond Williams in his book *Keywords,* ''nation'' and its word cluster are commonly endowed with the straightforward meaning of a *political* forma- tion. Frontiers, passports, visas, flags, one-man-one-vote, and other institutions of the State spring to mind, and to this can be added the ''official history'' promoted in the media and education systems.[144]

As such, the nation and the political are meant to be objective value-neutral scientific terms. This has its roots in French Enlight- enment discourses which asserted the absolute preeminence of popular sovereignty and the right to self-determination—ideas which were of enormous importance in the foundation of the United States, and, to a lesser degree, Australia and New Zealand. In practice, the nation as political formation requires codification in complex national and international laws which are not easily understood in lay terms and which resemble the kinds of discipli- nary apparatus assailed by European intellectuals in the Sixties and Seventies. In New Zealand's case, this definition has clearly been the dominant one.

Williams distinguishes the political definition of nation from another earlier one (which is still around), based on biological *racial* groupings.[145] The nation-as-racial-grouping serves as an emotional or spiritual alternative to the ultra-rational legal defini- tion described above. It has its roots mostly in German speculative and Romantic thought: the nation is a matter of the heart or spirit or blood, of the national will to unity, of asserting a sense of belonging to a place and a people who think, sound, and look like oneself, and it finds its most passionate expression nowadays when a legally defined nationalism is denied (South Africa, the Palestinians, the Armenians). Ironically, this denial is usually effected by means of exactly the same racial definition of nationalism. Thus South Africa resorted to ''passports'' and pass laws for its black population, and legal constraints based on grounds which would deny national identity outside blood lines and regulate travel inside the national frontiers. In New Zealand, this racial definition enjoyed some popularity in the later nineteenth century and early twentieth centuries (and was particularly directed at keeping out the Chinese), but it was steadily worn down by the healing powers of the official Myth of Integration. In the last few decades, "race" has given way to "ethnicity" within many social science discourses, and it has given way to "culture" within popular discourses.

Yet these two broad definitions—the political formation and the racial grouping—are in most cases mutually supportive and mutually contradictory: the nation-as-political-formation has to enlist the "will" to unity to function at all (via consensus or coercion), and the nation-as-racial-grouping has to enlist the "right" to self-determination in order to generate a momentum of resistance. Furthermore, both are based on the assumption that custody of the land can be legitimized by recourse to either history or the spirit. The political definition has evolved in the latter part of this century to signify a pluralist system—both intra- and inter-nationally—which in principle supervises and tolerates diversity within/on this land while continuing to exercise its power to constrain and coerce its own dissenting citizens. This is the tradition from which New Zealand nationalism and multiculturalism now receive their mandate. The racial definition, on the other hand, remains essentialist and oppositional and many of the functions associated with this definition have been invested instead in the term "culture," a term which has a history of being used in an oppositional sense. From this tradition come biculturalism, Maori nationalism, and Aotearoa.[146]

Official discourses have sought historically to legitimize themselves by having "culture" subordinated to "nation" (or the earlier "civilization") by confining it to the realm of the artistic. In the nineteenth century, debates around these terms used a class-based vertical model, wherein the desired aim was to ascend (transcend) through art to a higher unity within the universal process of human development. By contrast, the late twentieth-century conflict between nation and culture is based more on a horizontal model which is being stripped of its teleology and its depth metaphors. The scene of conflict nowadays takes place within the nation-state, against which culture is posed in essentialist defiance as rival for the same space. The consequence: each seeks to colonize the other. The pluralist nation-state (New Zealand) enlists the services of artists to promote "official culture," or "national culture," or "cultural nationalism," or even "biculturalism" when it is defined as non-political; essentialist groups (Maori, feminist, working class, and so on) are forced to assert their opposition to the State under the rubric of "culture," which is somehow supposed to be different from official culture yet which desires its political power. Ultimately, nation (New Zealand) and culture (Maori/Pakeha) each serve to justify the other in a circular double bind. As Edward Said has written: "Culture serves authority, and ultimately the national State, not because it represses and coerces but because it is affirmative, positive, and persuasive."[147]

It may be asked, are there other names and terminologies that are more relevant, more potent, for discussing the current situation in New Zealand? Certainly there are no strong alternatives in the English language. So it is not a question of abandoning the nation-culture opposition because each is hopelessly contaminated by the other. Nor is it a question of forcing them apart again analytically. Neither term in these binarisms has any intrinsic value over its reciprocal Other. Privileging a national identity over a cultural identity quickly leads to patriotism's excesses; privileging a cultural identity runs into the bind of renouncing the struggle for power and signals the retreat into hermeticism. It is a question, I think, of simply accepting the terminology for what it is: rhetorical weaponry.

Logically, this trajectory has led to the increased adoption of Maori terminology—mana Maori, taha Maori, wairua Maori, and so on—in an attempt to theorize an essential cultural difference or center outside international or Pakeha New Zealand culture, based on (among other things) a separate language and territorial or whakapapa (familial) affiliations. But the Maori were/are oppositional or essentialist or marginalized only when posed against a Pakeha New Zealand center; they were/are not oppositional or essentialist or marginal *per se,* as is implied by totalizing theorists (both Pakeha and Maori) who wish to ontologize Otherness and Difference. Essentialism is but the inverse of pluralism and relativism, whereby the tendency for each to become transformed into its Other is strategically repressed. Therefore, substituting perspectival or religious metaphors for carving and decoration has not produced any closer proximity to a "true" or "realistic" representation of what Maori culture actually is or would be. What it has done is provide a grammar, language and imaginative vocabulary for constructing and maintaining a Maori difference, and this strikes me as a political strategy.

Finally, there can of course be no authentic definitions for these terms, only competing ones, and I opted to discuss some of them in my last five chapters. I tried to demonstrate how they provide for different tactical responses to the double bind of representation which inheres in the various oppositions which have organized debate: New Zealand/international world, New Zealand/ Aotearoa, Pakeha/Maori, history/culture, nation/culture, and so on. If chapter 11 suggests that I clearly favor the option of irony, then this derives from my belief that the current language in which New Zealand's cultural and political debates are being carried out is fast becoming exhausted. The naming game is all about coming up with new languages, new vocabularies, new genres, and in the end, that, I believe, is what makes it all so interesting.

APPENDICES

APPENDIX A: GLOSSARY

The English translations for the following Maori terms are naturally problematic. Basically I have adapted the translations used by Herbert Williams in *A Dictionary of the Maori Language* (Wellington: Government Printer, 1971) and Michael King's more informal *Being Pakeha* (Auckland: Hodder & Stoughton, 1985).

Aotearoa	New Zealand, Land of the Long White Cloud
ariki	chief, leader of a federation of tribes
aroha	love for the many, caring, compassion
haka	dance and chant of welcome or defiance
hangi	earth oven and its contents
hapu	section of a large tribe or clan
hikoi	march, trek
hongi	press noses as physical introduction
hui	assembly, meeting
iwi	people, tribe
karakia	prayer, charm, incantation
karanga	welcoming call
kaumatua	male elder
kawa	etiquette, protocol
korero	speak, talk, address, conversation, story
kuia	female elder
makutu	curse, spell
mana	spiritual power, prestige, authority
manuhiri	visitors
Maori	person native to New Zealand
Maoritanga	Maori culture
marae	open space in front of a meeting house
matakite	second sight
mauri	ethos, life force
moko	tattoo

ngati	tribal prefix
pa	village community
Pakeha	person of European descent
poi	dance performed with small flax ball on string
powhiri	welcome
taha Maori	Maori dimensions of life
tangata whenua	people of the land, hosts
tangi	ceremony of mourning
taniwha	water spirit
taonga	sacred property
tapu	sacred, prohibited
tipuna	ancestor
tohunga	expert, priest
tukutuku	panels inside meeting house
turanga-waewae	a place to stand, a sense of belonging, a home marae
urupa	cemetery
utu	satisfaction, equity
wahine	woman
waiata	song
wairua	spirit
wero	challenge
whaikorero	formal marae speech-making
whakama	awkward, shy
whakapapa	genealogy
whenua	land, country

APPENDIX B: FILMOGRAPHY

*These films are discussed at more length in the text.

PART I: MAORILAND

Chapter 1: Noble Savages in Hollywood

* The Romance of Hine-Moa	UK Gaumont	1925/27	Silent	11m
* Under the Southern Cross	USA Universal	1928/29	Silent	64m
* Hei Tiki	USA Markey	1930/35	Sound	73m

Chapter 2: The Birth of a Nation

The Betrayer	Aust Smith	1921	Silent	---
The Birth of New Zealand	NZ Reynolds	1922	Silent	---
My Lady of the Cave	NZ Hayward	1922	Silent	---
The Adventures of Algy	Aust Smith	1925	Silent	---
* Rewi's Last Stand	NZ Hayward	1925	Silent	---
* The Te Kooti Trail	NZ Hayward	1927	Silent	90m
On the Friendly Road	NZ Hayward	1936	Sound	---
* Rewi's Last Stand	NZ Hayward	1940	Sound	64m

Chapter 3: Romances in Maoriland

The James McDonald films:

* Gisborne Hui Aroha	1919	Silent	10m
* Scenes at the Rotorua Hui	1920	Silent	24m
* Scenes of Maori Life on the Whanganui River	1921	Silent	48m

* Scenes of Maori Life on the East Coast		1923	Silent	26m

NZ Government Publicity Office 1922–1930:

* Whakarewarewa		1927	Silent	8m
* The Maori As He Was (parts II, IV, & V)		1928	Silent	3x10m
Valley of Enchantments		1930	Silent	10m
* New Zealand's River of Romance		1930	Silent	10m

NZ Government Publicity Office & Filmcraft 1930–1936:

Ka Mate!		1934	Sound	11m
Maori Days		1934	Sound	10m
* Amokura		1928/1934	Sound	13m
Maoriland Movielogues 5		1934	Sound	10m
Maoriland Movielogues 8		1935	Sound	10m
* Holiday Haunts		1935	Sound	10m

NZ Government Film Studios:

Maoriland Movielogues 9		1936	Sound	10m
Maoriland Movielogues 14		1939	Sound	11m

Independents, 1901–1940:

Royal Visit By Duke & Duchess of Cornwall & York to NZ	Salvation Army	1901	Silent	2m
Poi Dances at Whakarewarewa		1910	Silent	2m
Prince of Wales in Maoriland	H.C. Gore	1920	Silent	6m
Historic Otaki	NZ Moving Picture Co.	1921	Silent	10m
Journey Into Rua's Stronghold	Coubray	1928	Silent	4m
* Rotorua NZ: Penny Diving	Movietone News	1930	Sound	2m
* The Maori: Everyone Bathes on Washing Day	Movietone News	1930	Sound	2m
''Koura Fishing''	Movietone News	1930	Sound	1m

Maoris Demonstrate Their Goodwill and Loyalty at Waitangi	Movietone News	1934 Sound	2m
Waitangi Celebrations	Soundscenes	1934 Sound	7m
"Manley Canoe Film"	Manley	1937/40 unassembled	

PART II: NEW ZEALAND

Chapter 4: Government Newsreels and the Integration Myth

* One Hundred Crowded Years   1940   Sound   53m

The Weekly Reviews 1941–1950:   (all B&W; 6–10m)
                                            SE = Special Edition

* 112	Ruatoria . . . Ceremony in Honor of Maori V.C.	1943	SE
168	Wanganui . . . Funeral of Mr H.T. Ratana, MP	1944	
171	Children's Maori Display	1944	
190	Ngaruawahia Regatta	1945	
209	Rotorua . . . Maori Battalion P.O.W.s Return	1945	
221	Kawhia . . . A Golden Jubilee	1945	
* 232	Maori Battalion Returns	1946	SE
* 257	East Coast . . . District Nurse	1946	
264	Arts . . . Maori Carving	1946	
280	Patterns in Flax	1947	SE
321	Ruatoria . . . A Maori Gathering	1947	
* 324	Maori School	1947	SE
* 332	Backblock Medical Service	1948	SE
340	Waitangi Ceremony	1948	
368	Rotorua . . . Memorial Hostel Opened	1948	
378	Maori Art in London . . . The Oldman Collection	1948	
389	North Otago . . . Maori Cave Painting	1949	
395	Interview . . . Sir Peter Buck; Lakes at Tutira	1949	
* 402	Maori Rehabilitation . . . New Farms Beside the Wairoa	1949	

420	War Memorial . . . Meeting House Opened	1949		
439	Ngaruawahia . . . Games Athletes Entertained	1950		
446	Canterbury Museum . . . Moa Hunter Relics	1950		
458	Funeral of Sir Apirana Ngata	1950		

Also included:
Maori Village   1945

The NZ Mirrors 1950–1954:   (all B&W; 7–11m)

1	Natural Heating at Rotorua	1950 from WR	392
2	Moa Bones . . . Important Find	1950 from WR	396
3	Ngaruawahia Regatta	1950 from WR	190
5	Tutira Legends	1950 from WR	395
9	Ancient Art	1951 from WR	389
10	Modern Maori Farmers	1951 from WR	402
11	Muttonbirders; Maori Art Treasures	1951 WRs	308; 378
13	Maori Oven at Whakarewarewa; Wood Carver	1952	
14	Dances . . . Long Poi; Buried Village	1952	
15	What's Cooking in Korea?	1953 from PP	3
21	Pony Club Poems: A Ride to Rotorua; Bookman and Artist	1953	

The Pictorial Parades 1952–1971:   (all 9–14m)

3	K-Force Christmas	1953	B&W
4	H.M.N.Z.S. Bellona	1954	B&W
17	A Royal Tour Special—Northland to Waikato	1954	B&W
18	A Royal Tour Special—On the Road to Rotorua	1954	B&W
23	Pumicelands	1954	B&W
36	Ardmore Teachers' Training College	1955	B&W
74	"Canoedling" on the Waikato	1958	B&W
76	Moa Hunters	1958	B&W
103	Howard Morrison Quartet	1960	B&W
106	Waiwhetu: New Meeting House	1960	B&W
108	Waitomo	1960	Col

109	Christchurch: First in 100 Years	1960	B&W
* 114	Visit to Motiti	1961	B&W
116	Pakeha Concert Party	1961	B&W
128	Science, Patron of the Arts	1962	B&W
136	Rotorua: The New City	1963	B&W
141	Steaming Valley	1963	Col
173	New Meeting House at Mangere	1965	B&W
199	Tauranga Hui	1967	B&W

Other Weekly Reviews on Maori themes include numbers 67, 88, 124, 274, 275, 296, 298, 308, 392, and 396, as well as four on the Maori All Blacks, numbers 362, 363, 410, and 459. Some of the Weekly Reviews were reedited for use in the NZ Mirror series and the NZ Diary series. The latter ran to six episodes of approximately 20 minutes each. NZ Diary 4 reused Weekly Review 171 and NZ Diary 6 reused Weekly Review 190.

Chapter 5: Cracks in the Wall—The Social Problem Documentary

Tourism Romances:

Meet New Zealand	NFU	1949 B&W	47m
(aka) Introducing New Zealand	NFU	1955 B&W	—
Thermal Wonderland	NFU	1950 Col	12m
Land of Hinemoa	Lee Hill	1950 B&W	10m
The Maori Ancient and Modern	Robert Steele	1950 Col	14m
Rotorua Radius	NFU	1953 Col	21m
The New Zealanders (1)	NFU	1959 Col	43m
The New Zealanders (2)	NFU	1961 Col	22m
Taupo Moana	NFU	1963 Col	20m
Rotorua Lookabout	NFU	1968 Col	22m

Historical Romances:

* The Legend of the Wanganui River	NFU	1952 B&W	16m
Pumicelands	NFU	1954 B&W	16m

Kotuku	NFU	1954B&W	12m
Hot Earth	NFU	1954B&W	18m
People of the Waikato	NFU	1956B&W	17m

Social Problem
   Documentaries:

* Aroha	NFU	1951B&W	18m
* Tuberculosis and the Maori People of the Wairoa District	NFU	1952B&W	25m
* The Maori Today	NFU	1960Col	15m
As the Twig is Bent	NFU	1965B&W	20m
To Live in the City	NFU	1967B&W	30m
English Language Teaching For Maori and Island Children	Hayward Films	1971Col	23m

Chapter 6: Segregation Begins—The Arts and Culture Documentary

Song and Dance:

* Dances of the South Pacific	Pacific Films	1954B&W	17m
* Songs and Dances of Maoriland	Robert Steele	1959Col	14m
* Maori Arts and Culture No.1: Carving and Decoration	NFU	1962Col	29m
NZ Maori Rhythms	NFU	1963B&W	12m
Mauriora Maori Show	NFU	1963Col	14m
Songs of the Maori	NFU	1963Col	19m
Songs of Their Forefathers	NFU	1964B&W	26m
* Arts of Maori Children	Hayward Films	1965Col	19m
Maori Theatre Trust Entertainment	NFU	1968B&W	6m
Taku Toa	NZBC	1970Col	27m
Mawai Hakona	NFU	1979Col	12m

Animation:		all color	
Hatupatu and the Bird Woman	(Fred O'Neill)	1963	7m
Legend of Rotorua	(for the NFU)	1967	9m
The Great Fish of Maui		1967	8m
Maui—the Half-God	Sieben/Everitt	1977	8m
Rangi and Papa—the Maori Creation Myth	Robert Jahnke	1979	8m
Te Utu	Robert Jahnke	1980	7m
Kahukura and the Fairy Fishermen	Sieben/Everitt	1981	9m
Parallel Line	Larry Nelson/ NFU	1981	7m
Rau-Tapu—Magic Feather	Nicki Dennis/ NFU	1984	8m
Te Rerenga Wairua	May/Wylie	1984	16m
History and the Maori Cultural Essence:		(all color)	
* Into Antiquity: A Memory of the Maori Moko	Reynolds	1971	16m
Two Weeks at Manutuke	NFU	1971	22m
Matenga: Maori Choreographer	Hayward Films	1972	30m
Two Artists	NFU	1972	9m
* Te Rauparaha	NFU	1972	19m
* Tahere Tikitiki	NFU	1974	39m
Children of the Mist	NFU	1974	30m
Marae	NFU	1974	21m
Every Bend . . . a Power	Beryl te Wiata	1976	23m
Two Rivers Meet	Trilogic	1977	36m
Te Ohaki O te Po	Pacific Films	1978	33m
Aku Mahi Whatu Maori	Pacific Films	1978	28m
* Te Kuiti-tanga: the Narrowing	NFU	1980	50m
* Maori	NFU	1981	27m

* The Adze and the Chainsaw	NFU		1981	25m
* Te Maori: A Celebration of the People and Their Art	NFU/T.Horton Associates		1985	58m

Miscellaneous:

Legend of Birds	NFU	Col	1960	22m
The Years Back: The Twentieth Century	NFU	B&W	1973	36m
Four Faces of New Zealand	NFU	Col	1978	14m
The New Zealanders	NFU	Col	1978	30m

Chapter 7: The Pakeha Pilgrimage Documentary

The Tangata Whenua Series:	Pacific Films	1974	
* The Spirits and the Times Will Teach			46m
* The Great Trees			42m
* Waikato			40m
* Tuhoe Ringatu			30m
* Turangawaewae—A Place to Stand			50m
* The Carving Cries			40m

Other Pilgrimage Documentaries:

Island of Spirits	NZBC	1974	32m
* Te Matakite O Aotearoa	Steven/TV 2	1975	64m
Princess te Puea	South Pacific TV	1979	59m
* Denny	TVNZ	1979	25m
Letter From a Marae	TVNZ	1981	30m
* Race Against Time	Main/ Thomson/ TVNZ	1983	52m
The Importance of Being Maori	Australia/ ABC	1984	29m

The Beginners' Guide to Visiting a Marae	TVNZ	1984	30m
* Maori: The New Dawn	UK/BBC	1984	50m

Social Problem Documentaries:

* South Auckland: Two Cities	TVNZ	1982	50m
Give Me a Love	TVNZ	1986	50m

Others:

Adventures in Maoriland	Steven/TVNZ	1981	50m
Shadows on the Land	TVNZ	1985	30m

PART III: AOTEAROA

Chapter 8: The Politics of Silence

Pacific Films:

* Broken Barrier	Mirams/ O'Shea	1952	71m
* Runaway	O'Shea	1964	80m
* Don't Let It Get You	O'Shea	1966	80m
* Pictures	Black/O'Shea	1981/83	88m

Chapter 9: The Politics of Blame

* The Governor	Aberdein/ Isaacs/	1977	
I: The Reverend Traitor	TV 1		91m
IV: He Iwi Ko Tahi Tatou			78m
* Just Passing Through	Rymer	1985	50m
* The Quiet Earth	Murphy	1985	91m
* Mark II	Anderson/ TVNZ	1986	70m

Chapter 10: The Politics of Repression

* Sylvia	Firth	1985	98m
* Among the Cinders	Haedrich	1984	99m
* Other Halves	Laing	1985	102m
* Arriving Tuesday	Riddiford	1986	90m
* The Lost Tribe	Laing	1983/85	97m

Chapter 11: The Politics of Irony

* Utu	Murphy	1983	124m
* Came a Hot Friday	Mune	1985	105m
* Kingpin	Walker	1985	89m

Chapter 12: Maori Filmmaking in the Eighties

* Bastion Point: Day 507	Mita/Narbey/ Pohlmann	1980	26m
* Patu	Mita	1983	110m
* The Makutu on Mrs Jones	Parr	1984	25m
* Ngati	Barclay	1987	88m

APPENDIX C: PHOTO CREDITS

The author gratefully acknowledges the following agencies for allowing reproduction of their photos with permission.

SCNZFA Stills Collection, New Zealand Film Archive
NANZ   National Archives of New Zealand
NZFC   New Zealand Film Commission

Page
25   SCNZFA
26   SCNZFA
28   SCNZFA
30   SCNZFA
31   SCNZFA
32   SCNZFA
40   SCNZFA, © Auckland Museum, 51/17, RLS (2)
42   SCNZFA, © Mitchell Library, State Library of New South Wales, Alfred Hill Collection, ML MSS 528: PIC. ACC 5360, at H6790. Neg.# 320/1,2.
45   SCNZFA, © Mitchell Library, Neg.# 321
     SCNZFA, © Mitchell Library, Neg.# 320/3
51   NANZ
56   Museum of New Zealand, Neg.# B10452
57   Museum of New Zealand, Neg.# B1643
58   Museum of New Zealand, Neg.# B153
59   Museum of New Zealand, Neg.# B428
60   Museum of New Zealand, Neg.# B160
68   NANZ
69   NANZ
74   NANZ
75   NANZ
77   NANZ
78   NANZ
90   NANZ, NFU Stills Collection #1 W3939
92   NANZ, NFU Stills Collection #2 W3939
93   NANZ, NFU Stills Collection #4 W3939

252	NZFC
255	NZFC
257	NZFC
262	*New Zealand Herald*
263	*New Zealand Herald*
264	*New Zealand Herald*
266	Merata Mita
268	NZFC
271	NZFC
273	NZFC
275	SCNZFA
	NZFC
276	NZFC

APPENDIX D: NOTES

1   Salman Rushdie, *The Satanic Verses* (New York: Viking Penguin, Inc., 1989), p. 21.

2   Charles Newman, *The Post-Modern Aura: The Act of Fiction in an Age of Inflation* (Evanston: Northwestern University Press, 1985).

3   Roland Barthes, *S/Z*, translated by Richard Miller (New York: Hill & Wang, 1974).

4   J.R.R. Tolkien, *The Lord of the Rings* (New York: Ballantine Books, 1981).

5   I am alluding here to Salman Rushdie's excellent essay, "Outside the Whale," an attack on the late imperial fantasies known as the "Raj Revival" in British films and television programs during the early 1980s. Rushdie does not find the imperial dream at all "glamorous." See *American Film* (Jan.–Feb. 1985), p. 73.

6   Michael King, *Being Pakeha* (Auckland: Hodder and Stoughton, 1985)

7   Gregory Bateson, *Steps to an Ecology of Mind: Collected Essays in Anthropology, Evolution, and Epistemology* (San Francisco: Chandler, 1972), p. 217.

8   Readers will find it fairly easy to make an analogy here between the double-bind situation faced by other cultures and peoples and the situation confronted by feminist intellectuals. For more specific references to the feminist/female double bind vis-à-vis the Maori, refer to my discussions of the "erotic/exotic," *Broken Barrier, Runaway,* and *Just Passing Through.* Also see notes 22, 50, 106.

9   See the following: Michael King, *Being Pakeha* (note 6); David McGill, "Do Pakehas have a Culture?" *NZ Listener,* April 19, 1986; Carroll Wall, "Te Pakeha: the Search for White Identity," *Metro,* November 1986; *Sites* No. 13, Spring 1986; Angela Bellara, *Proud to be White?* (Auck-

land: Heinemann, 1986); and Jock Phillips, *A Man's Country?* (Auckland: Penguin, 1987). Also see *Illusions* No. 1, Summer 1986, pp. 32–33. David Harlan also referred to New Zealand's oedipal theme in *The Atlantic Monthly,* September 1986, p. 16.

10   Sir Apirana Ngata, ''Anthropology and the Government of Native Races in the Pacific'' in *New Zealand Affairs,* by Ngata et al. (Christchurch: L.M. Isitt, 1929), p. 23.

11   I am influenced here by the writings of Edward W. Said, particularly *Orientalism* (New York: Vintage, 1979).

12   *The Film Daily Year Book* (New York & Los Angeles: John W. Alicoate, 1927), p. 971.

13   *The Film Daily Year Book* provides short but informative analyses of developments in the New Zealand film industry from the 1920s onwards.

14   Internal memos of the Ministry of Internal Affairs, July 24, 1936.

15   Alfred Grace may have initiated the tradition with his *Hone Tiki Dialogues* (1910). They were followed by the Reverend V.C. Fussell's *Letters from Private Henare Tikitamu* (1917) and by Pat Lawlor's *Maori Tales* series (1927–1930). The most insightful and generous critic of such works, as indeed on all Pakeha writings on the Maori, is Bill Pearson. His two most influential essays on the subject are ''Attitudes to the Maori in some Pakeha Fiction'' in *Fretful Sleepers and Other Essays* (Auckland: Heinemann, 1974; orig. 1958); and ''The Maori and Literature 1938–65'' in *The Maori People in the Nineteen-Sixties,* ed. Erik Schwimmer (Auckland: Blackwood & Janet Paul, 1968), pp. 217–256.

16   Quoted in Erik Barnouw, *Documentary: A History of the Non-Fiction Film* (London: Oxford University Press, 1974), p. 45. Barnouw provides a useful introduction to Flaherty in his chapter titled ''Explorer.'' Flaherty was also involved to varying degrees in *White Shadows in the South Seas* and Murnau's *Tabu.*

17   Inevitably, many strange blunders occurred regardless; for example, the two tribes in *The Romance of Hine-Moa* are known as the Arawas and the Ngati (in Maori, ''ngati'' is only a tribal prefix), with the chief of the latter being named

Whakane, an erroneous spelling of Whakaue (which is the name of a Rotorua hapu or sub-tribe).

18   The American expeditionary films were generally better than the British; for example, *Grass* (1925), *Chang* (1927), and *Samba* (1928) are all quite good. For a sample of the British films, see Rachael Low, *The History of the British Film 1918–1929* (London: Allen & Unwin, 1971), pp. 287–90. They have titles like *Climbing Mount Everest* (1922), *From Senegal to Timbuktu* (1924), *The Vast Sudan* (1924), *To Lhasa in Disguise* (1924), *Nionga* (1925), and *Jungle Woman* (1926). The last two begin mixing in overtly fictional elements.

19   These two films are relatively enjoyable in retrospect, but there were much worse travesties—for example, *Congorilla* (1929) and the other films by Mr. and Mrs. Martin Johnson. In this tradition I would also place Jacopetti's *Mondo Cane* (1963), the films of South African filmmaker Jamie Uys, notably *The Gods Must Be Crazy* (1980/83), and the US/New Zealand co-production, *Savage Islands* (aka *Nate and Hayes*) (1983).

20   *White Shadows in the South Seas,* for example, is replete with familiar images of America in the 1920s— bootlegging, epidemics, fear of social disorder. For a discussion of the allegorical dimension in ethnographic narratives, see essays by Mary Louise Pratt, James Clifford, and Michael M.J. Fischer in *Writing Culture: the Poetics and Politics of Ethnography,* ed. by James Clifford and George E. Marcus (Berkeley: University of California Press, 1986).

21   *The Compound Cinema: the Film Writings of Harry Alan Potamkin,* selected, arranged and introd. by Lewis Jacobs (New York: Columbia University, 1977; orig. 1934), p. 488.

22   For example, see *Hinemoa: the Leap-Year Pantomime* by Paul Peritas in *Memories of Maoriland,* ed. by Isaac Selby (Melbourne: Tytherleigh Press, 1925). This prefigures the annexation of Hine-titama/Hine-nui-te-po by Pakeha feminists in the 1980s (see my chapter 9 discussion of *Just Passing Through*).

23   The most influential work in this area is still Bernard

Smith, *European Vision and the South Pacific 1769–1850*
(London: Oxford University Press, 1960). Smith uses four
main tropes in critiquing the relationship between European art and science and explorations and colonial projects
in the South Pacific: the Noble Savage, Ignoble Savage,
Comic Savage, Romantic Savage. Other writers have also
used the Dying Savage or Dying Race, a trope which comes
after the time period covered in Smith's book. For more
recent writers it has been more a question of wrestling with
a Cerebral Savage, for example Claude Lévi-Strauss in *The
Savage Mind* (London: Weidenfeld and Nicholson, 1972,
3rd ed.; original in 1962); Clifford Geertz, *The Interpretation of Cultures* (New York: Basic Books, 1973) pp.
345–59; and in New Zealand, K.R. Howe, ''The Fate of the
'Savage' in Pacific Historiography,'' *The NZ Journal of
History,* October 1977, pp. 137–54. For general information on these tropes, see George Boas, ''Primitivism,'' in
*Dictionary of the History of Ideas: Studies of Selected
Pivotal Ideas,* Vol. III, ed. Philip P. Wiener (New York:
Charles Scribner's Sons, 1973), pp. 577–98. For other
works specific to the Maori and Polynesians, see Bill
Pearson's introduction to Roderick Finlayson's *Brown
Man's Burden and Later Stories* (Auckland: Oxford University Press, 1973), and *Rifled Sanctuaries: Some Views of
the Pacific Islands in Western Literature to 1900* (Auckland: Auckland and Oxford University Presses, 1984);
Leonard Bell, *The Maori in European Art* (Wellington:
Reed, 1980), pp. 2–6; and Michael King, *Maori: A Photographic and Social History* (Auckland: Heinemann, 1983),
pp. 2–4. It is also interesting to see Maori intellectuals such
as Donna Awatere ironizing such tropes; for example, part
3 of *Maori Sovereignty* (Auckland: Broadsheet, 1984) is
titled ''Beyond the Noble Savage.''

24   Raymond Williams notes that the widespread usage of
racial classifications among British intellectuals dates from
around mid-19th century, associated with the writings of
Gobineau and Darwin, when it moved out of physical
anthropology into social and political thought and popular
prejudice. See *Keywords* (New York: Oxford University
Press, 1983; orig. 1976), pp.248–50. Also see John Sten-

house, "The Wretched Gorilla Damnification of Humanity" in *The NZ Journal of History,* October 1984, pp.143–62. Even influential public figures such as Dr. T. M. Hocken (after whom the Hocken Library is named) could argue that evolution meant that whoever could best use the land (a value judgment in itself) was entitled to have it, irrespective of its original inhabitants. See *The Early History of New Zealand* (Wellington: Government Printer, 1914).

25   For reviews of *The Romance of Hine-Moa,* see *The New York Times,* Oct. 1, 1929, and *Variety,* Oct. 2, 1929.

26   For U.S. reviews of *The Devil's Pit,* see *The New York Times,* Oct. 14, 1929, and *Variety,* Oct. 16, 1929. Also see *The Evening Post,* Aug. 3, 1929, p. 7.

27   For U.S. reviews of *Hei Tiki,* see *The New York Times,* Feb. 2, 1935, and *Variety,* Feb. 5, 1935.

28   In film, Rudall Hayward was the first to reverse this tradition with *To Love a Maori* in 1972, a film about the love between a Maori man and a Pakeha woman.

29   Prior to the premiere at the Strand Theatre, the story of the film had been serialized in both *The New Zealand Herald* and *The Auckland Weekly News.* Other publicity made much of Tina Hunt (Monika) being "Rotorua's Most Famous Beauty" and daughter of the popular Guide Susan. See *The Auckland Weekly News,* Sept. 1927, and *The Auckland Star* Nov. 16, 1927, p. 27. Other film personalities of the time included Chief Mita Taupopoki who appears in *Rewi's Last Stand* (1925), *The Maori as He Was, Scenes at the Rotorua Hui, Poi Dances at Whakarewarewa* and *The Betrayer*; and Paora Tomati who appears in *Under the Southern Cross, The Romance of Hine-Moa, Rewi's Last Stand,* and *The Maori as He Was.*

30   See the articles of November 11, 1927 in *The Christchurch Star,* the *Auckland Sun, The Dominion, Whakatane Press,* and *The Auckland Weekly News,* plus *The Auckland Weekly News* of November 17, and a review in the *Sun* on November 18. At one stage, with imaginations running wild, there was even talk of intercepting the film at the Customs Post Office if the filmmakers tried to smuggle it out of the country.

31   There is a brief review in the British *Monthly Film Bulletin,* June 30, 1949, p. 98. The film is described as a "melodrama of the Maori Wars" and the reviewer most liked the "native dancing or fighting." Also see Russell Campbell's "In Order that They May Become Civilized: Pakeha Ideology in Rewi's Last Stand, Broken Barrier and Utu" in *Illusions,* No. 1, Summer 1986.

32   Hayward later married Ramai te Miha, the actress who plays Ariana in the film. According to her (personal communication), the tragic ending was intended; it should not be confused with the happy ending in the novelization by A.W. Reed (Wellington: A.H. & A.W. Reed, 1939). After the war, the Haywards shot a film in Britain on race relations titled *The World Is Turning Toward Coloured People.*

33   In Robert Sklar, "Rudall Hayward, New Zealand Film-Maker" *Landfall,* 98, 1970, p. 152.

34   Claude Lévi-Strauss, *Triste Tropiques* (Harmondsworth, Middlesex: Peregrine Books, 1984, orig. in French 1955). Also see V.L. Smith, (ed.) *Hosts and Guests: the Anthropology of Tourism* (Philadelphia: University of Pennsylvania, 1977); Oriel Pi-Sunyer "Review Article: Tourism and Anthropology," in *Annals of Tourism Research* VIII (2) (Menomonie: University of Wisconsin, 1981), pp. 271–84; James Clifford and George E. Marcus (eds.), *Writing Culture* (note 20); Henry Louis Gates, Jr., (ed.) *Critical Inquiry,* Autumn 1985, an issue on " 'Race,' Writing and Difference."

35   The standard Cook's Tour sequence around the turn of the century was: Auckland and environs, Te Aroha, Okoroire, Rotorua and environs, Wairakei and Taupo, Tokaanu, Pipiriki and the Whanganui River, Wellington, Picton, Nelson, Buller Gorge, West Coast, Christchurch, Mount Cook and back, Dunedin, Lakes Wakatipu, Wanaka, Te Anau and Manapouri, and the West Coast Sounds. See *New Zealand as a Tourist and Health Resort* (Auckland: Thomas Cook & Son, 4th ed., 1902).

36   This particular quotation is from C.N. Baeyertz, *Guide to New Zealand: the Scenic Paradise of the World* (Dunedin: 1908), p. xi. For a sample of other travel guidebooks of the

time, see James Cowan's *New Zealand, or Ao-Tea-Roa: Its Wealth and Resources, Scenery, Travel-Routes, Spas and Sport* (Wellington: NZ Government Department of Tourist and Health Resorts, 1908), and *Travel in New Zealand: the Island Dominion: Its Life and Scenery, Pleasure-Routes and Sport* (Auckland: Whitcombe and Tombs, 1926, two vols.).

37   E.W.G. Craig, *Man of the Mist* (Wellington: A.H. & A.W. Reed, 1964), p. 9. Best's fascination with the Maori was transposed into his voluminous writings. His Fall foreshadows the similar trajectory followed much later by the poet, James K. Baxter, in the Fifties and Sixties. The book also contains short discussions of background information on the four McDonald films, in particular the Whanganui River film, pp. 186–88.

38   The titles of Goldie's paintings include "The Passing of the Maori," "The Last of Her Tribe," "One of the Old School," "The Last of the Chivalrous Days," "Weary with Years," and "A Noble Relic of a Noble Race."

39   G.H.L. Pitt-Rivers, *The Clash of Culture and the Contact of Races* (London: 1927), p. 1.

40   Pitt-Rivers, p. 217.

41   Pitt-Rivers, p. 219.

42   There have been a number of films on the Maori preserved and restored by the NZ Film Archive. Perhaps the most notable are the McDonald films but others include the Manley collection, reel 1 of *The Romance of Hine-Moa* (from Britain), *The Adventures of Algy, The Maori as He Was* (from Denmark), and a section of *Historic Otaki*. Funding and assistance for such projects has come from the NZ Film Commission, the Federation of Film Societies, the Lottery Board and the Minister for the Arts, Television New Zealand, the National Film Unit, a small number of corporations and film producers, and other interested parties. A number of overseas archives were involved in these recovery programs, including the Australian National Film Archive, the National Film Archive of Britain, the American Film Institute collection at the Library of Congress in the U.S., and Danske Filmmuseum in Denmark.

43   For listings of the films produced by the NZ Government

Publicity Office between 1922 and 1941, see Jonathan Dennis and Clive Sowry, *The Tin Shed* (Wellington: The NZ Film Archive, 1981).

44 "Venturesome daring" is from A.H. Reed's popular *The Story of New Zealand* (Wellington: A.H. & A.W. Reed, 1945), p. 427. There were 11 editions published between 1945 and 1965.

45 Around 1940 the canon consisted of (among others) J. C. Beaglehole, F. L. W. Wood, J. B. Condliffe, and W. P. Morrell in history, Raymond Firth and Sir Peter Buck in anthropology; and Mason, Fairburn, Hyde, Curnow, and Glover in literature. See Keith Sinclair's summary on pp. 269–70 of *A History of New Zealand* (Harmondsworth, Middlesex: Penguin, 1959), and his "Review Article" in *The NZ Journal of History,* April 1978, pp. 69–74. The canon after 1940 was focused more precisely on the Promethean activity of a national identity, beginning with E. H. McCormick's *Letters and Art in New Zealand* (Wellington: Dept. of Internal Affairs, 1940), published as part of a series commissioned by the Government to mark the New Zealand Centennial; M. H. Holcroft's essays (collected under the title *Discovered Isles: A Trilogy* (Christchurch: Caxton, 1950); and the prose of Frank Sargeson and John Mulgan. Particularly worth noting are Allen Curnow's *A Book of New Zealand Verse 1923–45* (Christchurch: Caxton, 1945) and *Penguin Book of New Zealand Verse* (London: Penguin, 1960). Finally, there was also the establishing of *Landfall* by Charles Brasch in 1947.

46 Morrell's *New Zealand* may have been the first overtly "nationalist" history in that it was the first to tell the history of New Zealand as the growth of a nation (London: Ernest Benn, 1935), p. xi.

47 Erik Barnouw (note 16) dates the newsreel from 1910 when Pathé and Gaumont started producing them. As far as New Zealand is concerned, most of the newsreel companies began work in the 1920s. Clive Sowry has compiled three filmographies for the National Film Unit's newsreel productions after 1941: "Made at Miramar: An Index to NFU Productions 1941–1978" (n.d.); "New Zealand Mirror:

Item Title Index'' (1986); and ''Pictorial Parade: A Guide to Contents'' (1985).

48   Stanhope Andrews, *Here & Now,* December 1952, p. 8.

49   P.J. Downey, ''Documentary Film in New Zealand,'' *Landfall,* December 1955, p. 343.

50   Most of the racial/cultural distinctions I discuss can equally be applied to gender distinctions. For example, the early *Weekly Reviews* emphasize the unity between Maori and Pakeha and between men and women. This changes noticeably during the late 1940s, in *Weekly Review 402,* for instance. As far as the cultural phenomenon of ''mateship'' is concerned, there has been surprisingly little literature and film in New Zealand which reflects it—*Goodbye Pork Pie, Carry Me Back,* and *Came a Hot Friday* perhaps. Many more novels and films have followed the Man Alone/ Pioneer Myth with its alienated male hero at odds both with himself and the world.

51   Helen Paske, ''Dreams in Black and White,'' *NZ Listener,* Aug. 8, 1981, p. 14.

52   Much of this *Weekly Review* also appears in the National Film Unit's anthology film, *The War Years* (1983). Reprinted from the original negative, the latter version is better edited for dramatic intensity than the original. See Paske, pp. 14–15; Peter Wells review, *NZ Listener,* August 6, 1983; David Young, *NZ Listener,* July 16, 1983, 87, 89; Nicholas Reid, *A Decade of New Zealand Film* (Dunedin: John McIndoe, 1986), pp. 88–92.

53   Andrews (note 48), p. 8.

54   The scientific expedition films include *White Island* (1947), *Campbell Island* (1947), and *Fiordland* (1949). All were shot in remote places where few tourists would dare to venture, but they include some beautiful landscapes. Early tourism romances proper include *Trout Fishing in the Tongariro* (1950), *Fighting Fins* (1951), *Waikaremoana* (1951), *Waitomo* (1952), *Mount Cook* (1953), along with the more general kind with ''New Zealand'' in their titles, including *Meet New Zealand* (1949) and *The New Zealanders* (1959).

55   ''New Zealand'' tourism romances of the period include *Amazing New Zealand* (1963), a prize winner; *This is New*

Zealand, shown at Expo 70; *Here's New Zealand* by Neuline, *It Is Called New Zealand* (1972), and others. Two recent such films include Ian John's *Here's New Zealand* and George Andrews' *Treasures from the Land* (1984). They all have euphemistic "Maori" sections.

56 Articles on film during the 1950s: M.K. Joseph, "Documentary Film in New Zealand" in *Arts Year Book 6* (1950); Robert Allender, "The National Film Unit" in *Landfall,* December 1948, pp. 320–7; Robert Allender, "Disordered Cinema" in *Landfall* 20, December 1951, pp. 296–304; P.J. Downey, "Documentary Film in New Zealand" in *Landfall,* December 1955, pp. 343–48; Maurice Shadbolt, "John Feeney and the National Film Unit" in *Landfall* 47, Sept. 1958, pp. 226–232. Immediately after the war there was an upsurge internationally in critical writing—*The Penguin Film Review* (1946-) and *The Hollywood Quarterly* (1945-), among others, began publishing at this time and New Zealanders made contributions to them. In New Zealand itself, the Censor Gordon Mirams published his reflections on the cinema in *Speaking Candidly* (Hamilton, 1945).

57 Shadbolt (note 56), p. 226.

58 Department of Internal Affairs Historical Branch, *Introduction to New Zealand* (Wellington: Whitcombe and Tombs, 1945), p. 213.

59 Joseph (note 56), pp. 12, 16–17.

60 Some examples (most of which I have not seen) include: *White Walking Stick* (1950), for the Blind Institute; *Elysian Bus* (1951), a drama about traffic accidents; *Trees* (1952), a three-minute color cartoon on forest fire prevention; *The Treatment of Cerebral Palsy in New Zealand* (1956), for the Health Department; *This Dog Is Dangerous* (1956), on hydatids; *Born in New Zealand* (1957), on Sir Truby King and the Plunket Society; *Letter to the Teacher* (1957), about correspondence schools; *Watch Out in the Water* (1963), for the Water Safety Council; and *One in a Thousand* (1964), on the intellectually handicapped. Some of the other films were also released as *Pictorial Parades; One Hundred Years,* for example, which celebrated the centenary of the Red Cross, was also *PP. 183.* Others were

financed by corporations like Unilever, Shell, Caltex, and Dunlop. The independent companies—Pacific Films and Neuline Films—were actually dependent on the corporations for their economic survival.

61   Keith Sinclair, *A History of New Zealand* (see note 45), and W.H. Oliver, *The Story of New Zealand* (London: Faber & Faber, 1960).

62   Their crucial chapters as far as a national identity is concerned are Sinclair's "New Zealanders and Britons" and "Epilogue: the Search for Identity," and Oliver's final chapter "Like and Unlike." This may be compared with Shrimpton and Mulgan naming their book of 1921, *Maori and Pakeha: A History of New Zealand* (Auckland: Whitcombe & Tombs), and Reeves evoking a Maori name for his 1899 history, *The Long White Cloud* (London: Horace Marshall & Son, 1899, 2nd ed.).

63   Besides the topographies provided here, there were obviously others, for example, the geological and archaeological climaxed in the television series, *Landmarks* (1981) by Kenneth Cumberland; and the anthropological lingered in Margaret Orbell, *The Natural World of the Maori* (Auckland: Collins, 1985), later a television series (1987). David Simmons and Gordon Ell specialized in the archaeological in *The People Before* (early 1980s) and *Shadows on the Land* (1985). Anne Salmond refashioned the mythological in the guise of epistemology; see her essay, "Maori Epistemologies" in *Reason and Morality,* ASA Monograph 24, ed. Joanna Overing (London & New York: Tavistock Publishers, 1985).

Significantly, the late 1950s and early 1960s were watershed years for New Zealand literature: Janet Frame's *Owls Do Cry* (1957), Ian Cross' *The God Boy* (1958), Sylvia Ashton-Warner's *Spinster* (1958), Bruce Mason's *The Pohutukawa Tree* (1960), Noel Hilliard's *Maori Girl* (1960), and Barry Crump's *A Good Keen Man* (1960). Shortly after came work from Ronald Hugh Morrieson, Hone Tuwhare, and Maurice Shadbolt.

In critical writings, there was Bill Pearson's essay "Fretful Sleepers" in *Landfall* (1952), republished in *Fretful Sleepers and Other Essays* (note 15); also Robert Chapman's essay

"Fiction and the Social Pattern" in *Landfall* VII (1953), republished in Wystan Curnow (ed.), *Essays on New Zealand Literature* (Auckland: Heinemann, 1973).

64 These lines appear for the first time in a later revised edition of *A History of New Zealand* (London: Allen Lane, 1980), p. 329, suggesting a confidence not felt so strongly back in 1959.

65 Sinclair, *A History of New Zealand* (note 64), p. 330. Recently, Sinclair has adopted a revisionist approach to the national historical model he helped publicize—see *A Destiny Apart: New Zealand's Search for National Identity* (Wellington: Allen & Unwin, 1986), esp. chapters 4, 6, & 7.

66 This is supported by the fact that the main period of "realism" in New Zealand short story writing occurred between the late 1930s and the early 1960s, the first of the two periods I distinguished. From the 1960s until the mid-1970s, the realistic short story was largely replaced by the realist novel, which suggests a national identity largely achieved, but the short story made a comeback in the late 1970s as the national psyche began to unravel. This would seem to be consistent with the thesis advanced by Lawrence Jones in "The Persistence of Realism," *Islands* 20, Dec. 1977.

67 I am thinking here of James Ritchie (the Rakau studies), Erik Schwimmer, Margaret Orbell, Ans Westra, John Turner, Gordon Walters, Jane and Bernie Hill (*Hey Boy!*), and others. For a critique of this position see Peter Ireland, *NZ Listener,* July 19, 1986, pp. 30–32.

68 Ronald Bowie produced some of the National Film Unit's most interesting "Maori" films, including *Maori Arts and Culture No.1: Carving and Decoration, New Zealand Maori Rhythms, Mauriora Maori Show,* and *As the Twig Is Bent.*

69 There are exceptions of course. *Ralph Hotere* (1974) treats that artist as though he were a "New Zealander" rather than a "Maori New Zealander," an auteur who works in a national and internationalist art scene; and *Gottfried Lindauer in New Zealand* (1975) is concerned with Pakeha representation of the Maori in portrait painting, but it opts

for an auteurist treatment and eschews the wider historical perspective associated with imperialism and colonialism.

70   The Howard Morrison Quartet performed on the New Zealand Broadcasting Corporation's opening night in 1960 and Maori singers were featured constantly on television during the 1960s, but it was always with the implicit understanding that they were New Zealanders first and Maori second. By the early 1970s, John Barningham had produced *Pupiri Ra,* a six-part series of Maori music and dance, and Bryan Easte had produced *Taku Toa,* a color film of traditional performances, aimed mainly at overseas release. Such recordings recurred infrequently throughout the 1970s. As far as art and culture documentaries are concerned, the NZBC in the mid-1960s produced *Towards the Past,* a series of outside broadcast programs on New Zealand museums. Auckland's contribution was ''Hotanui,'' featuring the meeting house in Auckland's museum, and the work of a Maori carver at Mangere marae. Two other programs by Dr. Roger Duff at the Canterbury Museum discussed the moa and the Maori migration fleet (Robert Boyd-Bell, *New Zealand Television: the First 25 Years* (Auckland: Reed Methuen, 1985), pp. 195–6.

71   According to Rangi Walker in *The NZ Listener,* May 29, 1982, an early version of the script was written by Witi Ihimaera but emasculated by his superiors at the Ministry of Foreign Affairs and the National Film Unit.

72   Such collaborations can be fruitful and they encourage overseas observers; for example, anthropologist James Clifford has remarked that the Te Maori-Mobil collaboration was ''a fantastic case of mutual appropriation''—in *Discussions in Contemporary Culture, Number One,* ed. by Hal Foster (Seattle: Bay Press, 1987), p. 150.

73   Michael King, *Being Pakeha* (note 6), p. 109.

74   King, p. 108.

75   King, p. 110.

76   For a brief but useful discussion of these distinctions, see Raymond Williams' *Keywords* (note 24), pp. 146–7.

77   The series is also available in shorter ''thematically'' based versions which in some cases contain material not used in the six longer versions. The following titles are listed with

a parenthetical reference to the titles for the longer versions they are associated with: *He Powhiri* (GT), *He Wawata* (T), *Kuia* (S), *Mauri* (W, CC), *Moko* (S), *The Mountain, the River, the Land* (GT, W, S), *Parihaka* (no longer available—from *The Prophets*), *Piko Piko* (GT), *Poukai* (W), *Rongopai* (CC), *The Sheltering Branches* (GT), *Tokomaru Bay* (T, GT), *Turangawaewae Marae, Wananga* (GT, W).

78   King, p. 109.

79   King, p. 111

80   King, pp. 120–24.

81   In the film Rangihau's wording differs slightly from this; he refashioned it for this quotation from Michael King, *Maori: A Photographic and Social History* (note 23), p. 202.

82   King has given his views in *Being Pakeha* (note 6), pp. 102–126. However, there is something of a paradox here. While Barclay has been more concerned with the introspection of Maoritanga, he has (with the feature film *Ngati*) moved into fiction story-telling, a mode of representation which is relatively outward-directed and expansive. King, on the other hand, has turned from biography to autobiography (in *Being Pakeha*), a mode which tends toward implosion. These opposite trajectories may also be observed in Barclay's *Aku Mahi Whatu Maori* (*My Art of Maori Weaving*) (1978) for Pacific Films, and King's *Princess Te Puea* (1979) for South Pacific Television.

83   For a substantial analysis of these films see Russell Campbell, "The Discourse of Documentary" in *Illusions* 4, Summer 1987, pp. 10–16.

84   There was a similar tendency in short fiction films, for example, Roger Donaldson and Ian Mune's *Big Brother Little Sister* (1976), Sam Pillsbury's *Against the Lights* (1980), and Mike Walker's *Kingi's Story* (1981).

85   Dean, *The NZ Listener,* July 20, 1985, p. 25.

86   Donna Awatere, *Maori Sovereignty* (note 23). For extended critical responses to the book, see Geoff McDonald, *Shadows Over New Zealand* (Christchurch: Chaston, 1985), an ultra-conservative critique; and John Knight, "Shadow Over New Zealand?" in *Sites* 14, Autumn 1987, pp.86–101, a sophisticated critique informed by literary theory.

Interestingly (and perhaps embarrassingly), both these works are written by Australians, not New Zealanders!

87   John O'Shea, personal communication.

88   The critic was F.A. Jones but I have been unable to trace the magazine. Interestingly, Mirams' and O'Shea's previous film was a documentary on exactly this topic.

89   Charles Brasch was editor of *Landfall* from its inception in 1947. Many of his editorials in the late 1940s and 1950s argued his thesis of romantic nostalgia.

90   Also see Nicholas Reid, *A Decade of New Zealand Film* (note 52), pp. 79–83.

91   For example, see *The Otago Daily Times,* May 27, 1983, and *The Auckland Star,* May 28, 1983.

92   See Hardwicke Knight, *Burton Brothers: Photographers* (Dunedin: John McIndoe, 1980).

93   Knight, pp. 34–5.

94   See *Accent,* March 1987; *Proud to be White* (note 9).

95   Said's "politics of blame" is from the essay "Intellectuals in the Post-Colonial World," in *Salmagundi,* Spring-Summer 1986, pp.44–6. This had also become the dominant theme of dissident New Zealand historians, as can be seen in the titles of the following books: Ian Ward's *The Shadow of the Land: A Study of British Policy and Racial Conflict in New Zealand 1832–1852* (Wellington: Historical Publications Branch, Department of Internal Affairs, 1968); Alan Ward's *A Show of Justice: Racial "Amalgamation" in Nineteenth Century New Zealand* (Canberra: Australian National University Press, 1974); Peter Adams' *Fatal Necessity: British Intervention in New Zealand, 1830–1847* (Auckland and Oxford University Presses, 1977); and Tony Simpson's *Te Riri Pakeha: the White Man's Anger* (Martinborough: Alister Taylor, 1979).

96   For a similar example, see Mario Vargas Llosa, "The Radical Romance of Latin America" in *Harper's,* November 1984, pp. 11–12.

97   Rorty, "On Ethnocentrism: A Reply to Clifford Geertz," *Michigan Quarterly Review,* Summer 1986, pp. 525–34.

98   Said, "Intellectuals in the Post-Colonial World" (note 95), p. 45.

99   Said, p. 54

100   Michael Neill, "Coming Home: Teaching the Post-Colonial Novel" *Islands* 35, April 1985, p. 53.

101   Neill, p. 52.

102   Peter Simpson, (ed.) *The Given Condition: Essays in Post-Colonial Literatures,* an edition of *Span* 21 (Christchurch: University of Canterbury, 1985).

103   In the 1980s, Pakeha journalists and photographers have been banned from some hui convened to discuss sensitive political issues such as media representation.

104   *The Governor* was accompanied by *Hunters' Gold* (1976), *The God Boy* (1976), *The McKenzie Affair* (1977), *Gather Your Dreams* (1978), *Children of Fire Mountain* (1979), and others. It has also served as the basis for later series such as *Pioneer Women* (1983) and *Legacy* (1987).

105   Keith Aberdein, *The Governor* (Wellington: Hamlet Books, 1977), p. 71.

106   The best-known such example is of course Laura Mulvey's "Visual Pleasure and Narrative Cinema," *Screen,* vol. xvi, No. 3 (1975). One of the best critiques of such "theoretical masochism" I have read is "The New Feminist Scholarship" by Jean Bethke Elshtain in *Salmagundi* (note 95), pp. 3–26.

107   Discussions like this have flared up periodically in *The NZ Listener* and *Landfall,* to no apparent end.

108   Allen Curnow, *A Book of New Zealand Verse 1923–45* (note 45), p. 47.

109   Robert Chapman and Jonathan Bennett (eds.), *An Anthology of New Zealand Verse* (London: Oxford University Press, 1956); Vincent O'Sullivan, *An Anthology of Twentieth Century New Zealand Poetry* (London: Oxford University Press, 1970); and Fleur Adcock, *The Oxford Book of Contemporary New Zealand Poetry* (Auckland: Oxford University Press, 1982).

110   Allen Curnow, *Penguin Book of New Zealand Verse* (note 45), p. 120.

111   Ian Wedde, *Penguin Book of New Zealand Verse* (Auckland: Penguin, 1985), p. 25.

112   Stead, "Wedde's Inclusions," *Landfall* 155, September 1985, pp. 298–99.

113   Wedde, p. 29

114 Mead, *Islands* 36, November 1985, p. 162.

115 Stead, *London Review of Books,* Dec. 5 1985, p. 4. Also see Keri Hulme's *The Bone People* (Auckland: Spiral in association with Hodder and Stoughton, 1985).

116 Hulme has referred to herself in this way, in Harry Ricketts, *Talking About Ourselves: Twelve New Zealand Poets in Conversation with Harry Ricketts* (Wellington: Mallinson Rendel, 1986), p. 24. In the same interview, she describes Wedde as an international voice and herself (in contrast) as a New Zealand voice.

117 Simon During, ''Postmodernism or Postcolonialism?'' *Landfall* 155, September 1985, pp. 373–74.

118 In 1961, MGM made *Two Loves,* aka *Spinster,* a film about Ashton-Warner which starred Shirley MacLaine.

119 Maurice Shadbolt, *Among the Cinders* (London: Eyre & Spottiswoode, 1965).

120 McCauley herself wrote the screenplay, the major changes from the novel being (1) a greater equalization of the two main characters (the novel is focused through its female protagonist); (2) less direct social commentary; (3) an urban ambience (Christchurch 1973 is replaced by Auckland 1983 and all rural scenes are excised); (4) considerably more ''glamor.'' Also see Brian Patrick MacDonnell, ''The Translation of New Zealand Fiction into Film,'' Ph.D. diss. (University of Auckland, 1986).

121 The report's title, *Race Against Time,* is designed to echo the film of the same name discussed in chapter 7. It was issued by the office of the Race Relations Conciliator, Hiwi Tauroa, in 1982.

122 See Fredric Jameson, ''Postmodernism, or The Cultural Logic of Late Capitalism,'' *The New Left Review* 146, July 1984; J-F. Lyotard, *The Postmodern Condition: A Report on Knowledge,* trans. Geoff Bennington and Brian Massumi (Minneapolis: University of Minnesota Press, 1984; orig. 1979 in French), pp. 31–37 and Fredric Jameson's foreword, pp. ix-x.; Charles Newman, *The Post-Modern Aura: The Act of Fiction in an Age of Inflation* (note 2); Simon During, ''Postmodernism or Postcolonialism?'' (note 117), a local interpretation; and Linda Hutcheon, *A Theory of Parody* (New York: Methuen, 1985).

123 Some Christian groups posit Aotearoa as the emotional and spiritual heart of secularized New Zealand in a reproof to modern Pakeha materialism in both its philosophical and consumerist sense. Others posit Aotearoa as a largely phantom world conjured up with the imagination where there is a dualism inherent in all things, a world of the Maori and a world of the Pakeha, where the former is likely to disappear under the latter like Joe Gillayley's mauri-god in Keri Hulme's *The Bone People* (note 115). These models are spatial and temporal respectively, but there is little difference between a Noble Savage and a Dying Savage. They are nostalgic for (an illusory) lost unity, and they force Maori intellectuals to counter it with the argument that Maori culture is "alive" and well within the present. Many of the *Te Maori* debates turned on this issue.

124 Sidney Moko Mead (ed.), *Te Maori: Maori Art from New Zealand Collections* (New York: Abrams, 1984), pp. 30–31.

125 Mead, pp. 31 & 63.

126 Mead, p. 32. The literature on the exhibition is now enormous. For a sample of just one source—*The NZ Listener*—see the following articles. 1984: Sept. 29, pp. 20–23; Oct. 27, pp. 10 & 45–46; Nov. 10, pp. 36–37; Nov. 17, p. 8. 1985: Jan. 26, p. 10. 1986: Aug. 16, pp. 75–76; Aug. 23, pp. 22–23; Sept. 13, p. 8; Oct. 25, pp. 8–10; Nov. 29, p. 105. 1987: June 27, pp. 40–41 & 70–71. Also see *Time,* Sept. 24, 1984, pp. 50–51, and note 72.

127 There are two versions of *Utu.* The director's cut is 124 minutes long and the producers' international cut is 101 minutes. The former is strictly in chronological order, the latter is structured around flash-forward sequences of the final "trial" and the differing claims to utu made by the various characters. As a matter of preference I like the New Zealand cut more.

128 David Chute, *Los Angeles Herald Examiner,* Oct. 20, 1984, B1.

129 Pauline Kael, *The New Yorker,* Oct. 15, 1984, p. 168.

130 Russell Campbell (note 31), p. 14.

131 See D.F. McKenzie, *Oral Culture, Literacy and Print In Early New Zealand: the Treaty of Waitangi* (Wellington: Victoria University Press, 1985), pp. 46–47.

132 The words are Nicholas Reid's, in *A Decade of New Zealand Film* (note 52), p. 127.

133 The major changes in the adaptation from novel to film are listed by Reid, pp. 118–28.

134 Reid, p. 128.

135 This throws into question the initiative of High Culture intellectuals to substitute "ethnic" for "racial" as a term of discourse. Yet that seems to be the intention of a number of New Zealand academics in the social sciences, as if ethnicity were somehow more scientific than race.

136 Quoted in Mikalsen, "Kingpin: Can There Be Only One?" *Illusions,* Winter 1987, p. 12.

137 Walker: "Willie was so desperate to find his father . . . that he was transferring his agony on to Riki's situation" (quoted in Mikalsen, p. 13).

138 Walker in Mikalsen, p. 15.

139 Walker in Mikalsen, p. 15.

140 When asked what a Maori film is, Barry Barclay has replied that it must be made by a completely Maori crew. He added that in 1987 this was at least five years off. See the interview in *Illusions* 5, 1987, p. 4.

141 Mita's other films include *Karanga Hokianga* (1979), a respectful documentary about Catholic Maori communities meeting at Hokianga which was commissioned by the Catholic Church; *The Hammer and the Anvil* (1980), a documentary history of New Zealand's trade union movement, co-directed with Gerd Pohlmann; *Keskidee-Aroha* (1981), a film which could never resolve its own shooting problems, co-directed with Martyn Sanderson; *The Bridge: A Story of Men in Dispute* (1982), a record of the Mangere Bridge strike, co-directed with Pohlmann. She has also worked on Chris Strewe's *Waitangi: The Story of a Treaty and its Inheritors* (1977); *Koha* (1980–1); Pohlmann's *Kinleith* (1981), Television One's *The Protestors* (1982), *South Auckland: Two Cities* (1982) and *Auckland Fa'a-Samoa* (1982); *Utu* (1983); *One of Those Blighters* (1982); *The Quiet Earth* (1984), and others.

142 W.H. Oliver & B.R. Williams, *The Oxford History of New Zealand* (London: Clarendon & Oxford University Press, 1981).

143 See Hayden White, "Getting Out of History" in *Diacritics,* Vol. 12, No. 3, 1982, p. 5.

144 Raymond Williams, *Keywords* (note 24), pp. 213–14.

145 Williams, p. 148.

146 Events in Fiji during 1987 and 1988 provide an interesting case of the essentialist/racial argument being used by indigenous Fijians to justify a military coup designed at least in part to prevent political/economic power from falling into the hands of Indian Fijians who, naturally enough, utilize arguments for pluralism, multiculturalism and parliamentary democracy.

147 Edward Said, *The World, the Text and the Critic* (Cambridge: Harvard University Press, 1983), p. 171.

INDEX

ABOUT THE AUTHOR

MARTIN J. BLYTHE is a New Zealander who is now resident in Los Angeles. He has an M.A. in English, 1st class honours, from the University of Auckland, and a Ph.D. from UCLA Department of Film & Television. He directed *Queen Street,* a drama for Television New Zealand in 1980; reviewed cinema for *The New Zealand Listener* and other publications in 1983 and 1984; completed in 1988 a doctoral dissertation titled *From Maoriland to Aotearoa,* on which this book is based; taught film at UCLA Extension from 1989 through the present; and has published articles in *Quarterly Review of Film and Video, East-West Film Journal,* and *The Independent.* He is currently Senior Manager, Promotions for Buena Vista International, the International Theatrical division of the Walt Disney Studios.